Mind

over

Matter

A Course in Abundance, vol 1

Mind

over

Matter

KIM MICHAELS

MORE TO LIFE PUBLISHING

www.morepublish.com

For foreign and translation rights,

contact info@ morepublish.com

ISBN: 978-9949-518-55-5

Series ISBN: 978-9949-518-53-1

The information and insights in this book should not be considered as a form of therapy, advice, direction, diagnosis, and/or treatment of any kind. This information is not a substitute for medical, psychological, or other professional advice, counseling and care. All matters pertaining to your individual health should be supervised by a physician or appropriate health-care practitioner. No guarantee is made by the author or the publisher that the practices described in this book will yield successful results for anyone at any time. They are presented for informational purposes only, as the practice and proof rests with the individual.

For more information:

www.ascendedmasterlight.com

www.transcendencetoolbox.com

CONTENTS

HOW TO USE THIS BOOK

The idea behind *A Course in Abundance* is to give you effective tools for shifting your consciousness. Many spiritual books give you understanding, and while this may be inspiring, it does not necessarily lead to practical change. The books in this course contain a unique combination of teachings and techniques for invoking spiritual light. The combination of teachings and exercises has the potential to help you go through a real transformation that will bring you to a higher level of your personal path.

The teachings and tools in this course are given by the universal spiritual teachers of humankind, also known as the ascended masters. The teachings in this course were given as direct, spoken dictations by an ascended master known as Mother Mary. She holds the Office of the Divine Mother for all people embodying on earth. The exercises invoke both Mother Mary and seven other representatives of the Divine Mother. If you are not familiar with the ascended masters and their teachings, it is recommended that you read the book *The Power of Self*, which explains who the masters are, how they can help you and how you can follow the path to self-mastery offered by the masters. You can also find information on the website: *www.ascendedmasterlight.com*.

The invocations following each chapter are meant to be read aloud by you. You can read them in a slow, meditative way or you can give them faster and with more power in your voice. There is no one right way to give the invocations, but they obviously cannot work unless you read them aloud. If you desire more detailed instructions for how to give invocations, please visit the website: *www.transcendencetoolbox.com*. You might also find it helpful to give the invocations along with a recording. You can purchase and download sound files of the invocations from the website: *www.morepublish.com*.

It is suggested that you start using this book by studying the first chapter and then giving the first invocation at least once, but preferably once a day for nine consecutive days. You can then move on to the second chapter and so on until you have worked through all eight chapters and invocations. Once you are familiar with the teachings, you do not have to read the chapter before giving an invocation, yet you will probably find that reading at least part of a chapter helps you get more out of giving the invocation. You can also do a longer ritual of giving each invocation up to 33 times.

Depending on your speed, it takes 15-25 minutes to give one invocation. This means you can give all eight invocations (one after the other) in around two hours, which is a very powerful ritual. You do not have to give the opening prayer or the sealing with each invocation. You give an opening prayer when you start and the sealing after you finish the last invocation.

Feel free to be creative in the use of the tools included in this book. For example, you can give the matrix for another person or persons, even for the healing of the collective consciousness.

If you make the effort to overcome your initial resistance and build a momentum on giving the invocations, you will likely find that it is one of the most powerful and effective spiritual tools you have ever used. By combining this tool with a willingness to look into your own psyche and let go of limiting beliefs, you can turn your life into an upward spiral that will expand your ability to manifest spiritual and material abundance. Truly, as the masters say, everything revolves around your free will. If you can accept that transcendence is possible for you, then the results *will* be manifest for you. Invoke, and ye shall receive.

Please be aware that this course is a very special gift from the heart of the Divine Mother. The words in the course are given as direct dictation, meaning that they contain subtle keys to unlocking your understanding. You will not get the full benefit from the course by reading it with the intellectual, linear mind. The course is designed to unlock your intuition, your inner mystical knowing, and thereby reconnect you to what you already know deep within your being. Studying the course can be approached as a process of worshiping the Divine Mother. If you approach the course with reverence, you will attain greater benefits.

You can use the course in a variety of ways, including using it as a meditative or contemplative tool. It is a powerful exercise to read the dictations aloud. It is perfectly valid to use it on your own, studying the dictations and giving the invocations. Yet it will give an accelerated benefit to use the course in a group setting. The course is not owned or controlled by any organization so it can be used freely by formal or informal groups. There is great benefit in a group of people meeting on a regular basis, studying and discussing one chapter and giving the corresponding invocation. Whenever two or three are gathered in the name of the Divine Mother, there she is in the midst of them.

Please note that for practical reasons, it has been necessary to publish this course in three separate books. In order to get maximum results, it is important that you follow the course in the order it was given. It is highly recommended that you start by working through Volume 1, then Volume 2 and finally Volume 3.

INTRODUCTION TO A
COURSE IN ABUNDANCE

Did you ever hear or read the words spoken by Jesus: "Fear not, little flock; for it is your Father's good pleasure to give you the kingdom" (Luke 12:32)? Did you ever think about those words and then look at your own life and wonder: "If it is the Father's good pleasure to give me the kingdom, how come I don't have God's abundance?" Did you ever think about those words and then look at the world and wonder: "If it is God's pleasure to give all people his kingdom, how come so many people live in abject poverty and have no opportunity to improve their lot in life? How come most people are poor while a small elite is so rich that it almost defies comprehension?" Did you ever wonder why God allows you to live without the abundance you desire and that he supposedly desires for you? Did you ever consider what you could possibly do to change the situation and experience the abundant life?

I am sure that you have, at some point in your life, considered these questions. Yet did you find an answer? If you did not find an answer, are you willing to look for an answer beyond traditional sources? Are you willing to look for an answer beyond the mental box in which your mind currently resides? If so, I recommend that you start by contemplating these questions: "Is it God who allows me to be poor and not have abundance or is it someone else? Is it God who prevents me from having his full abundance, or is it myself who rejects that abundance? Is it God who allows so many people on earth to be poor, or is it humankind as a whole that has rejected God's abundance and thereby created a state of lack and inequality on earth?"

I know these are very direct questions, and they might seem unloving. I assure you that I ask them in greatest love. I ask you to contemplate these questions in greatest love because I know that if you will openly contemplate these questions, you will inevitably find the answers that will empower you to inherit the abundance of God that is rightfully yours. In so doing, you will contribute to the movement that will inevitably lead to the point where the stranglehold of lack and inequality is broken on this planet. The floodgates of heaven can be opened and all people can receive God's abundant life. My questions are asked with the greater love that will not leave my children alone, trapped in poverty, lack and limitations. I would rather disturb their minds with a direct question, and in so doing hopefully jolt them awake to the reality that there is more to understand about life than what they currently know.

If you think you are deprived of the things you desire, then your state of lack is a prison. As all prisons, it has a door. If you can find that door and learn how to open it, you have the opportunity to escape the prison. If you do not believe there is a door, or if you do not know how to open that door, how can you possibly escape the prison cell in which you are currently trapped? You have no chance of escaping if you do not know how. The key to overcoming your current state of lack is to gain a greater understanding of what it will take to inherit

God's abundance. You can prove that when Jesus said that it is the Father's good pleasure to give you the kingdom, he was not making a false promise. He was making a true promise because Jesus had realized that there is a door out of the human prison. He had discovered that door. He had found the key that would unlock the door. Most importantly, he had done what it takes to walk through that door and therefore be free of the human condition, the human struggle. His entire life was dedicated to proving that it is possible to escape human limitations, and it was his hope that all other people would look at his life as an example of how they themselves could escape the prison – the mental prison – of the human state of consciousness, the consciousness of separation, limitation and lack.

***

I am come to help you discover the prison door. I am come to give you the keys that will open the prison door, for it truly has more than one lock. I am come to offer to take your hand and lead you through that door until you have escaped the prison and stand free to bask in the Sun of your true Being. Who am I to make such promises? In considering that your current situation is a prison and that you would like to escape that prison, who would you like to serve as your guide? There are numerous people who offer to be your guides. They promise that if you will only buy their services, their books or their classes, they will surely lead you out of the human prison. The problem is that they are still in a physical body, and thus they are still in time and space. They might have some understanding of how to escape the human prison but they have not yet applied that understanding to the fullest. If you would be guided by a Being who has applied the knowledge and who has escaped the human prison, then I am here to offer my service and my loving guidance. Who am I, then?

The central message given by Jesus was that you can escape the human prison and overcome even death itself. The central message of Jesus was that death is not the end, that you can find a new life – a new state of consciousness – in a higher realm. Jesus proved that you can escape the human prison permanently and that you can ascend to a higher realm. Although some Christians have been brought up to believe that Jesus was an exception, Jesus is not the only one who has escaped the human prison and who has permanently ascended to a higher realm. If Jesus was the only one who could follow this path, what would be the point of his coming to earth? What kind of God would send his only Son into this world to show you a path you could not follow? Would it not be adding insult to injury to show you that one person can escape the human prison but you cannot?

You have only two options: You can reason that God is not a loving God, or you can reason that behind the life and teachings of Jesus there is a hidden message, a message that all people have the potential to follow whereby they too can rise beyond this human prison and ascend to a higher realm. You can reason that either God sent Jesus to show you the way to his kingdom, a way you too can follow, or Jesus was lying when he said that it is the Father's good pleasure to give you his kingdom. You cannot have it both ways. You cannot logically reason that only Jesus can inherit the abundant life and at the same time consider Jesus a true savior and consider God a benevolent God. The human prison is made up of many beliefs that are illogical and contradictory, and it is indeed my intention to expose such beliefs in the coming chapters. If you will let me, I will lead you to a higher understanding of life, and thereby you will come to know the truth that will set you free. You can then walk through the prison door into your Father's kingdom of the abundant life. If you can accept the possibility that Jesus is not the only Being who has ascended to heaven, you might accept that I too have followed the path demonstrated by Jesus and I too have ascended to a higher realm. I was once in a human body, like the one you are currently wearing. I was known then as Mary, the mother of Jesus. After that lifetime as Mary, I did indeed win my permanent ascension to the spiritual realm. I am today an ascended being, and I have chosen to remain with earth in order to serve as a teacher, as a guardian, as a guide for you and those of your spiritual brothers and sisters who have not yet escaped the human prison.

Since my ascension I have not stood still. I have risen higher in the ranks here in heaven, for truly, as Jesus said: "In my Father's house are many mansions" (John 14:2). There are levels of attainment even in the spiritual world, and since my ascension I have attained a greater understanding, internalization and oneness with the consciousness and Being of the Mother aspect of God. I am today the representative of the Divine Mother for planet earth. You might consider this a spiritual office, much like the offices you have on earth, such as mayor of a city, governor of a state or leader of a nation.

I come as the representative of the Divine Mother to extend my hand in the deepest love, the most profound, unconditional and nurturing love of the Divine Mother. I have no other desire than to see all of God's children receive their rightful inheritance, which truly is the abundant life. It is an absolute truth that it is God the Father's good pleasure to give you the kingdom of the abundant life. You do not have to wait for that abundant life until you ascend to heaven. You can inherit and experience, you can claim, that abundant life right here on earth, as Jesus truly demonstrated by turning the water into wine and by multiplying the loaves and fishes.

***

This course is a gift from my heart that I offer to you with complete purity of motive and with nothing but love in my heart. This is my gift, given to you freely in the hope that you will receive it freely and without prejudice, without any preconceived opinions concerning what the Mother of God should say or should not say. It is my goal with this course to give you the keys to God's kingdom, the keys that open the prison door and help you go beyond all human limitations.

If your mind sets up limitations and conditions for what I *can* say and what I *cannot* say, then how can I possibly lead you beyond the prison of human limitations? If you use some preconceived opinion to reject my words or to reject this course, then you are demonstrating that you would rather remain in your current mental prison. You are not willing to open one particular lock, or maybe many locks, in the door that leads to the abundant life. Because I love you and because I respect that God the Father has given you free will, I will let you hold on to your preconceived opinions and conditions—if that is what you desire.

I ask only one thing of you. I ask you to be honest with yourself. I ask you to realize that if you use some preconceived human opinion to reject my words, you are doing so because you want to continue to experience limitations, suffering and lack. You are doing so because you are not truly willing to know what you need to know or do what you need to do in order to open the prison door and walk through that door. I am asking you to at least be honest with yourself. Please do not reject this course with the attitude that it is somehow wrong or of the devil. At least be honest with yourself and recognize that if you reject this course, you do so because you choose to maintain certain beliefs that are being challenged by this course. You have a perfect right to maintain such beliefs, you have a perfect right to choose to hold on to a limited world view rather than to accept the greater understanding that will empower you to open the prison door. I only ask that you recognize that this is a choice that you are making and that no one but yourself can truly force you to choose to cling to limitations.

It is the Father's good pleasure to give you the kingdom, and if you do not have his kingdom right now, there can be only one explanation. You have used some human beliefs or opinions to cling to a limited outlook on life. It is this limited outlook on life that prevents you from accepting the kingdom that God is offering you right now and has been offering you throughout your existence as a self-aware being.

It is God the Father's good pleasure to give you his kingdom, and it is God the Mother's good pleasure to give you that kingdom in the form of both spiritual and material nurturance in this world. I am come to offer you the truth that will make you free to accept the abundance of God the Father and the nurturance of God the Mother. This course will offer you that truth, yet it is up to you to accept it and to allow it to transform your consciousness, to transform your outlook on life, until you are free from your current limitations.

I say again, if you currently feel trapped in a prison of limitations and lack, then please realize that what keeps you in that prison is the beliefs and opinions that you have come to accept and that are out of alignment with the truth and the reality of God. If you are to ever escape the human prison, you can do so in only one way, and that is by being willing to look beyond the preconceived opinions and beliefs that you somehow think are true, infallible or beyond questioning. Only the truth will set you free and if you already knew the truth, you would be free right now. The only logical conclusion is that the truth is not found within your current mental box, meaning that if you are to ever find the truth, you must be willing to look beyond that box. If you are not willing to question the beliefs that keep you trapped in your current prison, there is no possibility of escape from that prison. The reason is not that escape is impossible; the reason is that you are choosing not to question, not to look beyond, your current beliefs. You are choosing to keep yourself in your current mental prison and you are refusing to acknowledge that there is something outside that box.

***

What I will do in this course is to offer you all of the keys you need in order to unlock the door that leads you out of the prison of human limitations, lack and suffering. I will offer you the very keys that I used to escape that prison myself. I will offer them by giving you the true meaning of the example and the teachings given by Jesus—in which he also demonstrated how to use the keys that will take you out of the human prison.

As has been said: "You can lead a man to water but you cannot make him drink," and the same is true for a woman. All I can do in this course is to offer you the keys to the prison door, the keys that will lead you out of human limitations and lead you into your Father's kingdom. It is up to you whether you will accept my offering and whether you will use it to actually unlock every lock that keeps the door sealed. I can only offer you the keys; I cannot force you to take them, I cannot force you to put them in the locks, I cannot force you to turn the keys, I cannot force you to open the door and I cannot force you to walk through it.

I have no desire to force you to come home to your Father's kingdom. I do have an infinite love for your lifestream, and I do have a longing to stand before you and greet you when you have walked through the door and now stand free as the pure spiritual being that God created in his image and likeness. I have a great desire to look deeply into your eyes and see in those eyes the joy of knowing that you are, once again, free—that you are home. I have a great desire to put my arms around you and to hold you tight so that I can feel the beating of your heart and you can feel the beating of mine. I long to share your joy as you realize that our hearts now beat to the same beat because we have become one in spirit. Your heart is no longer beating to the sound of a different drum, the drum – the humdrum – of human struggles, suffering and lack.

I offer you this course as a gift from my heart. Should you choose to reject it because of some idea that challenges a belief that you are not willing to question or give up, then I shall respect your choice. My love for you will not diminish but I will feel a tinge of sadness. I know that as long as you are trapped in human limitations, you will not be able to accept my love. You will not be able to accept the love of the Divine Mother and you will not be able to accept the kingdom of the Divine Father.

***

I make no excuse for the fact that this is a very long course and that I repeat myself, explaining the same point from more than one perspective. It is my goal to give you the ultimate course on how to manifest God's abundance in your life, and this simply cannot be done in a book of normal content and style or a course of normal length. I have no desire to give you a half-baked story that leaves out essential steps and thereby stops short of empowering you to break through and claim your full potential.

I also want to make it clear that this course is not written for the human intellect, for the analytical mind that loves to categorize everything. The intellect loves to compare every new idea to what it already knows and then put the idea into a small box with a label on it. It loves to fit everything into its existing world view, its existing belief system. Manifesting the abundant life cannot be accomplished through the human intellect but requires a higher form of reasoning. This course is written in a way that is specifically designed to activate the higher faculties of your mind, the faculties that are centered in your heart instead of in your head. If you study this course with your intellect, it will give you little of value. To get the full benefit, you need to activate your heart, your intuitive faculties, because it is through these faculties that you can think outside the mental box created by your intellect.

***

A major part of this course is the practical exercises, the invocations that you will find after each chapter. These invocations are designed to help you both challenge the imperfect energies and the limiting beliefs that exist in your subconscious mind and that block your ability to manifest abundance. By giving the invocations aloud, you will literally bring into your outer situation the spiritual light that has the potential to transform any limitation into a state of higher abundance. How exactly this works will be explained in great depth as the course progresses, but I want you to start using the invocations right away.

There is nothing mystical about these invocations. For thousands of years human beings have known how to invoke spiritual energy. Many spiritual and religious rituals were given to human beings in order to empower them to purify the misqualified energy that had accumulated in their minds. Due to the lower understanding that humankind had in the past, this fact has generally not been explained. If it *was* explained, the explanation was often hidden behind or distorted by orthodox doctrines.

Consider how you might have participated in a religious ceremony or ritual and felt uplifted afterwards. What happened was that the ritual invoked high-frequency spiritual energy, and as it entered your mind, it purified some of the misqualified energy that had accumulated there. It reduced the weight of misqualified energy that you are carrying around, and as a result you felt lighter, you feel uplifted. When people make the statement that it feels like they are carrying the weight of the world upon their shoulders, the reality is that they are carrying the weight of misqualified energy and they experience it as an almost physical burden that weighs them down. A religious ritual can temporarily relieve this burden, but if it is not powerful enough, the relief will last only for a short period of time. When the underlying belief is not removed, you immediately misqualify more energy and eventually feel as burdened as before.

What I give you in this course is a series of rituals, in the form of invocations, that are so powerful that if you use them diligently, you will not simply receive a temporary relief from the misqualified energies that burden you. You will enter an upward spiral that will purify so much energy – and at the same time potentially resolve so many self-defeating beliefs – that you will quickly pass a point of no return. You will know that your life has become an upward spiral, and as long as you keep moving forward, no force on earth has the power to stop that spiral. It is my goal with this course to inspire you to use the tools I will give you so that you anchor yourself so firmly on the upward path that you will have the inner knowing – which is beyond mere belief – that no power on this earth, neither your mortal self nor the prince of this world, can take you off the spiritual path. No power can force you back into the sense of struggle and suffering that you endured before you anchored yourself on the upward path of self-transcendence.

***

Many of the students of this course might not be familiar with the concept of giving invocations or other spiritual exercises. You might look at an invocation as a set of positive affirmations that are composed of two particular elements. One element is a series of affirmations that each deal with a specific dualistic lie, a specific dualistic illusion, concerning your sense of identity and your relationship to God. By reading these affirmations aloud, you are anchoring the higher truth they affirm in your subconscious mind, your energy field or aura. You will gradually begin to counteract the dualistic beliefs you have stored there. The other element of the invocation is the verses that rhyme and that are repeated after each of the individual affirmations. This element of repetition gives a powerful rhythm to the invocation. If you look at nature, you will see that rhythm is an integral part of God's creation. There are many spiritual people who know the power of rhythm, of repeating a particular ritual. You also see rhythm in the change of the seasons, you see it in music, and you will note that God used the power of sound to issue the command: "Let there by light!" By repeating an invocation, you generate wave upon wave of energy. By invoking such waves of high-frequency spiritual energy and directing them through the individual affirmation, you are sending light into your personal energy field where it will consume all misqualified energies.

You will have to put forth a great effort to follow this long course. I ask you in all sincerity to also take the step that will bring the fulfillment of your efforts. I am asking you to make a big commitment, and to make it with the absolute determination that you will see it through. What I am asking you to do is to give each invocation for nine consecutive days while studying the corresponding chapter. I am asking you to set aside time from your busy schedule and go into a room where you can remain private and undisturbed. Begin by reading a section of a chapter. It can be short or long as your time allows. Read to the point where you feel you have encountered an idea that has a message for you or an idea that you do not understand but that you sense is important. At that point, stop reading and start giving the invocation by reading it aloud with all the intensity of your heart flame.

I know that for many people this will require a sacrifice and it will require them to do something they have never done before. It might feel awkward in the beginning, but it will soon begin to flow naturally and you will feel that it becomes a joyful part of your day. If you want the full benefit from this course, it is absolutely essential that you give the exercises. Over the years, I have seen so many spiritual people who started reading some teaching on spirituality or abundance. They took it all into their minds and felt they had a great intellectual understanding, but they were reluctant to take actual physical steps in order to bring the abundant life into manifestation. Each of these people failed to achieve the results they desired. If you are to have results from this course, you cannot simply read the chapters. You cannot allow yourself to think that taking in from the book is enough. You must also give something out, and I have designed these invocations specifically to help you get out of any negative spirals you might be in, thereby putting your life into an upward spiral that neither your mortal self nor the prince of this world will be able to reverse. I ask you to seriously consider giving the invocations.

My beloved, I realize this is a big commitment, but if you will carry this through, your life will never be the same. You will literally realize that you have turned your life into an upward spiral, and you now have the understanding and the tools you need to continue that spiral and even accelerate it. As you do, you will manifest the truly abundant life in the form of both spiritual and material abundance. Consider very seriously how you can change your daily schedule in order to accommodate starting this vigil.

1 | WHY YOU DON'T ALREADY HAVE ABUNDANCE

Let us begin with a reality check. Let us look at the statement: "It is the Father's good pleasure to give you the kingdom." Although you may have heard that statement many times before, have you really spent the time and the attention to consider what this truly means? There really is only one meaning. It is the Father's good pleasure to give you the kingdom, and this must mean that God really wants you to have his kingdom. God really wants you to have the abundant life. It is his good pleasure to give it to you.

If you look at your life and see that you do not have abundance, you must reason that something has gone wrong. Something is preventing you from having the abundant life that God wants you to have. Now we can begin to reason together and consider what could possibly have prevented you from having the abundant life—if it truly is God's desire and God's will that you should have that abundance. What could possibly have gone wrong? What could possibly prevent you from having what God wants you to have? What could possibly prevent God's will from being a manifest reality on planet earth?

Let us now take a look at planet earth. There is great beauty in nature on this planet. Your scientists are continually discovering how intricate, how complex, and yet how wondrous this world is designed. There are so many interwoven and complex systems on earth that even the most materialistic scientists cannot help but once in a while feel a sense of wonder and awe over the intricacy, the beauty and the symmetry they discover in nature. If you are a spiritually inclined person, you will tend to agree with me when I say that this intricacy must have been designed by a mind that is very capable and that has great imagination and reasoning ability. What you see in nature is that God truly has designed a very beautiful and wondrous creation, a creation that has great abundance.

When you look at the area of human affairs, you see a different picture. Even though the human body is the most complex of all God's creations, human beings seem to have trouble figuring out how to use their bodies without destroying themselves, without destroying others or without destroying nature. Whereas you often see abundance and balance in nature, you do not see the same abundance or the same balance in human affairs. Think about the words of Jesus when he said that you are of greater value than the sparrows (Matthew 10:31). If God is capable of clothing and feeding the birds, he is surely capable of giving you everything you need. Many people on earth look at the birds with envy because the birds are free to fly wherever they like and they always seem to find food just for the taking. In contrast, many people are trapped by various circumstances and can hardly move. They must struggle their entire lives just to make a living and feed themselves and their children. Many people long for the carefree life of the birds and feel that, in contrast, their lives are one long struggle.

When you look at the beauty and the abundance that God has built into nature, does it seem logical to you that God would not be able to design a planet that can sustain human life with the same abundance and carefreeness that you see in the life of birds? Is there really any reason God should not be able to design a planet that can give you the same freedom and the same carefree living as you see in the life of the many creatures that have far less intelligence and, as Jesus said, far less value than yourself?

You have only limited options when you start reasoning this through in a logical manner. You cannot deny the reality that human beings do not have the abundant life. When you consider the concept that it is the Father's good pleasure to give you the kingdom, you must say that if God wants human beings to have the abundant life, then something must have gone wrong either on God's end or on your end.

One option is to reason that apparently God was able to create a wonderful and intricate planet that is able to sustain a carefree and abundant life for the birds and other creatures with less intelligence than humans. When it came to humans, God somehow was not able to engineer the planet so that it could sustain your life in the same abundance and freedom from care, lack or suffering. You can reason that God's ability to design must somehow be flawed, and when it came to human beings, he made a mistake. There are indeed many people who have reasoned this way. Some of them are religious people, and having been brought up to fear going to hell if they blaspheme God, they quickly push such thoughts aside. Others are willing to acknowledge the thoughts and some have even used them as a reason to reject all religion or reject the concept of God.

If you are inclined to think this way, I ask only one thing of you. The next time there is a clear night where you live, please go outside and look up into the night sky. Look up into the Milky Way and contemplate how many stars there are. You don't need to look up in a scientific book that tells you how many billions of stars scientist have calculated to be in existence. You just need to look with your eyes and see that there are more stars than you can count. Then, ask yourself: "If God was able to create a universe of such incredible vastness and complexity, does it seem logical that on this small planet, that we call earth, God was not able to provide an abundant and carefree life for the highest life form on this planet?"

My beloved heart, if you will contemplate this, I think you will realize the absolute truth that God is fully capable of designing planet earth in such a way that every human being on this planet can enjoy an abundant and carefree life with the same freedom as that enjoyed by the birds. The very fact that most people do not have this life cannot be caused by a problem on God's end. This leaves only one logical conclusion. The lack and the poverty found on earth must be caused by a problem on *your* end. Something must have happened on earth that prevents God's desire from being manifest here. Something must have happened that altered God's original design for this planet so that the highest and most complex life form often encounters a less abundant life than what is enjoyed by many of the creatures of far less intelligence.

***

You might find reason to question the image of God you have been given since childhood. You might consider these questions:

• If God truly is the almighty and infallible God that he is portrayed to be by many religions, and if it truly is God's desire that human beings have the abundant life, then how can it possibly be that God's desire is not manifest on earth?

• What could possibly prevent the desires of an all-mighty and all-powerful God from being manifest?

• If it is God's good pleasure to give people the king-dom, how could they possibly fail to have that kingdom?

You now reach another logical conclusion. Either there is something wrong on God's end or there is something wrong on your end. Either God has a flaw or the image of God upheld by many people on earth has a flaw. Once again, if God can create such an intricate and vast universe, is it likely that he is unintel-ligent? The logical conclusion is that there must be something wrong with the image of God that has been painted by certain religions on this earth. This leads us to a fruitful area of discus-sion because we can now begin to consider what might be miss-ing in the image of God that you have come to accept.

We have seen that God is quite capable of designing a very vast and complex universe. We have reasoned that a God who can create such an incredible universe is fully capable of creat-ing a small planet that can provide the abundant and carefree life for every human being living upon it. Despite the fact that God is able and willing, the current reality on planet earth does not reflect God's desire and God's ability. Something must have come between the design for earth that God holds in his mind and the reality that is currently outpictured on this planet. What could possibly prevent the desire of an almighty God from being manifest? It is logical that nothing can prevent God from having his will fulfilled. The only possible conclusion is that either God is not almighty or he has chosen to set aside, at least on a tem-porary basis, his almighty powers on earth.

This opens the possibility that God has given human beings dominion over the earth, as the Bible clearly states (Genesis 1:26). What does it mean that God told people to take dominion over the earth? Does it not seem reasonable to assume that God has given human beings an ability to not simply live on this planet and adapt to the natural circumstances, as you see in animal species? God has given human beings the ability to not simply adapt to their environment but to take dominion over that environment and to actively and consciously alter that environment to suit their needs. Human beings have the ability to choose how they will live. They are not simply slaves of their environment that must either adapt or become extinct.

All animal species are adapted to a certain type of environment. Although there is great adaptability in nature, there is a limit to how much an animal species can adapt to different types of environments. An animal does not have the awareness and the creative ability to consciously alter its environment or to insulate itself from that environment. Human beings do have that ability, and no animal species has the same ability to live in many different environments as is the case for human beings. God has given human beings abilities that are far beyond what is found in the animal kingdom. Human beings are more than simply sophisticated animals. Human beings are not simply highly evolved animals because humans are, to use a modern expression, a quantum leap above any animal species.

The logical conclusion is that God created human beings in his own image and likeness (Genesis 1:26). Humans have a consciousness and self-awareness so sophisticated that instead of simply adapting to their environment, they have the ability to imagine that their environment could be changed and that such a change could enable them to have more abundance than what their environment currently provides. Human beings also have the ability to freely choose that, instead of adapting to a particular environment, they will actively seek to change their environment. What sets a human being apart from animals is self-awareness, imagination and free will.

***

On the positive side, these creative abilities give human beings the potential to act as extensions of God on earth. This might give us a new view of the story of creation told in Genesis. It is explained how God spent six days creating the earth, the animal kingdom and human beings. On the seventh day, God rested. Could it possibly be that God "resting" means that God temporarily stopped his creative work on planet earth? He did this because he had created beings that were meant to act as his hands and feet on earth, as extensions of himself on earth, so that they could finish the creation of earth. Is it possible that God created human beings in his image and likeness because he wanted them to finish the creation of earth? Instead of passively living here, they could take active part in God's creation, they could feel that they played an active role and that they could assist in bringing God's kingdom into full manifestation on this planet.

I know these ideas go far beyond what you were told in Sunday school, and they go far beyond what your scientists are willing to even consider. These ideas can explain the reality that you see in your own life and in the lives of billions of people on this planet, namely that you do not have the abundant life. Somewhere deep inside, you know that you should have abundance, you know that life should be different, that life should be better than it is right now. You can understand this by looking at the flip side of the coin because the fact that God has given people imagination and free will has a dark side, a negative potential. It is possible that people can use their imagination to envision something that is less than what God wants for them. It is possible that they can use their free will to choose to manifest something on this planet that has less abundance than God's original design. God originally designed this planet to give human beings the same carefree living as enjoyed by animals. God wanted humans to build upon this foundation so they could create even more abundance for themselves than what nature is designed to provide. Human beings can also go in the opposite direction and tear down the foundation built by God whereby human society enters an unnatural state of lack that leads to poverty and inequality. If you will go deeply within your heart and consider these ideas, you will see that they can indeed explain why there is so much inequality, so much suffering, so much lack and so much poverty on this planet. These ideas can also explain why, deep within your heart, you have an inner knowing that this is not natural, that this is not right, that this is not what God intended, that this is not the way life is supposed to be.

We have now seen that it is truly the Father's good pleasure to give you the abundant life. This is the natural state of affairs on planet earth, namely that all human beings have abundance of every good and perfect gift. As Jesus said: "That ye may be the children of your Father which is in heaven: for he maketh his sun to rise on the evil and on the good, and sendeth rain on the just and on the unjust" (Matthew 5:45).

***

The conclusion is that human beings have done something to obstruct the natural state of affairs on earth, to obstruct the flow of God's abundance and to prevent it from reaching every human being. Once you reach this conclusion and begin to accept it – in the inner reaches of your being as well as in your outer mind – you gain an entirely different perspective on life and the possibility of attaining the abundant life. Instead of thinking you are living on a planet where suffering and lack are somehow inevitable, the reality is that abundance is the natural state of affairs. This is what God wants, and he has designed a planet with the full capacity to provide that abundance. I know you have been brought up to think that what prevents the abundant life on earth is a lack of natural resources, but this is not so. God has designed this planet so that it has every resource necessary to provide the abundant life for all people. Mother Earth can provide this abundant life for more people than are currently living within her womb. The problem on earth is that human beings have used their minds, the power of their imagination and free will, to limit, to divert, to obstruct the natural flow of God's abundance.

When you reach that conclusion, you can take your thoughts about the abundant life in a new direction. You can begin to consider how you can personally stop obstructing the natural flow of God's abundance so that you can truly inherit your Father's kingdom and experience the abundant life while you are still here on earth.

You can take two approaches to the abundant life. One is the passive and one is the active approach. When you take the passive approach, you might accept that God wants you to have abundance but since you do not currently have it, your only option is to reason that for some unknown, mystical, unknowable reason God does not want to give you the abundant life right now. Since you cannot understand why – and you cannot explain why because there is no logical explanation – your only option is to simply wait and hope that, at some future time, God will change his mind and give you the abundant life. This puts you in a waiting position, and it turns you into a helpless victim of circumstances and forces beyond your control.

When you take the active approach, you reason that it is natural for you to have abundance. If you do not have it, something is blocking it. If you can find out what is blocking it, you might be able to remove those blocks and then God's abundance will naturally start flowing into your life. My beloved, if you can accept this possibility, you are truly ready to receive the next keys to the kingdom that I will give you in the following chapters.

2 | I INVOKE MY CREATIVE POWERS

In the name I AM THAT I AM, Jesus Christ, I call to all representatives of the Divine Mother, especially Maraytaii and Mother Mary, to help me overcome all sense of being powerless or being a victim of factors beyond my control. Help me accept my creative powers and see the factors that block the flow of my God-given creativity, including...

[Make personal calls.]

1. The universe will give me abundance

1. It really is the Father's good pleasure to give me the abundant life, both spiritually, psychologically and materially.

O Cosmic Mother, sound the gong,
that calls me home where I belong.
I know you love me tenderly,
and in that knowing I am free.

**Maraytaii, I resonate
with song that opens cosmic gate.
Your melody makes me vibrate
my sense of self I recreate.**

2. God really wants me to have the abundant life. It is God's
good pleasure to give it to me.

O Cosmic Mother, hold me tight,
I resonate with your own light.
Your music purifies my heart,
your love to all I do impart.

**Maraytaii, I resonate
with song that opens cosmic gate.
Your melody makes me vibrate
my sense of self I recreate.**

3. Something has prevented me from receiving the abundance
that God wants me to have.

O Cosmic Mother, we are one,
your heart is like a blazing sun.
My being can but amplify,
the sacred sound you magnify.

Maraytaii, I resonate
with song that opens cosmic gate.
Your melody makes me vibrate
my sense of self I recreate.

4. God has designed a very beautiful and wondrous creation, a creation that has great abundance.

O Cosmic Mother, I now hear,
the subtle sound of Sacred Sphere.
As I attune to Cosmic Hum,
the lesser self I overcome.

Maraytaii, I resonate
with song that opens cosmic gate.
Your melody makes me vibrate
my sense of self I recreate.

5. I acknowledge how many stars there are in the sky and how vast the universe is.

O Cosmic Mother, take me home,
I am in sync with Sacred OM,
The sound of sounds will raise me up,
so only light is in my cup.

Maraytaii, I resonate
with song that opens cosmic gate.
Your melody makes me vibrate
my sense of self I recreate.

6. A God who could design such a complex universe surely could also design planet earth so it is able to give me the abundant life.

O Cosmic Mother, I will be,
a part of cosmic symphony.
All that I AM, an instrument,
for sound that is from heaven sent.

**Maraytaii, I resonate
with song that opens cosmic gate.
Your melody makes me vibrate
my sense of self I recreate.**

7. God has designed the material universe so that it is capable of providing me with everything I need for my growth in self-awareness.

O Cosmic Mother, I now call,
to enter sacred music hall.
I will be part of life's ascent,
towards the starry firmament.

**Maraytaii, I resonate
with song that opens cosmic gate.
Your melody makes me vibrate
my sense of self I recreate.**

8. Nothing has gone wrong on God's end, meaning the problem is found at the level of human beings.

O Cosmic Mother, tune my strings,
my total being with you sings.
Your song I now reverberate,
as cosmic love I celebrate.

Maraytaii, I resonate
with song that opens cosmic gate.
Your melody makes me vibrate
my sense of self I recreate.

9. I take responsibility for the fact that God is not withholding abundance from me, meaning I must be rejecting it without knowing it.

O Cosmic Mother, I love you,
your love song keeps me ever true.
You fill me with your sacred tone,
and thus I never feel alone.

Maraytaii, I resonate
with song that opens cosmic gate.
Your melody makes me vibrate
my sense of self I recreate.

2. I am a co-creator with God

1. There is something missing from the common image of God, and I desire to know the reality of God.

O Cosmic Mother, sound the gong,
that calls me home where I belong.
I know you love me tenderly,
and in that knowing I am free.

**Maraytaii, I resonate
with song that opens cosmic gate.
Your melody makes me vibrate
my sense of self I recreate.**

2. God has given us human beings dominion over the earth
and the creative ability to actively and consciously alter the
environment.

O Cosmic Mother, hold me tight,
I resonate with your own light.
Your music purifies my heart,
your love to all I do impart.

**Maraytaii, I resonate
with song that opens cosmic gate.
Your melody makes me vibrate
my sense of self I recreate.**

3. My Creator created me in its own image and likeness, meaning
I have a sophisticated self-awareness, imagination and free will.

O Cosmic Mother, we are one,
your heart is like a blazing sun.
My being can but amplify,
the sacred sound you magnify.

**Maraytaii, I resonate
with song that opens cosmic gate.
Your melody makes me vibrate
my sense of self I recreate.**

4. My creative abilities give me the potential to act as an extension of God, as God's hands and feet.

> O Cosmic Mother, I now hear,
> the subtle sound of Sacred Sphere.
> As I attune to Cosmic Hum,
> the lesser self I overcome.

> **Maraytaii, I resonate**
> **with song that opens cosmic gate.**
> **Your melody makes me vibrate**
> **my sense of self I recreate.**

5. I am designed to be a co-creator with God on earth and finish the creation that God started.

> O Cosmic Mother, take me home,
> I am in sync with Sacred OM,
> The sound of sounds will raise me up,
> so only light is in my cup.

> **Maraytaii, I resonate**
> **with song that opens cosmic gate.**
> **Your melody makes me vibrate**
> **my sense of self I recreate.**

6. I was not created to live passively on earth but to play an active role of bringing God's kingdom into full manifestation on this planet.

O Cosmic Mother, I will be,
a part of cosmic symphony.
All that I AM, an instrument,
for sound that is from heaven sent.

Maraytaii, I resonate
with song that opens cosmic gate.
Your melody makes me vibrate
my sense of self I recreate.

7. I acknowledge that deep inside I know I should have abundance, I know that life should be different, that life should be
better than it is right now.

O Cosmic Mother, I now call,
to enter sacred music hall.
I will be part of life's ascent,
towards the starry firmament.

Maraytaii, I resonate
with song that opens cosmic gate.
Your melody makes me vibrate
my sense of self I recreate.

8. I can use my imagination to envision something that is less
than what God wants for me.

O Cosmic Mother, tune my strings,
my total being with you sings.
Your song I now reverberate,
as cosmic love I celebrate.

**Maraytaii, I resonate
with song that opens cosmic gate.
Your melody makes me vibrate
my sense of self I recreate.**

9. I can use my free will to choose to manifest something on this planet that has less abundance than God's original design.

O Cosmic Mother, I love you,
your love song keeps me ever true.
You fill me with your sacred tone,
and thus I never feel alone.

**Maraytaii, I resonate
with song that opens cosmic gate.
Your melody makes me vibrate
my sense of self I recreate.**

3. Abundance is natural

1. I have the potential to build on God's foundation and manifest even more abundance than what nature is designed to provide.

O Cosmic Mother, sound the gong,
that calls me home where I belong.
I know you love me tenderly,
and in that knowing I am free.

**Maraytaii, I resonate
with song that opens cosmic gate.
Your melody makes me vibrate
my sense of self I recreate.**

2. Human society has entered an unnatural state of lack that leads to poverty and inequality.

> O Cosmic Mother, hold me tight,
> I resonate with your own light.
> Your music purifies my heart,
> your love to all I do impart.

> **Maraytaii, I resonate**
> **with song that opens cosmic gate.**
> **Your melody makes me vibrate**
> **my sense of self I recreate.**

3. I know in my heart that inequality, lack and suffering is not natural, is not right, is not what God intended.

> O Cosmic Mother, we are one,
> your heart is like a blazing sun.
> My being can but amplify,
> the sacred sound you magnify.

> **Maraytaii, I resonate**
> **with song that opens cosmic gate.**
> **Your melody makes me vibrate**
> **my sense of self I recreate.**

4. The natural state of affairs on planet earth is that all human beings have abundance of every good and perfect gift.

> O Cosmic Mother, I now hear,
> the subtle sound of Sacred Sphere.
> As I attune to Cosmic Hum,
> the lesser self I overcome.

**Maraytaii, I resonate
with song that opens cosmic gate.
Your melody makes me vibrate
my sense of self I recreate.**

5. Human beings have obstructed the natural state of affairs on earth, have obstructed the flow of God's abundance.

O Cosmic Mother, take me home,
I am in sync with Sacred OM,
The sound of sounds will raise me up,
so only light is in my cup.

**Maraytaii, I resonate
with song that opens cosmic gate.
Your melody makes me vibrate
my sense of self I recreate.**

6. I consciously abandon the belief that I am living on a planet where suffering and lack is inevitable. I accept that abundance is the natural state of affairs.

O Cosmic Mother, I will be,
a part of cosmic symphony.
All that I AM, an instrument,
for sound that is from heaven sent.

**Maraytaii, I resonate
with song that opens cosmic gate.
Your melody makes me vibrate
my sense of self I recreate.**

7. God has designed this planet with every resource necessary to provide the abundant life for all people.

> O Cosmic Mother, I now call,
> to enter sacred music hall.
> I will be part of life's ascent,
> towards the starry firmament.

> **Maraytaii, I resonate**
> **with song that opens cosmic gate.**
> **Your melody makes me vibrate**
> **my sense of self I recreate.**

8. I consciously decide that I am willing to see how I have personally used my imagination and free will to limit, to divert and obstruct the natural flow of God's abundance.

> O Cosmic Mother, tune my strings,
> my total being with you sings.
> Your song I now reverberate,
> as cosmic love I celebrate.

> **Maraytaii, I resonate**
> **with song that opens cosmic gate.**
> **Your melody makes me vibrate**
> **my sense of self I recreate.**

9. I see how I can personally stop obstructing the natural flow of God's abundance. I am inheriting my Father's kingdom and experiencing the abundant life while I am still here on earth.

O Cosmic Mother, I love you,
your love song keeps me ever true.
You fill me with your sacred tone,
and thus I never feel alone.

**Maraytaii, I resonate
with song that opens cosmic gate.
Your melody makes me vibrate
my sense of self I recreate.**

4. I take an active approach

1. I am transcending the passive approach of thinking that since I do not currently have abundance, it must mean that God does not want to give it to me right now.

O Cosmic Mother, sound the gong,
that calls me home where I belong.
I know you love me tenderly,
and in that knowing I am free.

**Maraytaii, I resonate
with song that opens cosmic gate.
Your melody makes me vibrate
my sense of self I recreate.**

2. I will no longer wait and hope that, at some future time, God will change his mind and give me the abundant life.

O Cosmic Mother, hold me tight,
I resonate with your own light.
Your music purifies my heart,
your love to all I do impart.

**Maraytaii, I resonate
with song that opens cosmic gate.
Your melody makes me vibrate
my sense of self I recreate.**

3. I am transcending the belief that I am in a waiting position or a helpless victim of circumstances and forces beyond my control.

O Cosmic Mother, we are one,
your heart is like a blazing sun.
My being can but amplify,
the sacred sound you magnify.

**Maraytaii, I resonate
with song that opens cosmic gate.
Your melody makes me vibrate
my sense of self I recreate.**

4. I consciously decide to take the active approach, and I accept that it is natural for me to have abundance.

O Cosmic Mother, I now hear,
the subtle sound of Sacred Sphere.
As I attune to Cosmic Hum,
the lesser self I overcome.

Maraytaii, I resonate
with song that opens cosmic gate.
Your melody makes me vibrate
my sense of self I recreate.

5. I accept that when I do not have abundance, it is because something in myself is blocking its flow into my life.

O Cosmic Mother, take me home,
I am in sync with Sacred OM,
The sound of sounds will raise me up,
so only light is in my cup.

Maraytaii, I resonate
with song that opens cosmic gate.
Your melody makes me vibrate
my sense of self I recreate.

6. I am seeing what is blocking abundance, and I am removing those blocks. God's abundance is naturally flowing into my life.

O Cosmic Mother, I will be,
a part of cosmic symphony.
All that I AM, an instrument,
for sound that is from heaven sent.

Maraytaii, I resonate
with song that opens cosmic gate.
Your melody makes me vibrate
my sense of self I recreate.

7. God has given me co-creative abilities, which means God will not give me the abundant life. I am using my creative abilities to flow with the River of Life.

O Cosmic Mother, I now call,
to enter sacred music hall.
I will be part of life's ascent,
towards the starry firmament.

**Maraytaii, I resonate
with song that opens cosmic gate.
Your melody makes me vibrate
my sense of self I recreate.**

8. I am uncovering and reactivating my co-creative abilities. I am using them to bring forth abundance for all.

O Cosmic Mother, tune my strings,
my total being with you sings.
Your song I now reverberate,
as cosmic love I celebrate.

**Maraytaii, I resonate
with song that opens cosmic gate.
Your melody makes me vibrate
my sense of self I recreate.**

9. I am receiving the keys to the kingdom and I am accepting the guidance of my ascended teachers.

O Cosmic Mother, I love you,
your love song keeps me ever true.
You fill me with your sacred tone,
and thus I never feel alone.

**Maraytaii, I resonate
with song that opens cosmic gate.
Your melody makes me vibrate
my sense of self I recreate.**

Sealing

In the name of the Divine Mother, I call to Maraytaii and Mother Mary for the sealing of myself and all people in my circle of influence in the creative flow of the Divine Mother, the River of Life. I call for the multiplication of my calls by all representatives of the Divine Mother, so that we form the perfect figure-eight flow of "As Above, so below." Thus, I accept that this is fully manifest, because the mouth of the Lord, the Divine Mother that I AM, has spoken it. Amen.

3 | FREE YOURSELF FROM IMAGES OF LACK

We have now seen that God is fully capable of designing a planet that can sustain human beings in a life of abundance. We have also seen that this state of abundance is not currently manifest on earth. We have reached the conclusion that the only logical explanation of this observable fact is that something has happened in human society that prevents, that blocks, the manifestation of God's will, which is that all of his children should have the abundant life. Our next logical step is to move on to consider what could possibly be blocking the abundant life on earth. In order to understand this, it will be necessary for you to have a greater knowledge of who you are and what you were designed to do before you were sent to a planet that is like a speck of dust in an endless universe. Who are you and why are you here on earth?

In order to answer these questions, I will have to go beyond what you have been taught by the two religions that dominate Western society, namely orthodox Christianity and materialistic science. Both of these belief systems claim that they have the ultimate truth about the

existence of God and the origin of the universe. If you prefer
to believe in one of these claims, then I am unable to teach
you the keys to the abundant life. The essential keys cannot be
found within the confines of either of these two belief systems.
You might wonder why this is so, and the answer is that if either
orthodox Christianity or materialistic science had been able to
provide people with the keys to the abundant life, then surely
that abundant life should have been manifest on earth long ago.
Only those who are willing to look beyond the mental boxes
created by these two belief systems, will find the true keys to
inheriting the abundance of their Father's kingdom.

In order to give you the next key, we need to step back from
the current situation on earth. In fact, we need to step outside
the entire material universe. Jesus said that his Father's house
has many mansions, and as I have mentioned before, there are
other dimensions, other levels, of God's universe. This is what
religious people have traditionally called the heaven world or the
spiritual realm. There are quite a number of these levels of the
heaven world, and given your current scientific knowledge that
everything is energy, it is easy to understand what sets these levels apart from each other. Your scientists know that the material
universe is not, as your senses tell you, made from two elements, namely matter and energy. The material universe is not
truly made from matter; it is made from energy because matter
is simply a form of energy. The importance of this fact is that the
entire matter universe is created from the same substance from
which the spiritual realm, the heaven world, is created. This is
what scientists call energy, but what the Bible calls light. Genesis
tells you how the creation of the universe began. It began with
a command issued by God when he said: "Let there be light!"
(Genesis 1:3) Because God is the Almighty, there *was* light.

Why did God begin the creative process by creating light?
Light, or energy, is a substance that has no form in itself but

that has the potential to take on any form. Even science agrees
with this. Current scientific theory, especially Einstein's famous
equation, $E=mc^2$, states that matter is simply energy that has
taken on visible form. Energy is seen as a form of vibration,
and science has detected many types of energy that can be put
on a scale from lower to higher frequencies. It is not difficult to
reason that the grosser forms of energy, that have taken on the
appearance of physical matter, vibrate in a lower spectrum of
frequencies than finer energies, such as X-rays (that can penetrate "solid" matter) or even finer energies such as thoughts. The
conclusion of these scientific observations is that the universe
was created from invisible, finer or more fundamental energy
that was lowered in vibration until it took on the appearance of
physical energy and physical matter. Scientists cannot currently
explain how this happens, but it will not be long before a scientific explanation will be discovered.

The difference between heaven and earth is a difference
in vibration. Planet earth and the entire material universe is
made from one basic substance that has the ability to take on
an infinite variety of different shapes, forms and characteristics.
This energy, or light, can have many different levels of vibration
so you can set up a scale of vibrations, ranging from slow to
fast, from dense to more pure. As you go from the lower vibrations to the higher vibrations, you will eventually reach a point
where there is an invisible dividing line. Once you cross that
line, you have stepped out of the material universe and into the
spiritual realm. As you keep going from the lower spiritual realm
into higher and higher vibrations, you encounter higher levels
of the spiritual realm. If you keep going to the highest possible
vibration in the entire world of form, you reach the pure light of
God beyond which is the Creator itself. This Creator is a conscious Being who started the creative process, of which you are
a part. The Creator is not the only or the ultimate aspect of what

human beings call God. If you truly step back from the world of form – the world that has been created by molding light into form, by molding formless light into form – you can begin to consider God's true Being. There are religions in this world that say that God, in the ultimate sense, is unknowable. There are religions who describe the ultimate God as "the void" because it has no form and no characteristics that can be described by any of the images or words found in this universe. You will note that the first of the ten commandments states: "Thou shalt have no other Gods before me" (Exodus 20:3). The true meaning is that you can never take unto yourself any particular form, any particular graven image, and claim that this image is a complete representation of God. In the ultimate sense, God is beyond the world of form created by God—the Creator is beyond the creation. As Jesus said: "The servant is not greater than his Lord" (John 13:16). You cannot use words and images from this world and project them upon the ultimate God and claim that you have now created an accurate or complete description of God. This is idol worship, and as we shall see later, it is one of the major problems that prevents the abundant life from being manifest on earth. It is still important to stretch the mind and consider God's Being.

What we *can* say, based on our previous discussion, is that there must be two aspects of God. God in the ultimate sense is all there is: "Without him was not any thing made that was made" (John 1:3), meaning that before anything was created, there existed only God. This God must be a complete and self-sufficient Being. God has no need to create a universe. If God is the Allness, why would God need to create a universe in which there are conscious beings who can know the existence of God? God in the ultimate sense has no need to be known or worshiped by human beings because God is the Allness and is therefore complete and completely self-sufficient. By the mere fact that you exist and that you live in a world that has form – and is therefore different from the Allness in which there is no form – we can see that the ultimate, the self-sufficient and formless, God cannot be the only aspect of God. There must be another aspect, which is what I have called the Creator. This is an aspect of God that desires to create, that desires to be more than the formless void. This is the aspect of God that has created the universe in which you live.

***

How did this God create the universe? The Creator created everything out of its own Being, for there was nothing else but God from which to create. The Creator is different from the formless God in that whereas the formless God is unchanging, the Creator is constantly growing, constantly expanding, constantly self-transcending. When Moses asked God for his name, the answer was: "YOD HE VAW HE," which is commonly translated into English as: "I AM THAT I AM" (Exodus 3:14). In reality, as some Bible scholars know, a more accurate translation is: "I WILL BE WHO I WILL BE." This translation captures the fact that God is true to his own commandments. He did not actually give Moses a name because he did not want people to use even a name to create a graven image, a static image, of God. Instead, the God on the mountain communicated the fact that God is forever changing, and thus God will be who he will be at any moment. In order to know God, you cannot cling to a particular image, you must flow with the self-transcendence of God, you must enter the River of Life that is the All of God's Being, including – but not limited to – the world in which you live.

In the Pure Being of God, in the formless God, there is no change. How could there be change in formlessness? How could there be progression in that which is complete within itself? In the Creator aspect of God, there is constant movement because this aspect of God exists for the purpose of creating and becoming more. What is the Creator? It is a self-aware Being who has three abilities. The first ability is self-awareness, the ability to know that it exists. The second ability is that of imagination, the ability to imagine a form that is not yet manifest in any universe. If there was no imagination in the Creator, how could God possibly create something new? The third ability enjoyed by the Creator is that of the ability to choose. When the Creator created the universe in which you live, it had to make choices. You look at the world in which you live, and you take so many things for granted. Why is the sky blue and not some other color? Why is the earth round and not some other shape? Your scientists are continually finding examples of how intricately and delicately the universe is designed. If the forces that hold the nucleus of the atom together were slightly different in strength, atoms could not hold together and matter would not exist. If the gravitational forces were slightly different, planets and suns could not stay in their orbits. Why are all of these things the way they are? Because when God designed this universe, your Creator made certain choices.

One of the choices made by your Creator was that your God did not want to create an entire universe alone. Your Creator decided to create self-aware beings as an extension of itself and to endow these beings with creative powers, with self-awareness, imagination and free will. That is why the Bible says that God created man in his own image and likeness. God created a number of self-aware beings and these beings are designed to serve as extensions of the Creator. They are designed to travel into the creation started by the Creator itself and to serve as co-creators who can build upon the foundation set by the Creator. We might say that the Creator creates from the outside and the co-creators create from the inside. You can reason about why the Creator did this, and there are many good reasons. The basic fact is that your existence proves that the Creator made this choice. God chose to create you as a self-aware being. You can know that you exist, you have the imagination that makes you able to ask questions about who you are, where you came from and why you are here.

These questions prove that you are not simply the product of a game of chance or a mindless process of evolution. The very fact that you can ask these questions proves that you are the offspring of a self-aware being. That is why you have the ability to imagine that which cannot be perceived by your senses. You also have the ability to formulate a concept or design in your mind and then use your physical body to build a house that is a perfect outpicturing of your mental idea. You have the ability to choose how to design your house. Neither of these abilities are found in the animal kingdom, from which some scientists claim you have evolved. That is why you are of greater value than many birds and that is why God has designed a universe that is perfectly capable of giving you the abundant life that is his true desire. Because the Creator has given you imagination and free will, because God has designed you to be a co-creator with him, the abundant life will not simply be given to you from an outside source. You must use your own imagination and your own free will to manifest that abundant life within your sphere of influence. You must decide to take dominion over the "earth," meaning your own mind and the material realm.

God has created a universe that is capable of giving you the abundant life, but he has not created a universe that will *automatically* give you that abundant life. God has not created you to be a mindless robot but to be a self-aware being with the ability to know who you are, where you came from and where you have the potential to go. I will later explain exactly where you have the potential to go, but for now it is enough to say that you have the potential to make the choice to either manifest the abundant life or to manifest a life of limitations, lack and suffering. You have the ability to choose and you have the ability to imagine, and through these two faculties, you are creating your own experience. You are creating what many people on earth mistakenly call "reality" but which is truly a mere mirage, projected onto the screen of life by the minds of human beings who have forgotten their true creative potential.

Before you can inherit your Father's kingdom, you must understand that you are truly created in the image and likeness of your Creator. This does not mean that the Creator has a physical body and looks like a human being. It does not mean that the Creator talks like Charlton Heston. It means that you are created with the ability to imagine that which is not manifest and the ability to decide which one of your mental images you will bring into physical manifestation, the very same abilities that were used by your Creator to create you and the universe in which you live.

***

We now see a potential answer to the question of what has gone wrong on your end, what has gone wrong on planet earth, that prevents God's desire of the abundant life for all from becoming a manifest reality. The answer is so simple, and it is my highest desire that all human beings could come to understand this one fact. The answer is that the abundant life is not manifest on earth because most human beings have not used their imagination and their free will, have not used their creative abilities, according to their highest potential. Instead of using their creative powers to manifest a life of abundance and to continually increase that abundance, human beings have used their imagination to envision a world with limited abundance, a world in which there is lack. They have chosen to accept this as the only possible reality on planet earth, and in accepting it, they have turned it into a temporary, yet illusory, reality. You now see that because God has given you imagination and free will and because God has not limited his gifts, he allows his children to create a temporary reality that is far less than the abundant life he had envisioned before he sent those children into the material world. In one sense even this is in accordance with the higher will of God because that higher will is that you travel into the world of form and gain experience concerning how to use your creative abilities in a way that is best for yourself and best for the whole of which you are a part.

If it is necessary that, as part of the learning process, you should suffer for some time in a state of lack and limitation, then God allows this to happen. God does not want you to be in a state of limitation. God does not want you to remain in a state of suffering for an indefinite period of time. It is always God's hope that you will eventually come to the point where you decide that you will no longer accept that suffering and lack are inevitable consequences of life on earth. It is always God's hope that some among humankind, and eventually all human beings, will awaken to the reality that life does not have to be suffering, that there is an alternative to the human prison. The alternative is to transcend the state of consciousness that has created the current conditions on earth.

Transcending this limited state of consciousness is precisely what every true religion and every true spiritual teaching is all about. Why do you think Jesus was sent to earth? It was to show you that you do not have to be limited by these human conditions. You can transcend them, you can transform the water of the human consciousness into the wine of a higher state of consciousness. You can multiply the loaves and fishes and thereby increase your material abundance through the power of your mind. You can even escape physical death and be resurrected into a higher state of consciousness, a higher form of life, in a higher realm.

The simple answer to the question of what has gone wrong, what has stopped God's abundance from being manifest on earth, is that human beings have misused their creative abilities. They have lost the clear vision of God's abundant life. Instead, most people have focused their imagination on a false image that is based on the concept that God's abundance is limited and that there is not enough for everyone. Only a few people can have abundance and the majority of the population must live in poverty. Humankind has been manipulated into using its free will to accept this false image and to accept it as inevitable. This is why the false image has become a temporary reality that for many people seem to be a permanent reality.

***

The key you need in order to experience the abundant life is the realization that you do not have to personally accept this false image, this pseudo reality. You can choose to separate yourself from that false image, you can separate yourself in consciousness. By transcending your current state of consciousness, you can rise and free your imagination and will so that you can finally accept the abundant life rather than the limited life. The essential key to inheriting your Father's kingdom is to realize that you must use your free will to purify your imagination so that you can create the abundant life instead of continuing to create a life of limitation and suffering. It is the Father's good pleasure to give you the kingdom, yet his design is to give you creative powers so that you can bring forth that kingdom from within yourself. If you want true abundance, you must contemplate and absorb Jesus' statement that: "The kingdom of God is within you" (Luke 17:21). You cannot look for an external God to give you the kingdom.

When you realize that you have the ability within yourself to recreate your life experience on earth, that you have the ability to recreate every aspect of your life experience on earth, you have taken the essential step on the path of returning to your Father's kingdom. I know full well that you have been programmed to believe that what you see around you is an inescapable reality and that you do not have the ability within you to free yourself from that supposed reality. Jesus came for one purpose only, namely to show you that this illusion is a lie and that you do have the kingdom of God within you. The reason is that God designed you in his image and likeness. God gave you imagination and free will. The only reason you are currently experiencing limitations, lack and suffering is that you, and a large number of the people on this planet, have used your imagination and free will to co-create that limitation and that suffering. When you begin to free your imagination and to use your free will in a way that is in alignment with the creative principles of God, you can recreate your life experience. When enough people do this, you can recreate the collective experience on this planet. You can literally co-create a reality that reflects God's true desire for this planet, a planet that sustains billions of people who all have the abundant life.

Through your life experiences and your upbringing on this planet, you have been programmed to think that the current limitations on earth are real and unavoidable. Perhaps some miracle from God can change it, but such a miracle obviously is not forthcoming. You have been programmed to think that you do not have the creative powers within yourself to recreate your life experience, and thus you are a slave of outer circumstances that are beyond your control. These are illusions, these are lies, that have nothing to do with the reality of God. The reality is that the Creator gave you its own creative abilities. God created you in his image and likeness so that you have the power within yourself to co-create the abundant life around you. Collectively, even a small number of human beings can recreate the abundant life on earth. This is the truth that Jesus came to bring, this is the truth that the Buddha came to bring, this is the truth that all true spiritual leaders, prophets and representatives of God have come to bring. When you realize this one truth, you can start walking a systematic, logical path that leads you step by step to the point of recreating your life in alignment with the abundant vision, the immaculate concept, held in the mind of God.

The rest of this course will be focused on giving you the understanding and the practical steps that you need in order to free yourself from all false images of God, all false images of yourself and all false images of the universe in which you live. I will help you be who you were designed to be. I will help you exercise your imagination and free will in a way that will give you the abundant life you desire and that will simultaneously bring about the abundant life for all other life forms on this planet.

***

It truly is the Father's good pleasure to give you the kingdom. The Creator wants you to feel that you are bringing about that kingdom through your own creative powers, that you are manifesting the kingdom through your God-given ability to be a co-creator with your God. This is God's desire, this is why God sent human beings into the earth with the command to "multiply" and "have dominion" (Genesis 1:28). He meant for you to multiply your creative abilities and to use your mind to take dominion over the matter universe itself so that you can bring into this matter universe the abundance of God. By you taking this dominion, the dominion of mind over matter, this matter universe can outpicture the perfection of God and therefore become, truly, the kingdom of God.

God has the ability to create a planet that permanently has the abundant life. God did not want to do this because how could you have learned from living on such a planet? You would have been reduced to an adaptive being, an animal, rather than a self-aware co-creator. God created a planet that had the potential to manifest the abundant life but did not yet have the abundant life in full physical manifestation. He then sent his sons and daughters into this world, and they had everything they needed – they had the creative abilities, they had the imagination and free will – to take dominion over this planet and bring God's abundance into physical manifestation. They could build on the foundation set by God so that through their own innate, God-given abilities the sons and daughters of God could build the kingdom of God on planet earth.

This is God's original plan, this is God's original desire, this is God's original design. Nothing has altered God's plan, nothing has altered the potential for planet earth to outpicture the perfection of God. On a temporary basis the sons and daughters of God have chosen to use their creative abilities to create suffering and lack rather than abundance. This has happened only because they have fallen into a state of ignorance so they do not recognize their full creative abilities. They do not understand the importance and power of their free will, they do not understand the vastness and the potential of their imagination, they do not understand that they don't have to be limited by imperfect images but that they can recreate even physical reality through the power of their minds.

The physical reality, the state of lack, that you experience on this planet, was not created by God—it was created by the collective consciousness of humankind. This was done through the power of the mind, namely by people imagining a state of lack and then using their willpower to accept it as permanent and inevitable. My beloved, please compare these concepts to one of the most important statements made by Jesus: "No servant can serve two masters: for either he will hate the one, and love the other; or else he will hold to the one, and despise the other. Ye cannot serve God and mammon" (Luke 16:13). The more spiritual interpretation of this statement is that "mammon" is a symbol for the human state of consciousness, the state of accepting lack and limitation as inevitable. This causes people to spend their entire lives accumulating the things of this world – mammon – instead of bringing forth abundance directly from God's infinite supply. Jesus was saying that you must choose which master you will serve, the false image of lack created by the collective consciousness or the reality of God's abundant life. Jesus was saying that you cannot serve both of these masters at the same time, which truly means that you cannot be in two mutually exclusive states of consciousness at the same time. You cannot remain true to God's abundant reality and at the same time accept the man-made images of lack and suffering. You must focus your mind on one "reality" or the other, and whatever image you focus upon is what you will bring into your physical experience. The matter substance itself will take on the forms that you hold in your mind. Your creative powers will bring about, in your physical experience, what you hold in your mind. If you want God's abundance, you must serve the true master of God's reality, and you must stop serving the false master of human illusions. You must do the work of freeing your imagination of all false images and beliefs. You must use your free will to choose to realign yourself with the creative principles that God used to define this universe.

Only by going through this transformation of consciousness, can you free yourself from the taskmaster who has currently imprisoned you in a box of limitations and suffering, a box that truly exists only in your mind and in the collective consciousness. The state of consciousness that most people currently accept as their reality is a state that Jesus called "death," meaning spiritual death. If you want to escape the human prison, you must choose the higher state of consciousness, the consciousness of life.

Ponder the statement from the Old Testament: "I call heaven and earth to record this day against you, that I have set before you life and death, blessing and cursing: therefore choose life, that both thou and thy seed may live" (Deuteronomy 30:19). God has given you the imagination that allows you to accept either a true image or a false image. God has given you the free will to choose which image you will bring into manifestation in this universe. You have – at this very moment – the potential to free yourself from the shackles of the consciousness of death and to enter into the consciousness of life, which is the only doorway that leads to your Father's kingdom. This state of consciousness is the Universal Christ Mind, and Jesus described it when he said: "I am the way, the truth, and the life: no man cometh unto the Father, but by me" (John 14:6).

Are you ready to follow me on a journey that will help you rediscover your true creative abilities and help you free yourself from the shackles of mortality and limitation that have been put upon you? Are you ready to rise and become the true son or daughter that you were designed to be when your Creator designed you in his own image and after his own likeness? If you are ready, then take my hand as I give you more keys to the abundant life.

4 | I INVOKE A NEW LIFE EXPERIENCE

In the name I AM THAT I AM, Jesus Christ, I call to all representatives of the Divine Mother, especially Nada and Mother Mary, to help me fully accept that God will not give me abundance from an external source. Help me learn to use my ability to bring forth abundance from inside myself and overcome all blocks to my ability to manifest abundance, including...

[Make personal calls.]

1. I choose abundance

1. The physical "reality," the state of lack, that we experience on this planet was not created by God. It was created by our collective consciousness.

> O Nada, blessed cosmic grace,
> filling up my inner space.
> Your song is like a sacred balm,
> my mind a sea of perfect calm.

With Nada's secret melody,
my mind remains forever free.
Conducting Nada's symphony,
eternal peace I do decree.

2. This was done by people imagining a state of lack and then using their willpower to accept it as permanent and inevitable.

O Nada, in your Buddhic mind,
my inner peace I truly find.
As I your song reverberate,
your love I do assimilate.

With Nada's secret melody,
my mind remains forever free.
Conducting Nada's symphony,
eternal peace I do decree.

3. I cannot serve God and mammon, I cannot be in the human state of consciousness, the state of accepting lack and limitation as inevitable, while at the same time having the abundant life.

O Nada, beauty so sublime,
I follow you beyond all time.
In soundless sound we do immerse,
to recreate the universe.

With Nada's secret melody,
my mind remains forever free.
Conducting Nada's symphony,
eternal peace I do decree.

4. I have the ability to imagine that which cannot be perceived by my senses, the ability to formulate a concept or design in my mind and then project it onto the basic light substance that will outpicture my mental idea.

> O Nada, future we predict
> where nothing Christhood can restrict.
> With Buddhic mind we do perceive,
> a better future we conceive.

> **With Nada's secret melody,**
> **my mind remains forever free.**
> **Conducting Nada's symphony,**
> **eternal peace I do decree.**

5. Because my Creator has given me imagination and free will, the abundant life will not be given to me from an outside source.

> O Nada, future we rewrite,
> where might is never, ever right.
> Instead, the mind of Christ is king,
> we see the Christ in every thing.

> **With Nada's secret melody,**
> **my mind remains forever free.**
> **Conducting Nada's symphony,**
> **eternal peace I do decree.**

6. I am using my own imagination and free will to manifest the abundant life within my sphere of influence. I am taking dominion over my own mind and the material realm.

O Nada, peace is now the norm,
my Spirit is beyond all form.
To form I will no more adapt,
I use potential yet untapped.

**With Nada's secret melody,
my mind remains forever free.
Conducting Nada's symphony,
eternal peace I do decree.**

7. I am making the choice to manifest the abundant life.

O Nada, such resplendent joy,
my life I truly can enjoy.
I am allowed to have some fun,
my solar plexus like a sun.

**With Nada's secret melody,
my mind remains forever free.
Conducting Nada's symphony,
eternal peace I do decree.**

8. I have the ability to imagine that which is not manifest and the ability to decide which one of my mental images I will bring into physical manifestation.

O Nada, service is the key,
to living in reality.
For I see now that life is one,
my highest service has begun.

With Nada's secret melody,
my mind remains forever free.
Conducting Nada's symphony,
eternal peace I do decree.

9. I am creating my own experience because I have the very same abilities that were used by my Creator to create me and the universe in which I live.

O Nada, we do now decree,
that life on earth shall be carefree.
With Jesus we complete the quest,
God's kingdom is now manifest.

With Nada's secret melody,
my mind remains forever free.
Conducting Nada's symphony,
eternal peace I do decree.

2. I rise above suffering

1. God does not want me to remain in a state of suffering for an indefinite period of time.

O Nada, blessed cosmic grace,
filling up my inner space.
Your song is like a sacred balm,
my mind a sea of perfect calm.

With Nada's secret melody,
my mind remains forever free.
Conducting Nada's symphony,
eternal peace I do decree.

2. Life does not have to be suffering. I am transcending the state of consciousness that has created the current conditions on earth.

O Nada, in your Buddhic mind,
my inner peace I truly find.
As I your song reverberate,
your love I do assimilate.

With Nada's secret melody,
my mind remains forever free.
Conducting Nada's symphony,
eternal peace I do decree.

3. I am transcending all human conditions. I am transforming the water of the human consciousness into the wine of a higher state of consciousness.

O Nada, beauty so sublime,
I follow you beyond all time.
In soundless sound we do immerse,
to recreate the universe.

With Nada's secret melody,
my mind remains forever free.
Conducting Nada's symphony,
eternal peace I do decree.

4. I am transcending physical death, and I am resurrected into a higher state of consciousness, a higher form of life.

O Nada, future we predict
where nothing Christhood can restrict.
With Buddhic mind we do perceive,
a better future we conceive.

**With Nada's secret melody,
my mind remains forever free.
Conducting Nada's symphony,
eternal peace I do decree.**

5. I am transcending the false image of lack. I am separating myself from that false image, separating myself in consciousness.

O Nada, future we rewrite,
where might is never, ever right.
Instead, the mind of Christ is king,
we see the Christ in every thing.

**With Nada's secret melody,
my mind remains forever free.
Conducting Nada's symphony,
eternal peace I do decree.**

6. I am transcending my current state of consciousness. I am freeing my imagination and will, and I accept the abundant life rather than the limited life.

O Nada, peace is now the norm,
my Spirit is beyond all form.
To form I will no more adapt,
I use potential yet untapped.

**With Nada's secret melody,
my mind remains forever free.
Conducting Nada's symphony,
eternal peace I do decree.**

7. I consciously decide to use my free will to purify my imagination. I am creating the abundant life instead of continuing to create a life of limitation and suffering.

O Nada, such resplendent joy,
my life I truly can enjoy.
I am allowed to have some fun,
my solar plexus like a sun.

**With Nada's secret melody,
my mind remains forever free.
Conducting Nada's symphony,
eternal peace I do decree.**

8. God wants me to have abundance and God's design is to give me creative powers. I am bringing forth abundance from within myself.

O Nada, service is the key,
to living in reality.
For I see now that life is one,
my highest service has begun.

With Nada's secret melody,
my mind remains forever free.
Conducting Nada's symphony,
eternal peace I do decree.

9. I acknowledge the reality of Jesus' statement that the kingdom of God is within me. I will no longer look for an external God to give me abundance.

O Nada, we do now decree,
that life on earth shall be carefree.
With Jesus we complete the quest,
God's kingdom is now manifest.

With Nada's secret melody,
my mind remains forever free.
Conducting Nada's symphony,
eternal peace I do decree.

3. I recreate my life experience

1. I have the ability within myself to recreate my life experience. I am recreating every aspect of my life experience.

O Nada, blessed cosmic grace,
filling up my inner space.
Your song is like a sacred balm,
my mind a sea of perfect calm.

With Nada's secret melody,
my mind remains forever free.
Conducting Nada's symphony,
eternal peace I do decree.

2. What I see around me is not an inescapable reality. I am freeing myself from the temporary conditions on earth.

O Nada, in your Buddhic mind,
my inner peace I truly find.
As I your song reverberate,
your love I do assimilate.

With Nada's secret melody,
my mind remains forever free.
Conducting Nada's symphony,
eternal peace I do decree.

3. I am helping to co-create a reality that reflects God's true
desire for this planet, a planet that sustains billions of people
who all have the abundant life.

O Nada, beauty so sublime,
I follow you beyond all time.
In soundless sound we do immerse,
to recreate the universe.

With Nada's secret melody,
my mind remains forever free.
Conducting Nada's symphony,
eternal peace I do decree.

4. I have the creative powers within myself to recreate my life experience because the Creator gave me its own creative abilities.

O Nada, future we predict
where nothing Christhood can restrict.
With Buddhic mind we do perceive,
a better future we conceive.

With Nada's secret melody,
my mind remains forever free.
Conducting Nada's symphony,
eternal peace I do decree.

5. I am walking a systematic, logical path that leads me step by step to the point of recreating my life in alignment with the abundant vision, the immaculate concept, held in the mind of God.

O Nada, future we rewrite,
where might is never, ever right.
Instead, the mind of Christ is king,
we see the Christ in every thing.

With Nada's secret melody,
my mind remains forever free.
Conducting Nada's symphony,
eternal peace I do decree.

6. I am freeing myself from all false images of God, all false images of myself and all false images of the universe in which I live.

O Nada, peace is now the norm,
my Spirit is beyond all form.
To form I will no more adapt,
I use potential yet untapped.

**With Nada's secret melody,
my mind remains forever free.
Conducting Nada's symphony,
eternal peace I do decree.**

7. I am being who I was designed to be. I am exercising my
imagination and free will in a way that is giving me the abundant
life and that is bringing about the abundant life for all other life
forms on this planet.

O Nada, such resplendent joy,
my life I truly can enjoy.
I am allowed to have some fun,
my solar plexus like a sun.

**With Nada's secret melody,
my mind remains forever free.
Conducting Nada's symphony,
eternal peace I do decree.**

8. My Creator wants me to feel that I am bringing about the
abundant life through my own creative powers, that I am manifesting it by being a co-creator with my God.

O Nada, service is the key,
to living in reality.
For I see now that life is one,
my highest service has begun.

With Nada's secret melody,
my mind remains forever free.
Conducting Nada's symphony,
eternal peace I do decree.

9. I am multiplying my creative abilities and using my mind to take dominion over the matter universe itself. I am bringing into manifestation the abundance of God.

O Nada, we do now decree,
that life on earth shall be carefree.
With Jesus we complete the quest,
God's kingdom is now manifest.

With Nada's secret melody,
my mind remains forever free.
Conducting Nada's symphony,
eternal peace I do decree.

4. I choose life

1. I will not spend my life accumulating the things of this world. I am bringing forth abundance directly from God's infinite supply.

O Nada, blessed cosmic grace,
filling up my inner space.
Your song is like a sacred balm,
my mind a sea of perfect calm.

With Nada's secret melody,
my mind remains forever free.
Conducting Nada's symphony,
eternal peace I do decree.

2. I hereby choose which master I will serve. I no longer serve
the false image of lack created by the collective consciousness. I
serve the reality of God's abundant life.

O Nada, in your Buddhic mind,
my inner peace I truly find.
As I your song reverberate,
your love I do assimilate.

With Nada's secret melody,
my mind remains forever free.
Conducting Nada's symphony,
eternal peace I do decree.

3. I cannot be in two mutually exclusive states of consciousness
at the same time. I hereby choose to stop serving the false master of human illusions. I am serving the true master of God's
reality.

O Nada, beauty so sublime,
I follow you beyond all time.
In soundless sound we do immerse,
to recreate the universe.

With Nada's secret melody,
my mind remains forever free.
Conducting Nada's symphony,
eternal peace I do decree.

4. The matter substance itself will take on the forms that I hold in my mind. My creative powers will bring about, in my physical experience, what I hold in my mind.

> O Nada, future we predict
> where nothing Christhood can restrict.
> With Buddhic mind we do perceive,
> a better future we conceive.

> **With Nada's secret melody,**
> **my mind remains forever free.**
> **Conducting Nada's symphony,**
> **eternal peace I do decree.**

5. I am freeing my imagination of all false images and beliefs. I choose to realign myself with the creative principles that God used to define this universe.

> O Nada, future we rewrite,
> where might is never, ever right.
> Instead, the mind of Christ is king,
> we see the Christ in every thing.

> **With Nada's secret melody,**
> **my mind remains forever free.**
> **Conducting Nada's symphony,**
> **eternal peace I do decree.**

6. I am freeing myself from the taskmaster who has currently imprisoned me in a box of limitations and suffering, a box that truly exists only in my mind and in the collective consciousness.

O Nada, peace is now the norm,
my Spirit is beyond all form.
To form I will no more adapt,
I use potential yet untapped.

With Nada's secret melody,
my mind remains forever free.
Conducting Nada's symphony,
eternal peace I do decree.

7. The state of consciousness that most people currently accept as their reality is a state that Jesus called "death," meaning spiritual death.

O Nada, such resplendent joy,
my life I truly can enjoy.
I am allowed to have some fun,
my solar plexus like a sun.

With Nada's secret melody,
my mind remains forever free.
Conducting Nada's symphony,
eternal peace I do decree.

8. I am choosing – at this very moment – to free myself from the shackles of the consciousness of death. I am entering the consciousness of life, which is the only doorway that leads to my Father's kingdom.

O Nada, service is the key,
to living in reality.
For I see now that life is one,
my highest service has begun.

With Nada's secret melody,
my mind remains forever free.
Conducting Nada's symphony,
eternal peace I do decree.

9. In oneness with the Universal Christ Mind, I say with Jesus:
"I am the way, the truth, and the life: no man cometh unto the
Father, but by me"

O Nada, we do now decree,
that life on earth shall be carefree.
With Jesus we complete the quest,
God's kingdom is now manifest.

With Nada's secret melody,
my mind remains forever free.
Conducting Nada's symphony,
eternal peace I do decree.

Sealing

In the name of the Divine Mother, I call to Nada and Mother
Mary for the sealing of myself and all people in my circle of
influence in the creative flow of the Divine Mother, the River of
Life. I call for the multiplication of my calls by all representatives
of the Divine Mother, so that we form the perfect figure-eight
flow of "As Above, so below." Thus, I accept that this is fully
manifest, because the mouth of the Lord, the Divine Mother
that I AM, has spoken it. Amen.

5 | ACTIVELY RECEIVING ABUNDANCE

I am well aware that what I have told you in these first keys goes far beyond what you were taught in Sunday school. It goes far beyond what you would have been taught in any orthodox religion on this planet. I am also aware that those who are open to this course have already started realizing, deep within their hearts, that there is more to life than what they were told in school or Sunday school. They are willing to look beyond traditional mental boxes in order to find answers to their questions about life. Nevertheless, we need to address the simple fact that so many religions in this world promote an image of God that portrays him as being outside of yourself, as being some remote entity up in the sky. Unfortunately, some religions, especially in the West, portray that God as an angry and judgmental being.

Certain religious authorities have set themselves up in a position where they think they have the right to judge anyone who does not comply with what they believe is the only true teaching about God. Many of these people are quick to judge, and they claim that anyone who speaks about ideas that are not approved according to their interpretation of the Bible is speaking blasphemy or is a representative of anti-christ. They will even say this about the true spiritual teachers of humankind, the very Beings who have dedicated their lives to setting humanity free from the bondage of all graven images. At the core of any type of blasphemy is the denial of God. The image of God promoted by many religions is based on a very subtle denial of God. Any religion that promotes an image of an external God and claims that this is all there is to know about God, or that this is the only true image of God, is in fact promoting a philosophy that springs from the denial of God. It is most unfortunate that many Christian churches do indeed uphold this image of the external God, the angry God in the sky.

If Christians would read their Bible more carefully – with an open mind and heart – they would see that Jesus himself taught about a God that is not external. Jesus talked about a God that can be known on a personal basis, and he called that God "Father." He also talked about the Old Testament quote: "Ye are Gods" (John 10:34), and he made the statement that people should not look for the kingdom of God outside themselves because the kingdom of God is within you (Luke 17:21). When you add to this the fact that the Gospel of John clearly states that without God was not anything made that was made (John 1:3), you see that there is a greater understanding of God waiting for you behind the image of an external God in the sky. Only those who are willing to let go of their idols of the external God, will be able to know the true God. That God cannot be known through the outer senses or through the human intellect. That God can be known only through the inner sense – the innocence – of your intuition, which is the key to any spiritual or mystical experience. Through such an experience, you can know the reality of God, you can know the Presence of God right within yourself, as Jesus clearly promised. The truth that Jesus preached, a truth that has been obscured by orthodox doctrine, is that you are the offspring of God, you are a son or daughter of God, you are an individualization of God. You were created in God's image and likeness, and the key to finding your true identity is to go within and reconnect to your higher self, your spiritual self, or what we call the "I AM Presence." I like this name because it truly is this Presence that gives you the self-awareness that empowers you to know that "I am."

Before you can come to fully accept who you are and why you are here on earth, you need to be willing to let go of the image of the external God. There *is* a God who is the Almighty Creator of heaven and earth, and that God is a self-aware Being. The image that this God is a Being with a particular form, residing in some higher world, is a graven image that limits the reality of your Creator. Your Creator cannot be confined to a particular being residing in that higher realm, and the reason is simple. As the Gospel of John states: "Without him was not anything made that was made," which means that the Creator created everything out of its own substance and Being. The Creator is within everything that it has created. In order for you to fulfill your rightful role as a co-creator, you need to overcome the consciousness of separation, which denies God where you are—and thus it is truly the consciousness of anti-christ, the source of all blasphemy.

***

For thousands of years human beings have been programmed to worship a God that exists somewhere in heaven but is not found on earth. They have been brought up with a dualistic view of God, which says that you are *here* and God is *somewhere else.* You are separated from God by some impenetrable barrier, and the only way for you to be saved and get back to God's kingdom is to follow the dictates of an outer religion, which will then save you and take you home.

Jesus' primary goal was to shatter this image of the external God. He came to help people stop the idol worship and overcome the illusion that they are separated from their God and that they need something or someone from outside themselves in order to reconnect to their God and be saved. What do you think it really means when Jesus said that the kingdom of God is within you? It means that you do not need an outer church in order to reach the kingdom of God. You do not need an elite of a priesthood who claims that you can only be saved by following their every dictate. These are the exact priests that opposed everything Jesus did, and these are the priests, the false preachers, who killed my son and your spiritual brother.

In every age, there has been a small elite of human beings who are completely convinced that they know the absolute truth about God. What they consider the absolute truth is actually an illusion about the external God that is separated from his creation. This is indeed the central problem that you see on planet earth. This is where suffering, pain and limitations begin. Every limitation known to human beings begins with the mindset that you can divide God's creation into separate spheres and that in this sphere, the material universe, God is not found.

This very belief is truly the root of all evil because it allows the self-aware beings who are designed to be co-creators with God to set aside their true identity and to start thinking that they can do whatever they want in this universe and get away with it. It is the consciousness of separation, separation from the Allness of God's creation and thereby separation from other people, that gives rise to man's inhumanity to man. This very consciousness has allowed human beings to use their creative abilities, the abilities given to them by God, to create a world view that is entirely based on an illusion. Humankind has collectively used the imagination and free will given by God to create the illusion that the material world is so dense that God is not found here. This allows some people to believe that God's laws are not working in this world and that they have separated themselves from God's laws and created their own laws—they have become a law unto themselves. They think they have created their own reality where they can define the laws in their own favor so that they can do whatever they want without reaping the consequences, without reaping what they have sown.

This entire mindset obscures the reality of God from the view of human beings. The reality is that God is not mocked (Galatians 6:7) and that his laws are not affected by the beliefs of human beings. It was not that long ago that the Catholic Church promoted the belief that the earth was the center of the universe and that all the stars in heaven revolved around it. As you know today, that is not the case, and neither was it the case when everyone believed it to be true. The earth was not flat when everyone believed it to be flat. The reason being that believing does not make it so if that belief is in conflict with the reality of God. A belief may temporarily obscure the reality of God in the minds of those who worship the belief as fact, those who worship a graven image.

The reality is that when God created the material universe and created self-aware extensions of himself, self-aware beings who have imagination and free will, God was well aware that when he gave you unlimited imagination and free will, it was possible that you could use those faculties in a way that would be destructive to yourself and to other parts of God's creation. Many human beings are currently trapped in a state of consciousness in which they are so focused on themselves, what they see as their own identity, that they are literally unable to consider any other part of life. They are completely unwilling to consider how their actions affect other people. It should not be difficult for you to look at today's headlines and find examples of extreme selfishness, people who act as if other people do not matter and as if they can get away with doing anything they want because they have power or money. When God created you, he did not create you alone, he did not create the entire universe exclusively for *your* pleasure. God created many self-aware beings and they are all created out of God's own Being and substance. They are all part of what we in heaven call the Body of God.

The "Body of God" is a concept that you might keep in mind because you know very well that even though your little toe is a relatively insignificant part of your body, if you hurt that little toe, it will affect your general feeling of well-being. A sharp pain in your little toe can make your entire being feel very uncomfortable, and thus when you hurt other people, it will inevitably affect your life experience. When God created this universe, he did not design it exclusively for *you*. He designed it in such a way that all of his sons and daughters would have equal opportunity to learn from using their creative abilities. In doing so, God knew that he would have to build a safety mechanism into the very design of the universe. If a few of his sons and daughters forgot that they were part of the Body of God and started acting as if they were the only ones who mattered, then these few could not destroy all of their brothers and sisters or destroy the entire universe.

If a society had no laws that would hold people accountable for their actions, such a society would deteriorate into lawlessness and anarchy. Those who are the most aggressive, the most ruthless, and those who will not consider others, would have an unfair advantage over the honest and loving people. You need to ask yourself very seriously whether you believe God designed the entire universe to give an advantage to the unloving, dishonest and selfish beings or whether he designed the universe with a built-in safety mechanism that would ensure that those who become selfish cannot destroy the entire universe and cannot ultimately destroy or control their brothers and sisters.

***

Let me now explain one of the safety mechanisms that God built into the fundamental design of the universe in which you live. The Creator of your universe is an expanding force, an expanding Being. This is what we might call the Father aspect of God. It is the drive to become more, the drive to self-transcend, for without it nothing would have been created out of the All-ness of God—no form would have emerged from the formless and self-sufficient God. Your Creator, your God, is a consuming fire that consumes all unlike itself in an ever-expanding cycle of self-transcendence. An expanding force cannot create a form that is sustainable even for a second. If the universe had only the expanding force, nothing would be sustainable; everything would be a big explosion with no form whatsoever. Your scientists currently favor the theory of the Big Bang, which says that the entire universe started in a giant explosion. If indeed there was only the expanding force of the Father, then the universe would be one continuous explosion where no form could be sustained because it would instantly be blown apart by the expanding force. In order to create forms that are sustainable, God had to create a force that will balance the expanding force of the Father. That force is the contracting force of the Mother, and it was this force that was brought into existence when God said: "Let there be light." Light is the substance that can be molded into form, and once it is molded into a particular form, it will retain that form for some time.

Light is an expression of the contracting force of the Mother, and the entire universe in which you live is created through a harmonious and balanced interaction between these two basic

forces. The expanding force of the Father supplements the contracting force of the Mother, the expanding force of the Father
acts upon the light substance of the Mother and stirs it from
its ground state into a particular form. When only the expanding force of the Father acts upon the Mother Light, the form
created directly by the Father is sustainable indefinitely. When
God created self-aware extensions of himself, he knew full well
that these beings were inexperienced when it came to using
their creative powers. It was quite possible that they could use
their imagination to envision forms that were not beneficial for
themselves or for the whole. He also knew that whereas some
might create imperfect forms without realizing what they were
doing, others might actually misuse their free will to deliberately
rebel against God's design of this universe. God knew that it
was necessary that his sons and daughters went through a learning period in which they could expand their understanding of
who they are and how the world works. After learning this, they
could use their creative abilities to magnify the whole instead of
destroying the whole and themselves.

Once again, God wants the entire universe to serve not just
one individual being but to serve the entire Body of God. God
had to make sure that one individual being could not misuse its
creative powers to such an extent that it destroyed the universe
or a part of it, and therefore destroyed the platform of growth
for other sons and daughters of God. To accomplish this, God
built intelligence into the Mother Light. The natural tendency
of the Mother Light is to always be in a ground state, in a state
where no form is expressed. The Mother Light cannot create by
itself. It needs the force of a self-aware being who acts upon the
Mother Light by directing the expanding force of the Father.
Then the Mother Light takes on the form held in the mind of
the self-aware being, the co-creator. The Mother Light has a
tendency to always return to its ground state where there is no

manifest form. This is the safety mechanism that makes sure that no individual co-creator can misuse his or her creative abilities to the point of destroying the whole of God's creation.

***

What I will explain to you next is a subtle principle that the human intellect will find is difficult to grasp. If you will think with your heart and use your intuition, you will come to understand what I will now explain. I have told you that the Mother Light has a built-in force that causes it to maintain its ground state in which light exists but it has no distinguishable form; it is undifferentiated. What will it take to give that Mother Light form? It will take a conscious mind that has the creative abilities of God, namely imagination and free will. That conscious mind must be able to imagine a form, even though it is not yet manifest. The mind must have the power of will to impose that form upon the Mother Light and thereby stir that light away from its ground state. The Mother Light gives birth to an expressed form that can be distinguished from the ground state.

In the beginning, only God the Creator had this creative power. God used his creative powers to envision a universe, a world of form, that would become a platform of growth for his sons and daughters. In order to create anything that has form, God had to make certain choices. God can imagine many different types of universes, but when it comes to manifesting a particular universe, God has to choose how that universe will be designed. Scientists are continually discovering new facets of the delicate nature of the forces that hold this universe together, and this shows you that God made certain choices when he designed this universe. If those forces were to be disturbed even slightly, the entire universe could collapse in an instant. Your Creator created this universe with an unconditional love for you and a pure desire to create a world that would be the best possible platform for your growth. I realize that life on earth can be very difficult and painful and that many people have been brought up with a hidden or recognized anger against God. They have been brought up to see God as the external God, the angry God in the sky, who has unfairly imposed his will upon them and caused them to suffer. Some people have even suffered so much that they have come to the point where they are angry at God for the very fact that they exist.

None of the imperfections you see on earth were created by God and they were not part of God's original design for this universe. God originally envisioned a universe in which all of his sons and daughters would live in constant abundance, an abundance that they could increase through their own creative powers. God did not envision, even for an instant, the current conditions on earth. The suffering and pain that you see all over this planet is simply beyond God's imagination. He never envisioned that such conditions would exist in his world because, as the Bible says, his eyes cannot look upon iniquity (Habakkuk 1:13). Yet he also knew that in giving his co-creators imagination and free will, they could indeed create conditions that were not according to his vision.

I ask you to ponder in your heart the very reality that God had only the best and most loving intentions for the design of this universe. He did not design it to give you suffering, he did not design it to make you feel like a miserable sinner, he did not design it to make you think you are a mortal human being who will go to hell unless you follow the dictates of some outer church or an external deity. God designed the universe to serve as the best possible platform for the expansion of your creative abilities so that you could transcend yourself and become a god-free being who has complete awareness of who you are and how your actions affect the whole of which you are a part. You are not separate from that whole, you *are* the whole but a particular expression of it.

When God designed this particular universe, he made certain choices. Those choices defined the basic forces that hold the universe together. Behind those choices are certain creative principles, and the most fundamental of these principles was not even decided by your Creator. It is the principle that is built into creation itself because any creation, any manifest form, springs out of God's drive to be more. The universal principle of all creation is that creation never stops, that it is an ongoing process. The basic law of creation, the basic law of life, is that you cannot stand still, that no form can ever be permanent and that any self-aware being must continually transcend itself and become more by expanding its awareness of its creative powers, its true identity and its oneness with the whole of God's creation.

This is the driving force behind all creation, without which nothing would be created. Even though you have been given unlimited imagination and free will, you cannot use those creative abilities to create a particular sense of identity for yourself and then remain in that sense of identity forever. God has given you free will so God has given you the right to create the sense of identity that you are a miserable sinner, living on a planet dominated by suffering, and that you will go to hell unless you believe the dictates of an outer church created by other miserable sinners. The very life force itself demands that you cannot remain in that limited sense of identity forever. If you do attempt to hold on to that limited sense of identity, then the contracting force of the Mother will act as the safety mechanism that breaks down your limited, unbalanced creation—as it broke down the Tower of Babel (Genesis 11:4). This will happen because when you create a limited sense of identity, the contracting force will instantly begin to break down that identity and even the material forms that spring from your sense of identity. After some time, the contracting force of the Mother will inevitably win, and your sense of identity will be challenged. You will then be forced to confront the choice described in the Bible: "Choose you this day whom ye will serve" (Joshua 24:15). The question is: "Will you serve life, which means growth, or will you serve death, which means stillstand that ultimately leads to self-annihilation?" Your basic choice is self-transcendence or self-annihilation. That is why Moses said: "Choose life" (Deuteronomy 30:19). Choose to grow and expand your limited sense of identity.

***

I know these teachings can seem abstract so let me try to make them more practical by comparing them to something in your everyday experience. You know very well that the engineers who designed your car did so by using certain laws of nature, certain design principles. In order to design a car that does what you want it to do, they have to adhere to certain laws. The consequence of this is that in order to maintain your car at a functioning level, you have to follow certain maintenance procedures. Your car drives because the engine is made of metal parts that are able to withstand the pressure generated by the explosions in the cylinders. Those metal parts will wear down unless they are protected by a film of oil. The oil eventually wears down and becomes dirty so you need to change it at regular intervals. If you buy a new car and never change the oil, then one day the engine will simply stop working. You cannot blame this on the engineers who designed your car because they simply designed it according to the laws of nature. The inevitable consequence is that you have to change the oil in order to maintain the engine's ability to function. You routinely change the oil in your car without feeling that this is a restriction of your basic freedom to use your car.

The basic design principles used by your Creator are not a restriction of your creative freedom and your creative powers. Your car is designed to give you maximum freedom of movement, and you can go anywhere you want. As long as you follow a set of simple maintenance principles, your car will keep giving you that freedom for a long time. If you deliberately or unknowingly ignore those principles, your car will stop functioning and you will lose the freedom of movement that your car gave you. Likewise, the universe in which you live functions according to certain principles. As long as you follow those principles, as long as you use your creative powers within the parameters that God used to design the universe, you can continue to co-create more abundance for yourself. If you go against the very principles that your Creator used to design the universe, you will gradually create problems for yourself, you will generate consequences that will limit your creative powers.

This is indeed the one explanation for the many types of suffering and limitations you see on earth. This suffering is not the revenge of an angry God in the sky. It is the natural consequence of the fact that most human beings on this earth have misused their creative powers. They have used their imagination to build a false image which says that this earth is a limited world in which there is not enough abundance for all. They have used their will to accept that image as the only possible truth. They accept that their limitations, pain and suffering are indeed unavoidable and that they can do nothing to overcome them.

If you are to truly have the abundant life, you need to take the right approach to getting that abundance. You cannot take a passive approach and say that you are a victim, a helpless victim, of forces beyond your control. You cannot take the approach that it is up to the God in the sky to give you abundance or that your abundance depends on other people in this world. You need to take the approach that if you are to have abundance, you need to bring it into manifestation by using the creative powers given to you by God. The core of those powers is your imagination and your free will. You need to be willing to realign yourself, to realign your understanding and choices, with the basic principles that God used to create this universe. When you know those principles, you can use your imagination within the parameters of God's laws. In so doing, you will bring abundance into your life in a way that is sustainable and, in fact, can accelerate indefinitely.

It is the Father's good pleasure to give you the kingdom, and he designed this universe so that all of his sons and daughters can have the abundant life. This means that they are not confined to a certain amount of abundance but that their abundance is continually expanding. When everyone is expanding their individual abundance, the abundance of the whole is also expanded. When everyone is continually expanding their abundance, there is no contradiction or conflict between the individual and the whole.

***

The essential design of God's universe creates a very remarkable state of being. All beings created by God were created out of the Presence of your Creator. They are all extensions of God, individualizations of God, sons and daughters of God. The people you see on earth are extensions of the same God and therefore all are part of the whole of God, the Body of God. In God's original design and vision for this universe, all of his sons and daughters would know, from within themselves, the creative principles that God used to design this universe. This is explained in the Bible in the statement that God has put his laws in your inward parts (Jeremiah 31:33). God has coded the creative principles into the very fabric of your being, the very fabric of your spiritual self. As long as you are in contact with your I AM Presence, you know instinctively or intuitively how to express your imagination and free will in a way that is in alignment with God's creative principles. When you, as an individual being, express your creativity in alignment with God's principles, your actions will not only benefit yourself, they will benefit all other parts of life. In magnifying your own abundance, you are magnifying the abundance of the whole.

You live in this universe and you are not alone, you are not the only person on earth. What you see on earth today is intense conflicts between individuals and between groups of people. This is not God's original vision and design. In God's vision there is no conflict between individuals or between groups because there is no separation between the individual and the whole. This state of innocence, this state of grace, this state of paradise, can be maintained only as long as individual beings use their creative powers within the framework of the principles defined by their Creator. As long as a critical mass of the individuals on earth are using their creativity in harmony with the laws of God, more abundance will be brought into this world and therefore humankind will continually expand its abundance. When this is so, there is no conflict between the individual and the whole because everyone is constantly receiving more abundance and there is no sense of lack. When there is no sense that there is only a finite amount of riches, there is no need to take from others. Why take from other people when you can freely receive more directly from God?

Consider as a thought experiment that you were the owner of the magic lamp mentioned in so many fairy tales. Consider that you did not need anything from outside yourself in order to manifest whatever you desire. You simply rub the lamp, and when the genie jumps out of the bottle, you tell him your desire and he will instantly manifest it for you. If you had that magic lamp, would you ever consider using force, cunning or other means to take something from other people? If you knew that the genie would give you anything you desired just for the asking, why would you run the risk or go through the trouble to take it from others. Why would you seek to hold on to, and hoard, what you have? Of course you would never do this; you would simply use your magic lamp to get what you desire. Now imagine that all of your neighbors also had their own magic lamps. Would there be any conflicts in your community? Would there be any need for some people to exploit others? Would there be a need for some people to steal from others? Of course there wouldn't! Everyone would simply rub their lamps and manifest what they desire.

You actually have a magic lamp, but the genie in the bottle is not some external entity. The genie in the bottle is your own spiritual self, your I AM Presence. It is through this higher self that the Father, your Creator, will manifest his desire to give you his kingdom. Your I AM Presence is the storehouse for the laws of God, it is where God has deposited his laws in your inward parts. When you, meaning the conscious self, bring your desires, your imagination and your free-will choices into alignment with your I AM Presence – which is not an external entity but is the real you – God's abundance will be manifest in your life through that I AM Presence. You will not need to take it from other people or from Mother Nature, you will not need to use force in order to have God's abundance. It will happen effortlessly and from within.

I am not hereby saying that you will not need to interact with other people. It is truly God's desire that people work together in creating abundance. When people work together, their creative powers multiply each other and thus they can accomplish more by working in unison than each person could accomplish alone. I am not painting a picture of a society in which each person is an isolated individual and creates his or her own abundance without interacting with others. I am painting the picture of a society in which all people are in alignment with the creative principles used by God. They can pool together their creative powers in bringing forth greater abundance than has even been seen on earth, greater abundance than can even be envisioned by most people in their current state of consciousness.

This abundance is the true potential on earth. There are no limitations built into God's basic design for this planet. The only limitations are those that exist in the minds of God's co-creators, namely the self-aware beings that God gave dominion over the earth. God has given you the right to co-create this planet in any way you see fit. God has given you the right to create the current state of limitation and suffering, of exploitation, conflicts and war. If that is indeed the experience people want, then God will let them create that experience—at least for a time. The basic design of the universe mandates that you cannot maintain a limited state indefinitely. In creating that limited state, you are activating the contracting force of the Mother to gradually break down the limitations you have created. In reality, this is a safety mechanism so that you – an unlimited spiritual being with an infinite potential – cannot remain forever trapped in a state of limitation.

***

When you create something that is in alignment with the creative principles of God, your creation is sustainable. That which is in alignment with the laws of God does not have built into itself contradictory forces that break it down. When you create something outside of God's laws, you will have built-in contradictions, you will have opposing forces that lead to conflict. When a number of people misuse their creative powers to go against the laws of God, you will see conflict breaking out in society. Suddenly, you see groups of people come together in factions and define their very identities in opposition to each other. That is why you can see the sad state of affairs that two groups of people can kill each other in the name of the same God.

Your scientists have discovered this principle as the second law of thermodynamics, which states that in a closed system entropy will increase. Entropy means disorder, and your scientists have found that nature itself has a built-in force that will return all structure, all organized form, to its lowest possible energy state. This means that all structure is broken down into nothingness, into pure subatomic particles. This is the scientific discovery of the basic principle built into the Mother Light, namely, as I said earlier, that the Mother Light has an internal force that seeks to return any form to its ground state. Your scientists do not have the full understanding of this law because they are yet too focused on the material side of life. It is very true that the Ma-ter Light will seek to return all form to its ground state, yet the contracting force of the Mother does not work alone. When the expanding force of the Father fulfills its rightful place as the head of the household in a spiritual sense, then the creation will not be broken down by the contracting force of the Mother. A particular form can exist indefinitely—which is not the same as forever.

If you create something that is out of alignment with God's laws, the form you create will gradually be broken down by the contracting force of the Mother. If what you create is in complete harmony with the creative principles of God, your form will not be broken down; it will be sustainable and it will exist for an indefinite period of time. I am not saying it will exist forever because the expanding force of the Father mandates that all form must transcend itself and become more.

There is a vast difference between creating an imbalanced form that will be broken down into nothingness or creating a balanced form that will be expanded and become more. When you create imperfect forms, you are engaged in an uphill battle, and this is what leads to the sense of lack, struggle and suffering. You are always coming from behind, feeling that you never have enough and that all of the forces of this world are out to take away from you what you have. In contrast, when you are in harmony with God, you will never lose what you have, you will use it as a foundation upon which you can build more abundance.

This is the principle illustrated by Jesus in the parable of the talents (Matthew 25:14). When God designed planet earth, he built the foundation. It is up to human beings to build a castle on that foundation, it is up to the servants to multiply their talents. The talents that God gave human beings are their creative powers, their imagination and free will. If you bury those talents in the ground by going against the creative principles of God, then the contracting force will eventually break down even the foundation built by God. A planet can become barren so that it no longer sustains life. It is possible that humankind, either through pollution or nuclear war, can destroy all life on this planet and turn it into a barren planet. When human beings multiply their talents, they will maintain the foundation built by God. They can build upon it and bring forth something that has more abundance than what God created. This is the true desire of God.

God does not desire you to bury your talents in the ground; he desires you to use those talents to magnify your own life and thereby magnify the life of all other people on this planet, ultimately magnifying your Creator. After all, your Creator has embedded a part of itself in you so when you magnify that part, you magnify the whole, you magnify the Creator. When *you* become more, *God* becomes more through you and this is the driving force behind all creation.

There is a distinction between that which is in alignment with the creative principles of God and that which is out of alignment with those principles. The law of God states that nothing can remain the same. Everything must go one of two ways:

- It must accelerate, meaning that it self-transcends through the expanding force.

- It must decelerate, meaning that it self-destructs through the contracting force.

I hope you now see the need to realign yourself with the principle of perpetual growth so that you can use your creative powers within the safe framework of God's laws. I hope you can see the advantage of creating something that is sustainable and can continue to grow and give you more abundance and also give more abundance to all other people on this planet. If you see the importance of this and if you are willing to bring yourself into harmony with your God, then the next chapter will show you how to begin this process, this journey back to the heart of your Creator, this return to oneness with your source.

6 | I INVOKE CREATIVE FREEDOM

In the name I AM THAT I AM, Jesus Christ, I call to all representatives of the Divine Mother, especially Kuan Yin and Mother Mary, to help me attune to the creative principles used by God and overcome all blocks to my ability to manifest abundance, including...

[Make personal calls.]

1. I reclaim my innocence

1. I am transcending the serpentine mindset, which says that because God is not found in the material universe, we human beings can define our own laws.

O Kuan Yin, what sacred name,
fill me now with Mercy's Flame.
In giving mercy I am free,
forgiving all is magic key.

In Kuan Yin's sweet melody,
I am set free my Self to be.
In Kuan Yin's vitality,
I claim my immortality.

2. I am reclaiming my inner sense – my innocence – and I am experiencing the Presence of God right within myself. My true identity is my I AM Presence.

O Kuan Yin, I now let go,
of all attachments here below.
All pent-up feelings I release,
free from emotional disease.

In Kuan Yin's sweet melody,
I am set free my Self to be.
In Kuan Yin's vitality,
I claim my immortality.

3. God's laws are not affected by the beliefs of human beings.

O Kuan Yin, why must I feel,
that life falls short of my ideal?
All expectations I give up,
my mind is now an empty cup.

In Kuan Yin's sweet melody,
I am set free my Self to be.
In Kuan Yin's vitality,
I claim my immortality.

4. God created many self-aware beings and they are all created out of God's own Being and substance. We are all part of the Body of God.

O Kuan Yin, transcend the past,
as all resentment gone at last.
From future nothing I expect,
eternal now I won't reject.

In Kuan Yin's sweet melody,
I am set free my Self to be.
In Kuan Yin's vitality,
I claim my immortality.

5. Everything in the world of form is created out of a harmonious and balanced interaction between the expanding force of the Father and the contracting force of the Mother.

O Kuan Yin, uplifting me,
beyond Samsara's raging sea.
All safe inside your Prajna boat,
the farther shore no more remote.

In Kuan Yin's sweet melody,
I am set free my Self to be.
In Kuan Yin's vitality,
I claim my immortality.

6. When I co-create from the mindset of separation, the contracting force of the Mother will break down my creation, returning the Ma-ter Light to its ground state.

O Kuan Yin, your alchemy,
with miracles you set me free.
As I forgive, I am forgiven,
by guilt I am no longer driven.

In Kuan Yin's sweet melody,
I am set free my Self to be.
In Kuan Yin's vitality,
I claim my immortality.

7. I am expanding my understanding of how the world works. I am using my co-creative abilities to magnify the whole.

O Kuan Yin, all worries gone,
with nothing done, no thing undone.
Through separate self I will not do,
and thus I rest, all one with you.

In Kuan Yin's sweet melody,
I am set free my Self to be.
In Kuan Yin's vitality,
I claim my immortality.

8. My Creator created this universe with an unconditional love for me and a pure desire to create a world that is the best possible platform for my growth.

O Kuan Yin, your sanity,
now sets me free from vanity.
For truly, what is that to me;
I just let go and follow thee.

In Kuan Yin's sweet melody,
I am set free my Self to be.
In Kuan Yin's vitality,
I claim my immortality.

9. I am transcending all hidden or recognized anger against God. None of the imperfections on earth were created by God. God originally envisioned a universe in which I would increase my abundance through my creative powers.

O Kuan Yin, so sweet the sound,
that emanates from holy ground.
As I let go of ego's chore,
I find myself on farther shore.

In Kuan Yin's sweet melody,
I am set free my Self to be.
In Kuan Yin's vitality,
I claim my immortality.

2. I know the creative principles

1. God designed the universe to serve as the best possible platform for the expansion of my creative abilities. I am transcending myself and becoming a god-free being with awareness of how my actions affect the whole of which I am a part.

O Kuan Yin, what sacred name,
fill me now with Mercy's Flame.
In giving mercy I am free,
forgiving all is magic key.

In Kuan Yin's sweet melody,
I am set free my Self to be.
In Kuan Yin's vitality,
I claim my immortality.

2. The universe is designed based on certain creative principles. The most fundamental of these principles is the drive to be more.

O Kuan Yin, I now let go,
of all attachments here below.
All pent-up feelings I release,
free from emotional disease.

In Kuan Yin's sweet melody,
I am set free my Self to be.
In Kuan Yin's vitality,
I claim my immortality.

3. The universal principle of all creation is that creation never stops, that I cannot stand still. I am continually transcending myself and becoming more by expanding my awareness.

O Kuan Yin, why must I feel,
that life falls short of my ideal?
All expectations I give up,
my mind is now an empty cup.

In Kuan Yin's sweet melody,
I am set free my Self to be.
In Kuan Yin's vitality,
I claim my immortality.

4. I am transcending the ego-based tendency to use my creative abilities to create a particular sense of identity for myself and then remain in that sense of identity.

> O Kuan Yin, transcend the past,
> as all resentment gone at last.
> From future nothing I expect,
> eternal now I won't reject.

> **In Kuan Yin's sweet melody,**
> **I am set free my Self to be.**
> **In Kuan Yin's vitality,**
> **I claim my immortality.**

5. If I attempt to hold on to a limited sense of identity, the contracting force of the Mother will act as the safety mechanism that breaks down my creation in order to set me free.

> O Kuan Yin, uplifting me,
> beyond Samsara's raging sea.
> All safe inside your Prajna boat,
> the farther shore no more remote.

> **In Kuan Yin's sweet melody,**
> **I am set free my Self to be.**
> **In Kuan Yin's vitality,**
> **I claim my immortality.**

6. I am transcending the consciousness of death. I am embracing the consciousness of life, and I am constantly transcending my current sense of self.

O Kuan Yin, your alchemy,
with miracles you set me free.
As I forgive, I am forgiven,
by guilt I am no longer driven.

In Kuan Yin's sweet melody,
I am set free my Self to be.
In Kuan Yin's vitality,
I claim my immortality.

7. The universe functions according to certain principles. I am using my creative powers within the parameters that God used to design the universe, and I am co-creating more abundance for myself.

O Kuan Yin, all worries gone,
with nothing done, no thing undone.
Through separate self I will not do,
and thus I rest, all one with you.

In Kuan Yin's sweet melody,
I am set free my Self to be.
In Kuan Yin's vitality,
I claim my immortality.

8. The suffering on earth is not the revenge of an angry God in the sky. It is the natural consequence of the fact that most human beings on this earth have misused their creative powers.

O Kuan Yin, your sanity,
now sets me free from vanity.
For truly, what is that to me;
I just let go and follow thee.

In Kuan Yin's sweet melody,
I am set free my Self to be.
In Kuan Yin's vitality,
I claim my immortality.

9. I am transcending the passive approach to abundance and the illusion that I am a victim of forces beyond my control. I am using my co-creative abilities to bring abundance into manifestation in my life.

O Kuan Yin, so sweet the sound,
that emanates from holy ground.
As I let go of ego's chore,
I find myself on farther shore.

In Kuan Yin's sweet melody,
I am set free my Self to be.
In Kuan Yin's vitality,
I claim my immortality.

3. I take command over my creative powers

1. The core of my creative powers is my imagination and free will. I am realigning my understanding and choices with the basic principles that God used to create this universe.

O Kuan Yin, what sacred name,
fill me now with Mercy's Flame.
In giving mercy I am free,
forgiving all is magic key.

In Kuan Yin's sweet melody,
I am set free my Self to be.
In Kuan Yin's vitality,
I claim my immortality.

2. All beings created by God were created out of the Presence of my Creator. We are all extensions of God, individualizations of God, sons and daughters of God.

O Kuan Yin, I now let go,
of all attachments here below.
All pent-up feelings I release,
free from emotional disease.

In Kuan Yin's sweet melody,
I am set free my Self to be.
In Kuan Yin's vitality,
I claim my immortality.

3. God has coded the creative principles into the very fabric of my being, into my I AM Presence.

O Kuan Yin, why must I feel,
that life falls short of my ideal?
All expectations I give up,
my mind is now an empty cup.

In Kuan Yin's sweet melody,
I am set free my Self to be.
In Kuan Yin's vitality,
I claim my immortality.

4. I know instinctively and intuitively how to express my imagination and free will in a way that is in alignment with God's creative principles.

O Kuan Yin, transcend the past,
as all resentment gone at last.
From future nothing I expect,
eternal now I won't reject.

In Kuan Yin's sweet melody,
I am set free my Self to be.
In Kuan Yin's vitality,
I claim my immortality.

5. I am transcending all conflicts between me and other co-creators.

O Kuan Yin, uplifting me,
beyond Samsara's raging sea.
All safe inside your Prajna boat,
the farther shore no more remote.

In Kuan Yin's sweet melody,
I am set free my Self to be.
In Kuan Yin's vitality,
I claim my immortality.

6. I am in a state of innocence, a state of grace, a state of paradise, by using my creative powers within the framework of the creative principles defined by my Creator.

O Kuan Yin, your alchemy,
with miracles you set me free.
As I forgive, I am forgiven,
by guilt I am no longer driven.

In Kuan Yin's sweet melody,
I am set free my Self to be.
In Kuan Yin's vitality,
I claim my immortality.

7. I am transcending the sense that there is only a finite amount of riches, and thus I need to take from others. Why take from other people when I am freely receiving more directly from God?

O Kuan Yin, all worries gone,
with nothing done, no thing undone.
Through separate self I will not do,
and thus I rest, all one with you.

In Kuan Yin's sweet melody,
I am set free my Self to be.
In Kuan Yin's vitality,
I claim my immortality.

8. I recognize that I have a magic lamp. The genie in the bottle is not some external entity but my I AM Presence. It is through my Presence that my Creator will manifest his desire to give me his kingdom.

O Kuan Yin, your sanity,
now sets me free from vanity.
For truly, what is that to me;
I just let go and follow thee.

In Kuan Yin's sweet melody,
I am set free my Self to be.
In Kuan Yin's vitality,
I claim my immortality.

9. My I AM Presence is the storehouse for the laws of God. I am bringing my desires, my imagination and my free will into alignment with my I AM Presence. God's abundance is effortlessly manifest in my life through that I AM Presence.

O Kuan Yin, so sweet the sound,
that emanates from holy ground.
As I let go of ego's chore,
I find myself on farther shore.

In Kuan Yin's sweet melody,
I am set free my Self to be.
In Kuan Yin's vitality,
I claim my immortality.

4. I multiply my talents

1. I am effortlessly working with other people in creating abundance. We are multiplying our creative powers and accomplishing more by working in unison than each person could accomplish alone.

O Kuan Yin, what sacred name,
fill me now with Mercy's Flame.
In giving mercy I am free,
forgiving all is magic key.

**In Kuan Yin's sweet melody,
I am set free my Self to be.
In Kuan Yin's vitality,
I claim my immortality.**

2. We are pooling our creative powers in bringing forth greater
abundance than has ever been seen on earth, greater abundance
than can be envisioned by most people in their current state of
consciousness.

O Kuan Yin, I now let go,
of all attachments here below.
All pent-up feelings I release,
free from emotional disease.

**In Kuan Yin's sweet melody,
I am set free my Self to be.
In Kuan Yin's vitality,
I claim my immortality.**

3. There are no limitations built into God's basic design for this
planet. The only limitations are those that exist in the minds of
God's co-creators, namely the self-aware beings that God gave
dominion over the earth.

O Kuan Yin, why must I feel,
that life falls short of my ideal?
All expectations I give up,
my mind is now an empty cup.

In Kuan Yin's sweet melody,
I am set free my Self to be.
In Kuan Yin's vitality,
I claim my immortality.

4. I am aligning myself with the creative principles of God and therefore my creation is sustainable. I am transcending my internal entropy and I am free from the second law of thermodynamics.

O Kuan Yin, transcend the past,
as all resentment gone at last.
From future nothing I expect,
eternal now I won't reject.

In Kuan Yin's sweet melody,
I am set free my Self to be.
In Kuan Yin's vitality,
I claim my immortality.

5. The Ma-ter Light will seek to return all form to its ground state, yet when the expanding force of the Father fulfills its rightful place, my creation is sustainable.

O Kuan Yin, uplifting me,
beyond Samsara's raging sea.
All safe inside your Prajna boat,
the farther shore no more remote.

In Kuan Yin's sweet melody,
I am set free my Self to be.
In Kuan Yin's vitality,
I claim my immortality.

6. When I create imperfect forms, I engage in an uphill battle. This is what leads to the sense of lack, struggle and suffering. I am in harmony with God, and I am using what I have as a foundation for building more abundance.

O Kuan Yin, your alchemy,
with miracles you set me free.
As I forgive, I am forgiven,
by guilt I am no longer driven.

In Kuan Yin's sweet melody,
I am set free my Self to be.
In Kuan Yin's vitality,
I claim my immortality.

7. I am transcending the ego-based mindset that causes me to bury my talents in the ground. I am magnifying my own life and the lives of all other people on this planet, ultimately magnifying my Creator.

O Kuan Yin, all worries gone,
with nothing done, no thing undone.
Through separate self I will not do,
and thus I rest, all one with you.

In Kuan Yin's sweet melody,
I am set free my Self to be.
In Kuan Yin's vitality,
I claim my immortality.

8. When I become more, God becomes more through me and this is the driving force behind all creation. Everything must either self-transcend through the expanding force or self-destruct through the contracting force.

O Kuan Yin, your sanity,
now sets me free from vanity.
For truly, what is that to me;
I just let go and follow thee.

In Kuan Yin's sweet melody,
I am set free my Self to be.
In Kuan Yin's vitality,
I claim my immortality.

9. I am realigning myself with the principle of perpetual growth. I am using my creative powers within the framework of God's laws. What I co-create is sustainable and gives more abundance to all life on this planet.

O Kuan Yin, so sweet the sound,
that emanates from holy ground.
As I let go of ego's chore,
I find myself on farther shore.

In Kuan Yin's sweet melody,
I am set free my Self to be.
In Kuan Yin's vitality,
I claim my immortality.

Sealing

In the name of the Divine Mother, I call to Kuan Yin and Mother Mary for the sealing of myself and all people in my circle of influence in the creative flow of the Divine Mother, the River of Life. I call for the multiplication of my calls by all representatives of the Divine Mother, so that we form the perfect figure-eight flow of "As Above, so below." Thus, I accept that this is fully manifest, because the mouth of the Lord, the Divine Mother that I AM, has spoken it. Amen.

7 | ARE YOU CREATING HARMONY OR LACK?

God has designed a universe that is capable of producing an infinite amount of abundance, even on this little planet that you call earth. When God created the earth, he merely created a foundation. Then he sent you, and many other co-creators, into this world with the command to multiply your creative abilities. You are here to take dominion over the earth so you can build upon God's foundation and bring as much abundance into this world as you can imagine and accept. When human beings use their creative abilities in alignment with the basic principles that God used to design the universe, they will create abundance that is sustainable. They will do this in a way that does not take abundance from other parts of life but magnifies the total amount of abundance on earth. The whole of the Body of God on earth is magnified in the process. When people use their creative abilities correctly, there is no conflict between the individual and the whole because God's universe was designed to provide enough abundance for all.

The central question we now face is how you, a human being on planet earth, can learn to use your creative abilities in harmony with the design principles that God used to design this entire universe. The difficulty we face is that planet earth is not currently expressing the original design. Instead of building a castle upon the foundation built by God, humankind has, over many millennia, buried their talents in the ground. The contracting force of the Mother has started to break down even the foundation built by God. I know this can be difficult to accept for people who have grown up in a modern society. Some people have been brought up to believe in the Biblical version that the earth is only a few thousand years old, that everything is created by God, that God can create only perfection and therefore everything *must* be perfect. Other people have been brought up with the scientific theory of evolution, which states that evolution can go in only one direction, from less complicated to more complex life forms.

Because of the Law of Free Will, it is quite possible that a human civilization can reach a high point and then gradually deteriorate into a lower state. Many aspects of life on earth have been affected by the state of consciousness of humankind. This is true not only for human society but for Mother Nature herself. Do you really believe that a loving God, who has unlimited imagination and free will, would choose to create viruses, bacteria, parasites, venomous insects or toxic chemicals that destroy your bodies? Do you really believe that God created the many diseases found on earth? If God did not create them, who did? The answer is: humankind. Humankind has collectively created all of the imperfect conditions currently seen on earth, even the imbalances of nature.

Everything was created from God's energy, from the Mother Light. The Mother Light takes on form only by being stirred by a mind, a self-aware being who has the creative abilities of God, namely imagination and free will. When you accept this fact, you realize that everything on earth is a product of conscious minds. The original design of earth was created by a group of representatives of God, called the Elohim. These beings created a beautiful planet, and the beauty that is present in nature is only a faint reflection of the original beauty created by the Elohim. The planet they created had perfect balance in nature, and thus you did not see disease, you did not see earthquakes or violent storms. Since that original creation, succeeding generations of humans, succeeding civilizations, have influenced this planet and have taken it to a lower state than the original design. This has been done through the power of people's minds whereby they have imposed upon the Ma-ter Light imperfect images that are out of alignment with the creative principles used by God.

People have descended, or fallen, into a state of consciousness in which they no longer have any intuitive or conscious awareness of the laws of God, the laws that God put in their inward parts. This is what is illustrated in the Bible's account of the Fall whereby Adam and Eve were cast out of the Garden of Eden. The fruit of the knowledge of good and evil was the fruit of the knowledge of *relative* good and evil. When you lose contact with the reality of God, the laws of God, you become a law unto yourself in the sense that you no longer have a guiding rod for what is absolutely true and what is not true.

***

Anything that is in harmony with the laws of God is beneficial to the whole and sustainable, which one might call good. Anything that falls outside of those laws is self-destructive and detrimental to the whole, and therefore one might call it false or evil. When human beings lose this absolute guiding rod, they define their own concepts of good and evil. These concepts are not based on the absolute guiding rod of God's law. They are based on what human beings want to believe and what certain individuals want to be true so that they can fulfill their own self-centered desires without any consideration for the whole. Because people have defined good and evil to suit their ends, they feel perfectly justified in fulfilling their selfish desires.

When there is no absolute guiding rod, human beings will define good and evil as it suits their purposes, their selfish purposes. Various civilizations have had different definitions of good and evil. In most cases that which was not in accordance with the laws created by the ruling minority was automatically labeled as evil. Only that which was in alignment with the dictates of the ruling elite was labeled good or acceptable. In many cases the ruling minority was completely out of alignment with the reality of God and the creative principles of God. What they called good was not good in an absolute sense. It was only *relative* good because it was good only according to their self-centered definition, a definition that not only ignored the creative principles of God but also ignored the reality that only what is good for the whole is truly good for the individual.

It is important for you to contemplate – in your heart – where this concept originated. The story of the Garden of Eden illustrates that there came a point when Adam and Eve realized that they had done something that was against the laws of God. Instead of going back to God and confessing their actions and seeking forgiveness, they decided to hide from God (Genesis 2:8). God has given you free will so you have a right to hide from God, if you so desire. Because God respects his own law, and therefore respects your free-will choices, God cannot help you overcome that sense of separation. If you turn your back upon God, he will allow you to do so and God will not force you in any way. Once you have turned your back upon God, you can keep moving further and further away from God in your consciousness. God will not force you, God will not confront you, God will let you walk as far away as you desire. That is why humankind has been able to descend into the incredibly low state of consciousness that you saw outpictured at the time of the cavemen when humankind was barely above the animal level.

The caveman was not the beginning of humankind. There have been many previous civilizations that reached a high level of sophistication. Some of these civilizations were far more advanced technologically and culturally than even western civilization today. Through the misuse of their creative powers, they gradually descended into lower and lower states of consciousness and lower and lower states of outer existence. If you have ever studied some of the myths, or what scientists call myths, about past civilizations, you will know of which I speak. Although some of the details in these surviving stories have become obscured by the passing of time, it is true that there have been past civilizations on earth and that the caveman was not the beginning of humankind but only one of the low points to which humankind descended.

If you personally desire to change your life – in order to have the abundant life that God offers you freely – you cannot take a passive approach and expect that God will do it for you. You cannot even take the approach of praying to God to give you the abundant life. God has set up a universe in which you have the creative powers to manifest the abundant life by using those powers.

God will not create the abundant life for you; God wants you to co-create the abundant life for yourself. God wants you to know that you have done so through your own internal powers – the power of God within you – and that you have done so by aligning yourself with the creative principles of God. The conclusion is that the reason you do not currently have the abundant life is that you have descended into a state of consciousness, we might call it a state of ignorance, where you have lost touch with the creative principles used by God. The only way to escape your current sense of lack and attain the abundant life is by changing your state of consciousness.

***

My beloved, I would like you to take a few moments to ponder the many "get rich quick" schemes that are found in Western society today. Consider how many gurus out there promise you that by following their simple system or reading their book, you will create ultimate abundance and riches and you can make so much money that it defies common sense. I am sure that if you have been aware of the need to bring more abundance into your life, you have either tried some of these schemes or you have considered them. If you have tried them, you might have experienced that they simply do not work.

I have now explained to you why no "get rich quick" scheme can ever work in the long run. The simple reality is that your current state of lack and suffering is an outpicturing – in physical matter – of what is happening in your consciousness. If you want to change your *outer* reality – the reality that is formed by the Ma-ter Light – you need to first change your *inner* reality, the reality of your consciousness, the mental images you project upon the Ma-ter Light. Only when you go through the process of fundamentally and deeply changing your state of consciousness, will you see a real, true and lasting improvement of your outer situation.

This is a profound principle that you need to understand if you are to manifest the true abundant life that God offers you. The reason you do not have the abundant life manifest physically is that you have descended into a lower state of consciousness, in which you are not using, you are not able to use, the creative principles of God. What the "get rich quick" schemes promise you is that they have discovered some kind of shortcut that will give you the physical riches that you want without having to truly change your consciousness. Some of them do talk about changing your consciousness, but it is on a very superficial level. They claim that by following a few simple steps, or giving a few simple affirmations, riches will instantly start flowing your way.

If you have not already tired of following such empty promises, I am not the one who will stop you from going through that experience if you feel you need it. I am the loving Mother, the representative of the Mother of God. It is my desire to see you have the real abundance that cannot be bought for money and cannot be brought about through shortcuts. I also love God the Father and his Law of Free Will. The Law of Free Will basically states that if you separate yourself from him, God cannot give you guidance and therefore the consequences of your actions become your teacher. You learn through your own experiences.

The Law of Free Will states that if you feel the need for a certain type of experience, God allows you to create that experience for yourself. If you still have a need to experience poverty, limitations, lack, pain and suffering, who am I to override God's law and seek to force you to accept God's abundance? If you desire abundance, but are not willing to truly do what it takes to manifest God's real abundance, who am I to prevent you from running after the false gurus who offer you shortcuts? If you need the experience of following such a false guru – until you have been so thoroughly disappointed that you finally give up on the dream of a shortcut and say: "There must be a better way" – who am I to stand in the way of you having that experience? If you are at the point where you have decided that you no longer want these empty dreams or shortcuts and that you no longer want to continue to experience pain, lack and suffering, then I have something to offer you. What I offer you is a real path whereby you can change the totality of your consciousness.

You can bring your consciousness into alignment with the creative principles used by God. By doing so, you will bring your individual lifestream into harmony with the whole of the Body of God in both heaven and earth. The entire matter universe, the Ma-ter Light itself, will rejoice in filling your true desires. You will then see that abundance will come about not through some kind of magic, not through some kind of force outside yourself, but through the proper use – the balanced and harmonious use – of the creative powers with which God endowed you when your lifestream first came into being.

***

The path that I offer you is the real path to real abundance, not some kind of shortcut, not the way that seems right unto man, but the ends thereof are the ways of death (Proverbs 14:12). The key to following the real path is to realize that it is not the goal of the path to bring about some temporary riches here on earth. The goal of the path is a permanent change, a permanent change in consciousness, whereby you realign your consciousness with the original design that was held in the mind of God when your lifestream was created. This is the design of a true son or daughter of God, designed in the image and likeness of God, using his or her creative powers in perfect harmony with the whole. You magnify not only your own lifestream but the life experience of all life on earth, indeed all life in the entire universe.

This is the state of consciousness that Jesus was talking about when he said that unless you absorb the flesh and blood of the only begotten Son of the Father, you have no life in you (John 6:53). The deeper meaning of that statement is that when you are using your creative powers in harmony with the laws of God, you are in perfect alignment with the purpose of life and with the guiding principles of life. You are immersed in, you are a part of, the ever-flowing, ever-growing River of Life that encompasses all that the Creator has created. You are constantly moving with that River of Life, you are constantly transcending yourself, multiplying your talents and becoming more, thereby bringing about more abundance in your life. This is the true definition of life.

The spiritual definition of life is not whether your physical body is breathing or not breathing. That is a mortal, human definition of life. The real spiritual definition of life is that you are transcending yourself and becoming more. In becoming more you experience the abundant life, you are part of God's ever-moving flow of abundance, the River of Life. Only when you are in that river, do you have true spiritual life. When you step outside of that river – because you separate yourself from your own higher being, from your source, forgetting the laws of your Creator – you descend into a state of consciousness that from a spiritual standpoint is the consciousness of death. You are dead in a spiritual sense, and this is the deeper meaning of Jesus' statement.

How can you, once you have descended into a lower state of consciousness, rise back up and realign yourself with the creative principles of God? What is it that allows you to reclaim your true inheritance, your true identity as a son or daughter of God, and reconnect to the higher part of your being, the I AM Presence, that inward part of your lifestream (into which God has put his laws)? The intermediary that allows you to climb back from death to eternal life is the only begotten Son of the Father. It is sad to have to acknowledge the fact that most mainstream Christian churches have misunderstood the true spiritual meaning of many of Jesus' most profound statements. Because they were trapped in the consciousness of duality and the sense of separation, and because they were not willing to overcome that state of consciousness, they reasoned that Jesus was talking about himself, the outer person of Jesus. They reasoned that the *person of Jesus Christ* is the way, the truth and the life and thus the only key to salvation (John 14:6). Jesus was not talking about one particular being, he was talking about the true begotten Son of the Father, which is not any particular individual but a universal state of consciousness, namely the universal Christ consciousness. This is the state of consciousness that the Gospel of John calls the Word. In the beginning was the Word, and the Word was God and without Him was not anything made that was made.

***

My beloved, we have now reached the point where I can explain to you the true inner meaning of the Christ consciousness, the only begotten Son, the Word. As the first act of creation, your Creator created Light. Light is a substance that has no form, but it has the potential to take on *any* form. It will take on form not by its own internal powers but only when it is acted upon by an outside force, a self-aware being with creative powers.

In the beginning, God the Creator was the only force acting upon the Ma-ter Light. Naturally, everything the Creator created was in perfect harmony with the basic principles that the Creator had designed to ensure the sustainability of his creation. There was no need to be concerned with the possibility that the Creator might create something that violated his own principles, his own laws. When the Creator had brought about the basic design for the universe, the Creator decided to create a number of self-aware beings that were extensions of the Creator but did not yet have the full creative powers of a God. The idea behind doing this is that by creating extensions of itself, the Creator becomes more. When you transcend yourself and expand your awareness and your creative powers, you magnify the whole of God's creation.

The original design was that these self-aware beings would start out with limited creative powers. As they multiplied their talents by co-creating in harmony with the laws of God, he would reward them. As Jesus said: "Well done, thou good and faithful servant: thou hast been faithful over a few things, I will make thee ruler over many things" (Matthew 25:21). The inner meaning is that as you show your willingness to multiply your talents by co-creating in harmony with the laws of God, he will give you greater creative powers. You can rise in awareness and creative power until you come to the full realization that Jesus talked about when he said: "Ye are gods" (John 10:34).

You were created with limited creative powers and a limited awareness of the whole of God's creation because you were meant to travel into the world of form and use your creative powers on just one little planet, such as earth. You would gradually rise in creative ability and awareness until you could permanently ascend from the matter universe and become an immortal being in the spiritual world. From there you can grow even further and, truly, this growth can continue indefinitely.

When God created self-aware beings that had imagination and free will, it became possible that such beings could, either through forgetfulness or even through deliberate disobedience, go against God's creative principles. After all, if they could not go against God's law, they would not truly have *free* will. It now became possible that someone could create something that was out of alignment with God's laws and therefore would lead not only to the destruction of that particular lifestream, but potentially to the destruction of others depending on the creative powers of that lifestream. In order to avoid this, God built another safety mechanism into the very design of the universe.

That safety mechanism is what the Bible calls the Word or the only begotten son of the Father, but which I prefer to call the universal Christ consciousness.

This safety mechanism works in the following way. Your lifestream is designed to be a co-creator with God. You do not have the creative powers of your Creator, you have limited creative powers. They are essentially the same in quality, but not in quantity as the creative powers of your Creator. There is a difference in the sense that your Creator is the All and thus creates from within itself. You, on the other hand, are an individual, and therefore you are not the All, at least not yet. You create from inside the creation already created by God. The safety mechanism designed by God mandates that a co-creator can create something that is sustainable only through the agency of the Christ consciousness.

The Christ consciousness is an awareness of the laws of God that can never be compromised. The Christ consciousness is always one with the Father and with the Father's laws. When Jesus obtained the Christ consciousness, he exclaimed: "I and my Father are one" (John 10:30). When you, as an individual lifestream, have that awareness of the All and the laws of God, you realize that the individual you is not the true doer, is not the true creator. That is why Jesus said: "I can of mine own self do nothing" (John 5:30) and: "but the Father that dwelleth in me, he doeth the works" (John 14:10). Jesus knew that it was not his outer person, the physical person, it was not even the outer mind, the personality that human beings saw as Jesus Christ, that was the true doer, the true creator. It was the higher part of his being, the individualization of God, focused as the I AM Presence, that was truly creating. That Presence was creating only because it was using the energy and the laws of God to bring about form.

The Christ consciousness always knows that it is not a law unto itself, that it is a co-creator *with* God, that there is something greater of which it is a part. God has designed a set of principles that guide the growth of everything in this universe, and the Christ consciousness knows that when you create in harmony with those principles, your creation is sustainable and will magnify the whole. When you lose awareness of those principles, the contracting force of the Mother will cause your creation to self-destruct and this will potentially destroy other parts of the whole.

If you stay in the Christ consciousness, you can never fall into the lower state of consciousness in which you separate yourself from your God and his laws, in which you forget the laws that God has put in your inward parts and therefore become a law unto yourself. With the Christ consciousness you can never believe in the knowledge of relative good and evil and thereby define your own principles and think you can get away with fulfilling your selfish desires with no regard for how it affects the whole. This safety mechanism prevents you from permanently forgetting who you are, from where you came or forgetting the laws defined by your Creator.

This state of Christ consciousness is the natural state for any lifestream created by God. Because God gave you imagination and free will, it is possible that you can forget this natural state of awareness and thereby descend into the duality consciousness, the state of separation, where you no longer know your true origin. You might even come to believe that you are a mortal human being who is condemned by an angry God to live a life of pain and suffering and that there is nothing you can do about it by your own internal power.

***

Here is the central distinction that God created when he decided to create self-aware beings. The Ma-ter Light, the Mother Light, is what scientists call energy. Energy is vibration and you can start at the low vibrations of the material universe and go through successively higher vibrations in the spiritual realm until you reach the highest vibration of the pure light of God itself. That light has such a high vibration that no form is possible. There is no distinguishable form in the pure spiritual light. How does form come about? It comes about when a self-aware mind imposes an image, a matrix, upon the pure light and thereby causes it to take on a lower vibration than its ground state. For that to happen, the self-aware being must envision a form and then, through the power of the mind, impose that form upon the pure Ma-ter Light. Here is the essential safety mechanism. Only through the Christ consciousness, only through the agency of the Christ consciousness, can a co-creator impose an image upon the pure Ma-ter Light. Only an image that is in harmony with the laws of the Creator will affect the pure Ma-ter Light.

This works to ensure that only those who have the Christ consciousness can create something that is balanced and therefore sustainable. The Ma-ter Light has another built-in safety mechanism, namely that it always seeks to return to its ground state. When a form is created in harmony with the laws defined by the Creator, that form will be part of the River of Life, meaning that it will be part of the process of constant self-transcendence. A form is sustainable only through self-transcendence because growth is the basic law of creation. Any form that is not in harmony with the laws of God, that is not self-transcending and does not have the right balance between the contracting and expanding forces, will gradually be broken down by the contracting force built into the Ma-ter Light, the force that returns all imbalanced creations to the ground state. Any form which is created based on a graven image, an image that is not self-transcending, will inevitably be broken down by the contracting force. It is the contracting force that makes it possible to create form, but if you become attached to any form – if you start worshiping a graven image and refuse to self-transcend – you go outside the River of Life and become subject to the contracting force. You can maintain this unbalanced state only for a time because when a form is exposed to the contracting force – with no counterbalance from the expanding force – it will inevitably be broken down. The perversion of the Mother force will lead to self-annihilation.

In the highest levels of the spiritual universe are only beings who have the full Christ consciousness. They have created spheres of such beauty that hardly anyone on earth can imagine it. Some people have been blessed with spiritual or mystical visions or near-death experiences in which they have seen the beauty and the perfection of the spiritual realms or at least some of those realms. For anyone who has had such a vision, it is obvious that only a being with a much higher state of consciousness than what is common on earth could have imagined, could have envisioned, such states of beauty, such perfection. In heaven, in the spiritual realm, you can remain only as long as you are in the Christ consciousness. In the heaven world you find only beings who are in the Christ consciousness. This does not mean that a being in heaven does not have creative freedom, for truly within the context of God's laws you have unlimited possibilities for exercising your creative powers.

A being in heaven still has the option to go against the creative principles defined by the Creator of this world. If a being in heaven does so, that being can no longer remain in heaven and must then descend to a lower realm. This is precisely how the material realm came into being. After God and God's representatives had created a large number of levels in the heaven world, a new level of God's creation was brought into manifestation.

This level was made of energies that were lower than any of the energies found in the spiritual realm. It could be inhabited by beings who had chosen to go against the creative principles defined by God. These beings now had a place to go where they could exercise their creative powers and reap the consequences of their actions until they had experienced enough limitation and they finally turned back to God and said: "Oh my Creator, I want to come home."

The material universe was indeed created by representatives of God who used their Christ consciousness to envision a balanced and harmonious creation. They then imposed that vision upon the Ma-ter Light whereby it took on a lower vibration than any vibration found in the spiritual world. Although the material universe was created by beings who had the perfect Christ consciousness, the material universe was designed to allow beings to exist here that do not have the full Christ consciousness. That is why the Ma-ter Light used to create this universe can easily be molded into forms that are out of alignment with the creative principles of God. Those forms will not instantly self-destruct as they will do in the spiritual realm. They can exist on a temporary basis and will only be broken down after some time.

This is a very subtle concept that I know will be abstract for many people. There is value in stretching your mind to understand this. In the spiritual realm, the intelligence built into the Mother Light makes it impossible for any imperfect or unbalanced form to exist for any length of time. Anything that is out of harmony with the laws of God will instantly self-destruct, due to the contracting force of the Mother. In the material universe the contracting force of the Mother has been adjusted so that imperfect forms will not instantly self-destruct; they can indeed exist for some time. As scientists have discovered and expressed in the second law of thermodynamics, all imperfect forms will eventually break down. This universe allows those self-aware beings, who either ignorantly or deliberately have descended into a lower state of consciousness, to learn by experiencing the consequences of their actions. These beings will inevitably create some things that are out alignment with the laws of God. When they do so, they will not create the abundant life that you find in the spiritual realm. They will create a state of lack and limitation. It is God's hope that when these beings experience the limitations, the pain and the suffering that they have created, they will eventually tire of that experience and therefore voluntarily bring themselves back into alignment with God's laws.

We now see the distinction. If a being in the spiritual realm decides to rebel against God's law, anything it creates will instantly self-destruct. If the being had nowhere else to go, that being would instantly annihilate itself. What would the being learn from that experience? If the being was annihilated, no learning would be possible. God has set up a universe in which a being can go against God's creative principles without instantly destroying itself. It can continue an existence, continue an awareness. It can exist in the material realm, and in this universe it will experience the fruits of its actions, it will reap what it has sown. In so doing, it has the potential to learn that when you follow God's laws, you magnify both your own life and the lives of all others. When you go against those laws, you limit your own life and the lives of all others. The Law of Free Will is fulfilled in that the being has the potential to go against God's laws, and thereby experience pain, limitations and lack, until it has had enough of that experience and therefore decides to bring itself back into alignment with God's laws and recreate the abundant life that was God's original plan. The important distinction here is that in order to create something that is sustainable and that enhances both your own life and the lives of all other people on earth, you must create from the Christ consciousness. When you do not create from the Christ consciousness, what you create will limit your creative powers and will cause you to experience limitations, lack, suffering and pain. The pain and limitation is brought about because what you create with the lower state of consciousness will not be self-transcending. It will be based on a graven image, an image that does not grow. It cannot be sustainable – it will not have eternal life – and thus the contracting force of the Mother will begin to break down the forms that you have created. Although this will take some time, it is nevertheless an inevitable process that you cannot reverse from the lower state of consciousness. You can only reverse it by rising to the Christ consciousness.

In the spiritual realm the concepts of space and time do not have the same meaning that they have here on earth. When you are in heaven, you are in the Christ consciousness, and in the Christ consciousness you see yourself as one with the All. When you are one with the All, you are, in a sense, everywhere in the consciousness of God. If you, as an individual lifestream, have the potential to expand your awareness and be everywhere in the consciousness of God, then obviously the concept of space takes on a different meaning. On earth you experience space as a limitation. Your sense of self-awareness is centered around your physical body, which lives on a planet called earth, a planet that is like a drop in an infinite ocean. As long as you identify with that body, your sense of identity is limited in space. It exists only "here," it is centered around this body on this planet, and therefore you cannot be everywhere at the same time. This truly is a limitation in your mind more than it is an actual and unavoidable limitation. Your physical body cannot be everywhere in the physical universe, but your mind is not limited by the body. When you are in the spiritual realm, you are a part of the ever-moving River of Life that is the totality of God's creation, God's Being. When you are moving along with that River of Life, time does not have the same meaning as it has on earth. On earth, time is a limitation that focuses you on this present moment. It sets limitations for how long you can live because there is a limit to how long your dense physical body can continue to exist. As Jesus attempted to show humankind, even death is an illusion and can be conquered through the Christ consciousness.

One might say that the coordinates of time and space are not ultimately real. They are products of the fact that the material universe allows self-aware beings to create that which is out of alignment with the laws of God. The more you remove yourself from alignment with the oneness with God and with the laws of God, the more you limit yourself, the more you limit your awareness to a particular location in space. The more you set yourself apart from the awareness lifestreams had before the Fall and the further you move away from being in the flow of the River of Life, the more you limit yourself to a particular moment in time, the more your sense of identity becomes centered around a physical body with an incredibly short life span. The body's life span is so short that even common sense should show you that it could not possibly be God's design that you should live for only 70 years and then cease to exist as a self-aware being.

***

I am deliberately starting out with some very difficult and abstract concepts because only by building a foundation can we truly escape the duality consciousness that stands between you and the abundant life. In order to escape that consciousness, you need to have the larger view that has not been available on this earth, neither through orthodox Christianity nor through materialistic science. To set the proper foundation that allows you to follow the path I am offering, I have to give you this larger view. I have to take you out of the forest so you can see beyond the trees and see the forest itself—and therefore understand the greater purpose for which your world was created. You can understand that your lifestream, your consciousness, your sense of identity, is not confined to this material world with all of its limitations, pain and suffering. You have an alternative. You have the opportunity to rise above your current, limited state of consciousness, your limited sense of identity. You can come up higher and build a new sense of identity that is in alignment with the true design of your being.

My beloved, can you sense my fervor? What I am trying to convey to you here is that humankind has an incredibly limited understanding of its origin, an understanding that does not incorporate the realty of who you are. Neither science nor most religions currently offer you a true understanding of who you are, where you came from and why you are here. If you do not know who you are, how can you understand your purpose for coming to this earth? If you do not understand that purpose, how can you hope to bring yourself back into alignment with your original desires, the desires that made you come into this universe?

I have told you about the Law of Free Will. Contrary to the image of an angry and punishing God, painted by some religions, God is not angry and God never punished anyone. The Creator has unconditional love for each one of its sons and daughters, and that unconditional love can be seen very clearly in the Law of Free Will that gives you the possibility to go against the original creative principles, the original design, that your Creator had in mind when it created this world of form; when it created *you*. Only a God of unconditional love would allow you to go against his laws so that you could reject his abundant life and create a state of suffering and pain that was far below what your Creator envisioned for you. If God truly had been an angry tyrant, he would have prevented you from doing this. If God truly had

been a punishing God, he would have punished you by annihilating you the moment you stepped outside of his laws. Your
God is a loving God. The original love for you, held in the heart
of God, has not been diminished in the least by the fact that
you have temporarily chosen to turn your back upon God, to
reject his abundant life and to instead create for yourself a state
of limitation and suffering. God loves you in the exact same way
that he loved you when your lifestream was first created. God's
love is unconditional, and no matter what you might have done
on earth, you could never, ever lose that love.

Because you have free will, you can reject God's love.
Because you have unlimited imagination, you can create a false
image of God that portrays God as an angry and punishing God,
and you can accept that image as the absolute truth about God.
You can accept that you are not worthy to receive God's love
and that you are condemned to remain forever in your current
state of limitation and suffering, your current state of separation
from God's love and God's abundance. This is your right, but
at the very moment you decide that you will no longer hold on
to this limited sense of identity, that you will no longer reject
God's abundance, God stands ready to bring you back into his
kingdom, to give you the abundant life that is rightfully yours.
You only need to follow his creative principles to bring that
abundance into manifestation in your life experience.

God gave you free will. God gave you the right to go against
his laws if you so desire. God even designed an entire universe in
which you can go against his laws and still retain consciousness
and a sense of individuality, in which you can experience the
consequences of your actions, in which you can experience the
limited reality that you have created for yourself. Even though
God allows this, God remains ever hopeful that – one day –
you will decide to stop running away from his abundance. You
will stop limiting yourself. You will stop denying your creative

potential, your divine potential to become a true God, a true co-creator with God. God hopes that you will come home again and become a conscious co-creator with God so that you know who you are, you know where you came from. You are consciously exercising your creative powers with the goal to not simply fulfill your own self-centered desires but to magnify the whole of God's creation and thereby be part of the River of Life that truly is so magnificent that it is beyond the comprehension of most people on earth.

My beloved, I am here as a representative of God the Father. In the past I chose to descend to planet earth and take on a dense physical body. I have chosen to ascend back to the spiritual realm in order to demonstrate that it is possible to rise above all human limitations, even the last enemy called death. Because I have chosen to unite myself with the consciousness of the Mother of God, I have come to you as the loving Mother who has no other desire than to see the very best for her children. That is why I have come to offer you a genuine, a true and an everlasting path that can lead you back into your Father's kingdom, the kingdom that, as Jesus said, is within you because the kingdom is your own consciousness. It is truly in your consciousness that you decide whether you will experience the abundant life of God's kingdom or the not so abundant life created by those who have lost awareness of God's kingdom, have lost awareness of their true identity and of their creative powers. Instead of being conscious co-creators of God's abundant kingdom, they have become unconscious co-creators of the kingdom of lack.

God gave you unlimited creative powers in the sense that you cannot turn them off. Even when you lose awareness of God's laws, you are still co-creating and that is why, as the laws in most countries say: "Ignorance of the law is no excuse." Even if you do not know God's creative principles, you are still creating through the powers of your mind. When you use your imagination to envision imperfect and imbalanced images, you are imposing those images upon the Ma-ter Light. The Ma-ter Light outpictures those images and that is why you experience limitations, pain and suffering in the physical world on earth.

I have given you the overall picture of the reality of life on earth. Surely, there are many details that can be filled in. If you will contemplate what I have given you and what I will give you in the following keys, you will see that it is possible for you to rise above all human limitations. It is possible for you to walk out of the desert of human limitations until you stand on the bank of the River of Life, God's ever-flowing abundance. It is possible for you to give up, to surrender completely, the limited state of consciousness based on separation and duality. You can once again plunge yourself into the River of Life and become one with the whole of God's creation.

This does not mean that you lose your individuality. On the contrary, it means that you regain your true individuality— instead of the limited pseudo individuality you have built during your sojourn on earth. Once you reclaim your true individuality, you will know that you are not a limited, mortal, human being, that you are not a sinner by nature, that you are indeed a son or daughter of God and that you have the potential to co-create God's kingdom right here on earth. You will not only magnify your own life but magnify the lives of all other people until this planet is raised up and outpictures the same perfection, balance and harmony found in the spiritual realm. This is the true meaning of bringing God's kingdom to earth.

If you are open to my words, there is a very high probability that you descended to this earth for the specific purpose of bringing God's kingdom to this planet. You came here not because you had rebelled against God's will in a different realm, you came here because you desired to bring God's kingdom to earth. You came on a rescue mission to serve as an example for those of your brothers and sisters who had rebelled against God's laws and had therefore lost their way. You came here with the love that you wanted to see the Mother Light itself be set free from the imperfect images put upon it by these fallen beings so that it could be free to outpicture the perfection and the beauty that you know is its true potential.

My beloved, if you came here out of love, you will know the truth that I speak. If you came here for other reasons, but have tired of going against God's law and have reconnected yourself to the inner love of God, then you too will know the truth that I speak. You will know this if you focus on your heart center and feel a stirring, a vibration, even waves of light that rush over you and show you that the words I speak in this course, the words that are outside yourself, vibrate in perfect resonance with something within your heart.

I will later explain to you what that something is, but for now I ask you to focus your attention at the center of your chest, at the height of your physical heart, and feel if the words that I have given you have stirred something in you. If you feel that stirring, then you will know that you are on your way back to being the fullness of the conscious co-creator that you were designed to be from the very beginning. You will know the truth of the path that I am offering you. As we move on into the following chapters, you will begin to see that path unfold. This will give you new hope, new direction, new purpose and a sense of love for your Creator, for all life and for your Self as part of the River of Life.

8 | I INVOKE SPIRITUAL HARMONY

In the name I AM THAT I AM, Jesus Christ, I call to all representatives of the Divine Mother, especially Mother Mary, to help me develop the ability to discern what is in alignment with the reality of God and what springs from the duality consciousness. Help me transcend all blocks to my ability to manifest abundance, including...

[Make personal calls.]

1. I transcend duality

1. I am transcending the consciousness represented by the fruit of the knowledge of good and evil, meaning *relative* good and evil.

> O Blessed Mary's Song of Life,
> consuming every form of strife.
> As I attune to sound so fair,
> each cell is healthy, I declare.

O Mother Mary, generate,
the song that does accelerate,
my mind into a peaceful state,
God's perfect love I radiate.

2. I am transcending the ego-based consciousness of defining my own concepts of good and evil, defining my own "reality."

As life's own song I ever hear,
it does consume all sense of fear.
In tune with Mother's symphony,
from all diseases I AM free.

O Mother Mary, generate,
the song that does accelerate,
my mind into a peaceful state,
God's perfect love I radiate.

3. I am experiencing my I AM Presence, and it is my guiding rod for what is in harmony with the laws of God, beneficial to the whole and sustainable.

In Mother's love I do transcend,
and all my struggles hereby end.
For when with Mother's eye I see,
no imperfection touches me.

O Mother Mary, generate,
the song that does accelerate,
my mind into a peaceful state,
God's perfect love I radiate.

4. I hereby decide that I am willing to go back to God, to confess my actions and seek forgiveness. I am revealing everything to God.

> I see that healing must begin
> by finding Living Christ within.
> For as I see with single eye,
> each cell the light does amplify.

> **O Mother Mary, generate,**
> **the song that does accelerate,**
> **my mind into a peaceful state,**
> **God's perfect love I radiate.**

5. God will not create the abundant life *for* me. God wants me to co-create the abundant life for myself.

> In Mother's music I am free,
> from memories of a lesser me.
> My vision in a perfect state,
> that all my cells regenerate.

> **O Mother Mary, generate,**
> **the song that does accelerate,**
> **my mind into a peaceful state,**
> **God's perfect love I radiate.**

6. God wants me to know that I have created the abundant life through my internal power – the power of God within me – and that I have done so by aligning myself with the creative principles of God.

O Mother's Love, sweet melody,
from imperfections I AM free.
O Mother Mary, sound of sounds,
within my heart your love abounds.

O Mother Mary, generate,
the song that does accelerate,
my mind into a peaceful state,
God's perfect love I radiate.

7. I no longer want the empty dreams or shortcuts and I no longer want to experience pain, lack and suffering. I am walking the real path whereby I am changing the totality of my consciousness, bringing it into alignment with God's creative principles.

Through Mother's beauty so sublime,
transcending bounds of space and time.
All cells beyond the mortal tomb,
as they are whole in Mother's womb.

O Mother Mary, generate,
the song that does accelerate,
my mind into a peaceful state,
God's perfect love I radiate.

8. My individual lifestream is in harmony with the whole of the Body of God in both heaven and earth. The entire matter universe, the Ma-ter Light itself, is rejoicing in filling my true desires.

In resonance with life's own song,
in life's harmonics I belong.
The blueprint of my perfect state
does every cell reconsecrate.

O Mother Mary, generate,
the song that does accelerate,
my mind into a peaceful state,
God's perfect love I radiate.

9. I accept the abundance coming to me through the balanced and harmonious use of the creative powers with which God endowed me when my lifestream first came into being.

The tuning fork in every cell
is now attuned to Mother's bell.
From curse of death I AM now free,
I claim my immortality.

O Mother Mary, generate,
the song that does accelerate,
my mind into a peaceful state,
God's perfect love I radiate.

2. I embrace the Christ consciousness

1. It is not my goal to bring about some temporary riches here on earth. My goal is a permanent change in consciousness. I am realigning myself with the original design that was held in the mind of God when my lifestream was created.

O Blessed Mary's Song of Life,
consuming every form of strife.
As I attune to sound so fair,
each cell is healthy, I declare.

O Mother Mary, generate,
the song that does accelerate,
my mind into a peaceful state,
God's perfect love I radiate.

2. I am a true son/daughter of God, designed in the image and likeness of God. I am using my creative powers in perfect harmony with the whole. I am magnifying my own lifestream and the life experience of all life on earth.

As life's own song I ever hear,
it does consume all sense of fear.
In tune with Mother's symphony,
from all diseases I AM free.

O Mother Mary, generate,
the song that does accelerate,
my mind into a peaceful state,
God's perfect love I radiate.

3. I am using my creative powers in harmony with the laws of God. I am in perfect alignment with the purpose of life and with the guiding principles of life.

In Mother's love I do transcend,
and all my struggles hereby end.
For when with Mother's eye I see,
no imperfection touches me.

O Mother Mary, generate,
the song that does accelerate,
my mind into a peaceful state,
God's perfect love I radiate.

4. I am immersed in the ever-flowing, ever-growing River of Life. I am constantly moving with the River of Life. I am constantly transcending myself, multiplying my talents and becoming more, thereby bringing about more abundance in my life.

> I see that healing must begin
> by finding Living Christ within.
> For as I see with single eye,
> each cell the light does amplify.

> **O Mother Mary, generate,**
> **the song that does accelerate,**
> **my mind into a peaceful state,**
> **God's perfect love I radiate.**

5. The spiritual definition of life is that I am transcending myself and becoming more. I am experiencing the abundant life, I am part of God's ever-moving flow of abundance, the River of Life.

> In Mother's music I am free,
> from memories of a lesser me.
> My vision in a perfect state,
> that all my cells regenerate.

> **O Mother Mary, generate,**
> **the song that does accelerate,**
> **my mind into a peaceful state,**
> **God's perfect love I radiate.**

6. I was created as a self-aware being with limited creative powers. As I multiply my talents by co-creating in harmony with the laws of God, God will give me greater creative powers.

O Mother's Love, sweet melody,
from imperfections I AM free.
O Mother Mary, sound of sounds,
within my heart your love abounds.

**O Mother Mary, generate,
the song that does accelerate,
my mind into a peaceful state,
God's perfect love I radiate.**

7. I am gradually rising in creative ability and awareness until I
can permanently ascend from the matter universe and become
an immortal being in the spiritual world.

Through Mother's beauty so sublime,
transcending bounds of space and time.
All cells beyond the mortal tomb,
as they are whole in Mother's womb.

**O Mother Mary, generate,
the song that does accelerate,
my mind into a peaceful state,
God's perfect love I radiate.**

8. God built a safety mechanism into the design of the universe,
namely the Word, the only begotten son of the Father, the universal Christ consciousness.

In resonance with life's own song,
in life's harmonics I belong.
The blueprint of my perfect state
does every cell reconsecrate.

O Mother Mary, generate,
the song that does accelerate,
my mind into a peaceful state,
God's perfect love I radiate.

9. I am creating from inside the creation already created by God. I am creating something that is sustainable through the agency of the Christ consciousness.

The tuning fork in every cell
is now attuned to Mother's bell.
From curse of death I AM now free,
I claim my immortality.

O Mother Mary, generate,
the song that does accelerate,
my mind into a peaceful state,
God's perfect love I radiate.

3. I accept God's love for me

1. The Christ consciousness is an awareness of the laws of God that can never be compromised. The Christ consciousness is always one with the Father and with the Father's laws. In oneness with Jesus, I say: "I and my Father are one."

O Blessed Mary's Song of Life,
consuming every form of strife.
As I attune to sound so fair,
each cell is healthy, I declare.

O Mother Mary, generate,
the song that does accelerate,
my mind into a peaceful state,
God's perfect love I radiate.

2. I am not the true doer, for I can of mine own self do nothing. I co-create through the power of God within me, and I access that power through the Christ consciousness. Christ consciousness is the natural state for any lifestream created by God.

As life's own song I ever hear,
it does consume all sense of fear.
In tune with Mother's symphony,
from all diseases I AM free.

O Mother Mary, generate,
the song that does accelerate,
my mind into a peaceful state,
God's perfect love I radiate.

3. The true doer is the higher part of my being, the individualization of God, focused as my I AM Presence. My Presence is creating by using the energy and the laws of God to bring about form.

In Mother's love I do transcend,
and all my struggles hereby end.
For when with Mother's eye I see,
no imperfection touches me.

**O Mother Mary, generate,
the song that does accelerate,
my mind into a peaceful state,
God's perfect love I radiate.**

4. When a form is created in harmony with the laws defined by the Creator, that form will be part of the River of Life, meaning it will be part of the process of constant self-transcendence. A form is sustainable only through self-transcendence because growth is the basic law of creation.

I see that healing must begin
by finding Living Christ within.
For as I see with single eye,
each cell the light does amplify.

**O Mother Mary, generate,
the song that does accelerate,
my mind into a peaceful state,
God's perfect love I radiate.**

5. It is the contracting force that makes it possible to create form. If I become attached to any form, I go outside the River of Life and become subject to the force that returns the Ma-ter Light to its ground state.

In Mother's music I am free,
from memories of a lesser me.
My vision in a perfect state,
that all my cells regenerate.

O Mother Mary, generate,
the song that does accelerate,
my mind into a peaceful state,
God's perfect love I radiate.

6. I am in the Christ consciousness, and I see myself as one with the All. I am part of the ever-moving River of Life that is the totality of God's creation, God's Being.

O Mother's Love, sweet melody,
from imperfections I AM free.
O Mother Mary, sound of sounds,
within my heart your love abounds.

O Mother Mary, generate,
the song that does accelerate,
my mind into a peaceful state,
God's perfect love I radiate.

7. My lifestream, my consciousness, my sense of identity, is not confined to this material world. I am rising above my limited sense of identity. I am building a new sense of identity that is in alignment with the true design of my being.

Through Mother's beauty so sublime,
transcending bounds of space and time.
All cells beyond the mortal tomb,
as they are whole in Mother's womb.

O Mother Mary, generate,
the song that does accelerate,
my mind into a peaceful state,
God's perfect love I radiate.

8. I understand my purpose for coming to this earth. I am bringing myself back into alignment with my original desires, the desires that made me come into this universe.

> In resonance with life's own song,
> in life's harmonics I belong.
> The blueprint of my perfect state
> does every cell reconsecrate.

> **O Mother Mary, generate,**
> **the song that does accelerate,**
> **my mind into a peaceful state,**
> **God's perfect love I radiate.**

9. My God is a loving God. The original love for me, held in the heart of God, has not been diminished by anything I have done on earth. God loves me in the exact same way as when my lifestream was first created. I accept God's unconditional love for me.

> The tuning fork in every cell
> is now attuned to Mother's bell.
> From curse of death I AM now free,
> I claim my immortality.

> **O Mother Mary, generate,**
> **the song that does accelerate,**
> **my mind into a peaceful state,**
> **God's perfect love I radiate.**

4. I know my true purpose

1. I hereby surrender my limited sense of identity. I accept God's abundance. I am back into God's kingdom, and I am receiving the abundant life that is rightfully mine. I am following God's creative principles and bringing that abundance into manifestation in my life experience.

> O Blessed Mary's Song of Life,
> consuming every form of strife.
> As I attune to sound so fair,
> each cell is healthy, I declare.

> **O Mother Mary, generate,**
> **the song that does accelerate,**
> **my mind into a peaceful state,**
> **God's perfect love I radiate.**

2. I am a conscious co-creator with God. I know who I am, I know where I came from. I am consciously exercising my creative powers with the goal to magnify the whole of God's creation.

> As life's own song I ever hear,
> it does consume all sense of fear.
> In tune with Mother's symphony,
> from all diseases I AM free.

> **O Mother Mary, generate,**
> **the song that does accelerate,**
> **my mind into a peaceful state,**
> **God's perfect love I radiate.**

3. I am walking the path that leads me back to my Father's kingdom within me. It is in my consciousness that I decide whether I will experience the abundant life of God's kingdom or the not so abundant life created by those who have fallen into separation.

In Mother's love I do transcend,
and all my struggles hereby end.
For when with Mother's eye I see,
no imperfection touches me.

O Mother Mary, generate,
the song that does accelerate,
my mind into a peaceful state,
God's perfect love I radiate.

4. I am rising above all human limitations. I am walking out of the desert of human limitations. I am standing on the bank of the River of Life, God's ever-flowing abundance.

I see that healing must begin
by finding Living Christ within.
For as I see with single eye,
each cell the light does amplify.

O Mother Mary, generate,
the song that does accelerate,
my mind into a peaceful state,
God's perfect love I radiate.

5. I am giving up, I am surrendering the limited state of consciousness based on separation and duality. I am plunging myself into the River of Life, and I am one with the whole of God's creation.

In Mother's music I am free,
from memories of a lesser me.
My vision in a perfect state,
that all my cells regenerate.

O Mother Mary, generate,
the song that does accelerate,
my mind into a peaceful state,
God's perfect love I radiate.

6. I am regaining my true individuality. I am surrendering the
limited pseudo individuality I have built during my sojourn on
earth. I am a son/daughter of God and I am co-creating God's
kingdom right here on earth.

O Mother's Love, sweet melody,
from imperfections I AM free.
O Mother Mary, sound of sounds,
within my heart your love abounds.

O Mother Mary, generate,
the song that does accelerate,
my mind into a peaceful state,
God's perfect love I radiate.

7. I am magnifying my own life and the lives of all other people.
This planet is raised up and outpictures the same perfection, balance and harmony found in the spiritual realm. This is the true
meaning of bringing God's kingdom to earth.

Through Mother's beauty so sublime,
transcending bounds of space and time.
All cells beyond the mortal tomb,
as they are whole in Mother's womb.

O Mother Mary, generate,
the song that does accelerate,
my mind into a peaceful state,
God's perfect love I radiate.

8. I descended to this earth for the specific purpose of bringing God's kingdom to this planet. I came here because I desired to bring God's kingdom to earth.

In resonance with life's own song,
in life's harmonics I belong.
The blueprint of my perfect state
does every cell reconsecrate.

O Mother Mary, generate,
the song that does accelerate,
my mind into a peaceful state,
God's perfect love I radiate.

9. I came here with the love that I wanted to see the Mother Light itself be set free from the imperfect images put upon it by the fallen beings. The Mother Light is free to outpicture the perfection and the beauty that I know is its true potential.

The tuning fork in every cell
is now attuned to Mother's bell.
From curse of death I AM now free,
I claim my immortality.

O Mother Mary, generate,
the song that does accelerate,
my mind into a peaceful state,
God's perfect love I radiate.

Sealing

In the name of the Divine Mother, I call to Mother Mary for the sealing of myself and all people in my circle of influence in the creative flow of the Divine Mother, the River of Life. I call for the multiplication of my calls by all representatives of the Divine Mother, so that we form the perfect figure-eight flow of "As Above, so below." Thus, I accept that this is fully manifest, because the mouth of the Lord, the Divine Mother that I AM, has spoken it. Amen.

9 | BRINGING SPIRITUAL LIGHT INTO THE MATERIAL WORLD

My beloved heart, we have now reached a turning point in this series of discourses. I have given you a number of ideas that might seem esoteric and somewhat disconnected. Every idea, and even the precise wording of every idea, is designed to trigger inner memories that will bring you step by step closer to being able to remember and accept who you really are and why you are here on earth. In this chapter I will explain to you the very purpose of creation itself and the very purpose of your existence, even the specific purpose of your coming to this planet. This will give you the option of choosing between the high road of manifesting God's abundance or the low road of seeking to acquire earthly abundance. This is the difference between trying to take abundance by force or allowing God to give it to you freely.

I have explained to you that God has two aspects. One is the Creator and one is the Pure Being of God in which there are no differentiations. If you will go into your heart and consider my words, you will realize that the Pure Being of God is the Allness. The Pure Being of God is complete and self-sufficient. Within the Pure Being of God, there is no room for a form that is set apart from the Allness. In the Pure Being of God it is not possible to create any distinct form, to create anything that is separate from the Allness. Before any form can be created, there must be a space that is less than the Allness of God so that in the "empty" space distinct forms can be created, forms that are set apart from the Allness. Compare this to the sun where the light is so intense that only pure, white light can exist. Only at some distance from the sun is there room for light of different colors and shades.

I will now give you an image of creation, yet I want to make sure you understand that the image I give you is adapted to your current state of consciousness, in which your mind tends to think in linear terms. What I give you is a linear image, but I desire you to keep in mind that God's reality is not linear. Be careful not to take the image I give you and turn it into a graven image that you think gives a complete picture of God and God's creation.

I do not give this image in order to trap your mind in a particular view of God. I give you this image to set your mind free from the limited view of God that most people have in this world. I give you this image with the hope that you can eventually go beyond all needs to have a linear image of God and thereby experience directly the spherical, all-encompassing consciousness and Being of God.

In the Allness of God, there are no distinct forms. Neither do the concepts of time and space have any meaning in the Allness. In order to start the process of the creation of a world of form, the Creator withdraws itself and creates what some spiritual teachings have called the "void." When the Creator withdraws itself, it pulls itself into a single point. This is what scientists call a singularity, and they currently claim that the creation of the universe began when all matter was concentrated into a singularity. Imagine that you have the Allness of God, in which there is no space and no distinct forms. The Creator now draws itself into a single point, and around that single point it creates a void that is less than the Allness.

This void is like a gigantic empty space, shaped like an egg. Some people have had mystical visions in which they saw God's creation as the cosmic egg. I do not desire you to see creation as an egg surrounded by nothingness. I desire you to see that creation started when an egg-shaped void was created, and thus the void is surrounded by Allness. The void is itself empty space, meaning that it is devoid of any kind of form and of the Allness of God. One might say that it has nothing in it—neither the Allness of God nor any distinct forms. One might even say that it is darkness, in that it has no substance at all.

In the center of this original void is a single point that is a very high concentration of that portion of the Allness of God from which the void was created. This is the focal point for the second aspect of God, the individual Creator. The Creator has the drive to become more and thus fill the void, until the void once again becomes the Allness of God. What we have here is the cosmic dance that some have called the inbreath and the outbreath of God.

The Creator breathes in, concentrating itself into the singularity and creating the void. Then the Creator breathes out until the cosmic outbreath again fills the void. In the process of participating in this cosmic dance, of filling the void, the Creator grows in self-awareness. This growth in self-awareness is the entire purpose of creation. The growth in self-awareness does not apply only to the original Being that is the Creator, and I will shortly explain why.

***

The Creator exists as a single point, as the singularity, in the middle of the void—the void that is less than the Allness and therefore can be filled by forms created by the Creator. As the first act of creation, the Creator needs to create a substance that can be molded into any form. God said: "Let there be Light," and there *was* light. As Genesis records (Genesis 1:4), God separated the light from the darkness, meaning that God separated the light that can take on form from the darkness that fills that part of the void in which there is yet no form, no light. The overall purpose for the Creator's efforts is to expand the light until it fills the entire void and consumes the darkness, the darkness that is not evil but simply the absence of light.

This act of creation does not take place in an instant, for even though the Creator has Almighty power, the Creator does not use its power to fill the void instantly. The Creator is not filling the void only for its own sake. God is filling the void in a gradual manner in order to create the opportunity that self-aware beings, created by the Creator as extensions of itself, can serve as co-creators and help fill the void. In so doing, they too grow in self-awareness and become more aware of who they are, from where they came and where they have the potential to go. This is the true purpose of creation, a growth in self-awareness that causes even the Pure Being of God to become more because God becomes more through the self-awareness of individual Creators and their co-creators.

When your Creator began the creative work that has led to your existence and the existence of the material universe in which you currently abide, God started by creating a sphere that was set apart from the void. In that sphere was a certain amount of God's light. This light set it apart from the void, and it served as a basis for creating form. Your Creator did indeed create certain forms in that sphere of light, but your God did not fill that sphere completely with light. Your Creator created extensions of itself as self-aware beings and sent them into the first sphere with the command to multiply and take dominion. Multiply your creative abilities, multiply your light, multiply your self-awareness and then take dominion over the sphere in which you abide. Fill that sphere with light until it becomes truly the kingdom of light, the kingdom of God. What does it mean that a sphere is the kingdom of God? It means that everything radiates light and you can see the pure Mother Light behind all manifestations. You see God the Creator as the first cause behind all appearances and thus you can never lose the awareness of God.

When the first sphere had become filled with light to a critical intensity, the drive of God to become more mandated that another sphere was created. This second sphere encompassed a greater portion of the void, yet like the first it was not completely filled with light. Self-aware beings were sent from the first sphere into the second sphere with the command to multiply and take dominion. Some of the beings sent into this second sphere were indeed created directly as extensions of the Creator, yet most of them were created as extensions of the self-aware beings that had served as co-creators and had filled the first sphere with light. These were then the extensions of the beings in the first sphere, who were extensions of the Creator.

This basic process of creation has continued through many spheres, many cycles. The world in which you live, the material universe, is the latest extension of this creative process. It is indeed an extension of the entire process whereby God creates a new sphere that takes in more of the void and therefore separates it from the darkness by being filled with a certain amount of light. The material universe in which you live is not – as your senses tell you, as science tells you, and even as many religions tell you – set apart from God and the rest of God's creation. The material universe is not separated from God or from the spiritual realm by some impenetrable barrier. This universe is an extension of the spiritual realm, it is an extension of God. Although I have given you a linear image, the reality of God is not so linear. In the room where you are now sitting, there are many different radio waves that are penetrating the air. These waves have different frequencies, and that is why they can coexist in the same space without canceling out each other. So it is with the spheres created by God; they also coexist in the same cosmic space, in the same void, they simply have different frequencies.

At this very moment, I am not some being sitting up in a remote heaven, talking down to you. I am indeed right here with you. As I am dictating these words through one particular messenger, I have merged my Being with the consciousness of the messenger, even with his body. Because I have transcended the material universe, transcended time and space, I am not confined to a particular space or a particular time. If you are willing, I can assure you that as you read these words, your attention creates a bridge to my heart. If you are willing to let me enter your being, I can indeed cross that bridge and merge my Being with your own being. I can take you by the hand and show you the deeper reality behind my words, the reality that cannot be expressed in words because they are far too linear.

You are not separated from your Creator. As you are sitting here reading this course, your Creator is right here with you. Your Creator is omnipresent within its creation, and therefore you can never actually be separated from your Creator. You can only be separated from your Creator in your own mind because your mind creates the sense of separation. This sense of separation is nothing but an illusion, a mirage projected unto the screen of life by a certain part of your consciousness, a part that I will later expose for what it is.

***

Let me now return to my image of creation. My point for telling you that you are not separated from your Creator, or from the brothers and sisters who have gone before you and have ascended to heaven, is to make you realize that when God created the first self-aware beings, those beings were created out of the consciousness and Being of God. The first beings, which we might name Alpha and Omega (Revelation 1:8), the beginning and the ending, then created other beings who created other beings, and so forth and so on into many layers of creation, many congruent spheres of creation.

Each being that was created, was created out of the greater Being of its parents, and those parents were created out of the greater Beings of their parents. If you keep tracing this back to the beginning, you see that all self-aware beings were created out of the Being of the Creator itself. You are not some disconnected being that suddenly appeared out of nowhere. You are, in fact, an extension of, an individualization of, a greater Being that exists right now in the spiritual realm. This greater being is part of a hierarchy of spiritual beings that form what we might call the "Chain of Being," and it reaches all the way back to the Creator itself.

You are truly a part of this Chain of Being, you are an extension of the Creator, an individualization of the Creator, whereby God can enter into this particular sphere of his creation. God can complete his creative work from within creation itself and at the same time experience this particular sphere from the inside. I know it might take you some time to fully accept and understand it, yet if you will invite me into your heart, I will make it easier for you to accept your true origin and your true identity. When you accept this identity, your outlook on life will take a dramatic turn. You will realize that life is not meaningless, life is not empty. Life does indeed have a greater purpose, and you are part of a grand scheme that is aimed at creating the kingdom of

God right here on earth, thereby turning this planet into a world so beautiful that it will fulfill your deepest dreams, your deepest longings. You might have forgotten those longings, but I don't think you have forgotten the very fact that when you see the limitations, the pain and the suffering on earth, there is something inside of you that cries out and says: "This is not right, this is not the way things are supposed to be." This shows you that deep within you is the memory that there is more to life, that there is indeed a reason for being, a reason for your being here on earth.

This is important because you now see that life is worth living, that life has a greater purpose, and you also see that there is a greater purpose for creating abundance. You are not here to simply fulfill the temporary, human or carnal desires that center around your physical body and the sense of identity that is based on the body. You are more than the physical body, you are more than this lower sense of identity. You have a greater sense of identity, a greater part of your being, and you are here to express the fullness of that greater identity, that divine individuality. You are here to serve as a co-creator with God who can bring the light of God, the perfection of God, the harmony of God, the qualities of God into this world. You are here to be the light of the world (Matthew 5:14) and to turn this world into a kingdom of light, the light that consumes the darkness that is currently covering the land and creating all kinds of suffering, pain and lack that you know simply cannot be God's design or God's will.

***

Let us now consider more specifically why you are here on earth. When God creates a new sphere, God fills it with a certain amount of light. God, or rather God's representatives, do create a certain amount of forms. Planet earth was created by seven representatives of God who created this planet as a platform that was capable of sustaining life in a certain state of abundance and balance. It was never God's design that the earth should remain in that state. The drive behind all creation is the drive to be more, and God sent a number of self-aware beings into this world with the command to multiply and take dominion. What does it mean to multiply and take dominion? Ultimately, it means to multiply your self-awareness so you become aware of your ability to serve as a co-creator with God.

You become aware that your consciousness, your mind, has the ability to serve as the open door for bringing more of God's light, more of the high-frequency spiritual light, into the lower vibrations of the material universe. As that light is brought into this world, it consumes the darkness, and thereby this world becomes lighter and brighter and begins to express all of the perfection that is found in the spiritual realm. As the co-creators multiply their creative abilities, they become better at directing God's light through their minds, thereby using their minds to impose a perfect, a balanced and a harmonious image upon the light. It is this very process, of imposing a mental image upon the Ma-ter Light that creates form.

As a co-creator you have a twofold purpose. Your first purpose is to expand the connection with your I AM Presence that resides permanently in a higher realm. As you expand that connection, more and more light can stream through your consciousness. You are bringing more light into this world, raising the total amount of light that is available for creating form. This raises the potential of the earth for expressing God's abundance.

The true key to increasing the amount of abundance on earth is to increase the amount of light that is available in this realm. When you have drawn the light of God down from your I AM Presence, you can then, through the self-awareness that is focused in this realm, direct that light and use it to create forms that express more of God's abundance. The abundance becomes manifest as a physical reality that can be perceived even by the gross physical senses of the human body. What I have just told you is the master key to abundance. It is indeed the chief cornerstone that has been rejected by the builders (Matthew 21:42), that has been overlooked by most human beings. It has been overlooked by most of the gurus who claim that they can help people increase their worldly abundance. Why is what I have just told you so important? Please allow me some time to explain this because this one point is what will make or break your efforts to achieve the abundant life. If you do not understand the point I am trying to convey, you will never achieve true spiritual abundance. You might or you might not achieve material abundance, but that material abundance will never satisfy the inner longing of your being.

The all-important point about abundance is that everything in this material world, everything on planet earth, is created from God's light. It is created from spiritual light that was lowered in vibration until it vibrates within the spectrum of frequencies that make up the material universe. After it is lowered in vibration, it is then available to create form in this universe. The material universe is made from energies that vibrate within a certain frequency spectrum. You are a co-creator with God, and your sense of self-awareness is focused in this frequency spectrum. When you co-create, you use your mind to impose an image upon the Ma-ter Light. Before you can do this, there must be a portion of light that has been lowered into this realm so that it now vibrates within the material frequency spectrum.

Your mind has two abilities when it comes to working with God's light. Your mind can lower the vibration of spiritual light to the material frequency spectrum. Once the light is lowered in vibration, your mind can impose an image upon it that creates a certain form. Although these two abilities were designed to work together, it is possible for you to separate them in your mind. For example, many people have forgotten the ability to bring spiritual light into this world but still use their minds to impose mental images upon the light that is available in this frequency spectrum. Before any form can be created, a self-aware being must reach into the spiritual realm, establish a connection to his or her spiritual self and serve as the open door for bringing spiritual light into the frequency spectrum of the material universe. When planet earth was created, a certain amount of light was brought into the material frequency spectrum by the Elohim. After co-creators started embodying on this planet, no more light was brought in by spiritual Beings. It was now up to the inhabitants of earth to bring more light into the material spectrum. The total amount of abundance that can be created on earth is directly dependent upon the total amount of light that is available within the energy field of this planet. Most human beings have forgotten their ability to bring light into this world and they have created imbalanced forms with the light that was available. The contracting force of the Mother has actually reduced the amount of light below the level that was available when the planet was created. There is less abundance on earth today than when the Elohim created this planet.

***

Please make an effort to go within your heart and allow me to give you the understanding that cannot be expressed in words, yet can be triggered by the words I am giving you. During your upbringing, your mind has been programmed to believe that there is only a certain amount of abundance in this world. You have been programmed to believe that you live in a world that is defined by lack and limitations. For example, you have been told that there is only a finite amount of natural resources available on planet earth, and therefore it is possible that humankind can consume all of these resources and then have nothing left. Many sources have indeed sought to make you believe that this is an inevitable scenario, and thus you should accept certain limitations for your life and even for humankind as a whole. This concept is not unconditionally true, neither is it completely wrong. I am sure you have been told that there is only a certain amount of oil available on this planet. When humankind consumes all the oil, there will be nothing left and you will not be able to run your car or fly in an airplane. Some have attempted to create the image of a looming doomsday when humankind has consumed all of the resources on this planet and the entire planet becomes a barren desert that can no longer support life. My beloved heart, this doomsday scenario is indeed a possibility, but it is not the certainty that some portray it to be.

You know very well that new oil reserves are constantly being discovered. You also know that there was a time when there was no oil on this planet. Oil was produced because organic matter died and through the movement of the earth was buried and exposed to pressure that turned it into oil. Diamonds are created when ordinary coal is exposed to immense pressure in the crust of the earth. Since there is a very large amount of coal on this planet, there is truly a potential that an enormous amount of diamonds could be created. I know some will say that it will take millions of years to create more oil, and therefore humankind will run out of oil before the current oil supplies can be replaced through this natural process. Certainly, this is true, but I would remind you that oil has been around for thousands of years and has even been known to humankind. Yet 500 years ago oil was considered an insignificant natural resource and the reason was that humankind did not have the knowledge of how to make use of oil. People had not invented combustion engines or any of the other mechanical devices that make use of fossil fuel to produce goods or allow people to travel. It simply is not true that this planet has a finite amount of natural resources and therefore a finite amount of abundance. Only a few centuries ago oil was a largely worthless substance and it became valuable only because humankind increased its knowledge, its awareness, its understanding and therefore was able to create technology that made use of oil, turning it from a worthless substance into a valuable resource.

Where did this knowledge and understanding come from? Do you seriously believe that it came out of nowhere? Or are you open to the idea that some human beings reached beyond the material universe, established a connection to their spiritual selves and through that connection they were able to bring forth the ideas and the understanding that gave birth to new inventions and new technology? Certainly, there are some resources on this planet of which there is only a finite amount. Certainly, it is possible that humankind can run out of oil and therefore lose the ability to use technology that is based on burning oil. Before oil became a resource, humankind had more primitive technology that used other natural resources, such as wood and coal, that was converted into steam. You know very well that there is already technology that splits the atom and converts uranium into a resource more powerful than oil. Although I do not consider nuclear power a problem-free technology, it is quite possible that there are substances on this earth that are currently considered worthless but that, through the right knowledge and understanding, could become the basis for new kinds of technology that are far more powerful than the technology based on fossil fuels. It is quite possible that humankind can expand the amount of abundance currently found on earth. By multiplying their creative talents, by multiplying their understanding of the laws of God, the laws God used to design this universe, human beings can transcend their current level of awareness and truly become co-creators with God who can create abundance out of

what today seems worthless. Consider how sand that was use-
less was turned into silicon and became the basis for the entire
computer industry that has created immense abundance in many
aspects of life. Consider how people are already researching how
to use Hydrogen, the most prolific substance in the universe, as
the fuel to run technology. I encourage you to consider these
ideas and to realize that the scenario promoted by the doomsday prophets – of this planet becoming a barren desert – is only
possible if humankind stops all efforts to expand its creativity. If
people stop multiplying their talents, their creative powers, then
indeed human society will eventually consume the resources that
are available according to people's current understanding of natural law. This planet will one day be turned into a desert that can
no longer support life. This will happen only if people choose
to shut off their creative abilities, if they refuse to multiply their
talents and instead bury them in the ground—as a symbol for
their current level of consciousness.

***

Everything you see around you, even the physical matter
that might seem to have no connection whatsoever to the spiritual world, is made from spiritual light. Even your scientists
have recognized that solid matter is made from vibrating energy.
That vibrating energy is simply God's light, spiritual light, that
has been lowered in vibration. The amount of resources and
abundance that is currently found on planet earth is not determined by some arbitrary measure, nor is it a fixed amount that
was determined when the earth was created. The amount of
resources and abundance found on earth is in direct proportion to the amount of spiritual light that has been brought into
the material frequency spectrum by the self-aware beings living
on planet earth. Matter did not appear out of nowhere. It is a

product of the Mother Light being lowered in vibration until it reaches the frequency spectrum of physical matter. Contrary to what you have been brought up to believe, there is not a fixed amount of matter. God's co-creators can literally bring more light into the material frequency spectrum and expand the amount of natural resources on this planet.

Abundance is not a fixed quantity. It is quite possible for human beings to bring forth more abundance by making more efficient use of the natural resources that are currently available on this planet. It is even possible that human beings can bring more spiritual light into the material realm and thereby increase the amount of resources and abundance available on earth. This opens entirely new perspectives for the possibility of attaining the abundant life. You have, right within yourself, right within your own consciousness, the ability to reach into the spiritual realm, to connect to your I AM Presence, and to bring spiritual light into the material world. When you do this, you will increase the amount of abundance manifest in your life and you will do this without taking that abundance from any other part of life.

Please take some time to step back and truly consider what I am saying. What I am saying here is that when it comes to attaining greater abundance in your life, you can take three different approaches:

• The lowest and most primitive approach is to reason that there is only a fixed amount of abundance available in this world. Since not every human being is rich, it is obvious that the amount of abundance available in this world is not enough for everyone. If you are to become rich, you must take abundance from someone else whereby they become poor. Throughout most of known history, a small elite has subscribed to this view of a fixed amount of abundance. Such people have used aggressive means to set themselves up as a power elite with a monopoly on wealth and the control over resources. They have done this by basically enslaving the majority of the population to serve as the worker bees for milking the planet of its meager natural resources and concentrating them for the use of the power elite. This is an incredibly primitive approach to abundance. It is an approach that is based entirely on force, based entirely on the need to fight with others for a fixed and inadequate supply of abundance. It is an approach which is based on the philosophy of lack, the philosophy that makes it necessary to take abundance by force and thereby inevitably deprive other human beings of their abundance in order to concentrate wealth in the hands of a select few. This approach requires continued use of force because the elite cannot retain its wealth without continually defending it, not only against other people but even against the forces of nature that seek to take away from them what they seek to own. This approach to abundance is an uphill battle, a never-ending struggle.

•   A much higher approach to abundance is to reason that it is possible to create more abundance by increasing your understanding of the laws of nature. By coming up with new inventions and new technology, you can create wealth by turning worthless substances into valuable resources or by turning know-how into valuable technology. This is a far higher approach to abundance, yet it still does not address the fact that there is currently only a certain amount of energy available to human beings on earth. It too has a certain factor of limitation, and you currently see this in society. Many people know that the days of using fossil fuels to run humankind's technology are numbered. They know that wars have already been fought over oil and that there is a potential for even more devastating wars to be fought over oil or other resources. Despite the fact that many people see the need to bring forth new technology, that new technology currently is not forthcoming. This shows you that even the approach of seeking to create more abundance by using the resources that are already available has certain limitations. The limitation it has is that the true key to bringing forth more abundance is to bring more spiritual energy into the material frequency spectrum. As scientists say: "Everything is energy." The total amount of abundance available on planet earth is in direct proportion to the total amount of energy available in the energy system of this planet. The only way to truly expand abundance is to expand the amount of energy available on earth.

• The third approach to abundance is to combine the second approach of seeking greater understanding with the spiritual approach of reaching into a higher realm to bring more energy into the material frequency spectrum. The purpose of this course is to teach you how to make use of this approach to abundance.

***

You are standing at a dividing line, the dividing line between a mortal, human, force-based approach to abundance and a spiritual, immortal, love-based approach to abundance. You have a choice to make, and the choice is between the consciousness of lack and the consciousness of true abundance. It is the choice between the consciousness of death and the consciousness of life. The material universe was created from God's light. It was created by turning a part of the void into a distinct sphere and filling it with a certain amount of light that vibrates within a certain spectrum of frequencies. The initial light was not enough to displace the darkness, and thus the remaining darkness in the material world is the cause of the lack and suffering you see on earth. You cannot remove darkness from a room because darkness has no substance in itself. You cannot put it into boxes and throw it out the window. You can remove darkness only by replacing it with something that does have substance, namely light. The way to remove the darkness is to turn on the light, and the way to remove lack and suffering from earth is to bring more spiritual light into this world. This is part of the ever-flowing process of God's creation, the ever-flowing River of Life. God expands his creation and sends self-aware co-creators into it so that they can bring more light into that world and so that the world and its inhabitants can become more through self-transcendence.

The true design of God is that abundance is brought about as the result of bringing spiritual light from a higher realm into the world in which you live. You have the ability to do this because you were designed in the image and likeness of your God, you were designed with imagination and free will. Your mind can be the open door for God's light to stream into this world. By increasing the amount of spiritual light flowing through your consciousness, you will inevitably increase the amount of abundance that is available to you in the material world. God's safety mechanism is that you can only bring light from a higher realm when you attain some measure of the Christ consciousness.

This is the choice you have to make. You can take the first approach and seek to accumulate abundance by taking from the fixed supply that is currently available on earth. This makes it necessary for you to take abundance from other parts of life, thereby depriving them of it. It makes it necessary for you to defend the abundance you accumulate, and this process of taking and defending will continue for the rest of your life. If you have any doubt about what I am saying, then look at the lives of some of the richest people on this planet. They have accumulated wealth by taking it through force, and many of them spend the rest of their lives defending it. They never seem to have enough, they never seem to be happy. They never actually have the abundant life, they only have material abundance. They are not able to transform that material abundance into true spiritual abundance, true happiness and true peace of mind.

If this is what you want, you have the ability to do so. Your mind has the ability to impose an image upon God's light. The true way to accumulate abundance is to not simply take it by physical force. The reality is that your mind is always co-creating, your mind is always imposing mental images upon the Ma-ter Light. The question is where the Ma-ter Light comes from—the light that you are using to capture into your mental images. In God's original design, you are meant to maintain the connection to your I AM Presence so that you can bring spiritual energy, spiritual light, into this world. You then impose an image upon that light and create a physical form that becomes your abundance. This is literally like having your private genie in a bottle, a genie who can fulfill all of your wishes without taking anything from others.

When you lose the conscious connection to your spiritual self, you no longer have the open door for bringing spiritual light into this world—you have fallen from grace. You cannot draw down new light whereby you can create form. This does not mean that you can no longer use your mind's ability to impose images upon the Ma-ter Light. It *does* mean that you have to do this by taking the light that has already been brought into the material frequency spectrum.

When you retain the original connection to your I AM Presence, there is no limit to the amount of abundance you can manifest in your life. God is unlimited. God does not have a finite amount of light that is available for his co-creators. God has an infinite supply of light, the only limitation is how the co-creators multiply their creative abilities.

Your mind forms a pipeline between your conscious awareness and your I AM Presence. The size of the pipeline determines the amount of light that can flow through it. Originally, you were sent into this world with a certain size of your spiritual pipeline. You were meant to multiply your talents and thereby increase the size of the pipeline whereby God would give you more spiritual energy that would increase your creative powers. Most people have gradually forgotten their true origin, and they have lost their conscious connections to their spiritual selves. This has decreased the size of their pipelines to the point where there is only enough light flowing to keep them and their physical bodies alive. They do not have enough light to actually manifest abundance from within themselves. The only option left to them is to use the light that has already been brought into the material frequency spectrum and then impose images upon that light through the power of their minds. There is only a finite amount of energy available on planet earth, which means that for you to get more abundance, you have to take energy from other people.

This opens an entirely new perspective on human existence. I will give you a new understanding of what life on earth is all about and what is the driving force behind the human power struggle. Allow me to give you the next chapter that will show you what people are truly fighting for when they seem to be fighting for material possessions.

10 | I INVOKE SPIRITUAL ABUNDANCE

In the name I AM THAT I AM, Jesus Christ, I call to all representatives of the Divine Mother, especially Portia and Mother Mary, to help me transcend the force-based mindset of lack and adopt the mindset that God's abundance is unlimited. Help me transcend all blocks to my ability to manifest abundance, including...

[Make personal calls.]

1. I surrender the force-based mindset

1. I am choosing the high road of manifesting God's abundance. I give up the low road of seeking to acquire earthly abundance.

> O Portia, in your own retreat,
> with Mother's Love you do me greet.
> As all my tests I now complete,
> old patterns I no more repeat.

O Portia, opportunity,
I am beyond duality.
I focus now internally,
with you I grow eternally.

2. I surrender trying to take abundance by force and I am allowing God to give it to me freely.

O Portia, Justice is your name,
upholding Cosmic Honor Flame,
No longer will I play the game,
of seeking to remain the same.

O Portia, opportunity,
I am beyond duality.
I focus now internally,
with you I grow eternally.

3. I surrender the limited view of God that most people have in this world. I am experiencing directly the spherical, all-encompassing consciousness and Being of God.

O Portia, in the cosmic flow,
one with you, I ever grow.
I am the chalice here below,
of cosmic justice you bestow.

O Portia, opportunity,
I am beyond duality.
I focus now internally,
with you I grow eternally.

4. I am a self-aware extension of my Creator. I was sent into the material world with the command to multiply and take dominion. I am multiplying my creative abilities, multiplying my light, multiplying my self-awareness.

> O Portia, cosmic balance bring,
> eternal hope, my heart does sing.
> Protected by your Mother's wing,
> I feel at one with everything.

> **O Portia, opportunity,**
> **I am beyond duality.**
> **I focus now internally,**
> **with you I grow eternally.**

5. I am taking dominion over the material realm, filling it with light until it becomes the kingdom of God where everything radiates light and one can see the pure Mother Light behind all manifestations.

> O Portia, bring the Mother Light,
> to set all free from darkest night.
> Your Love Flame shines forever bright,
> with Saint Germain now hold me tight.

> **O Portia, opportunity,**
> **I am beyond duality.**
> **I focus now internally,**
> **with you I grow eternally.**

6. I see God the Creator as the first cause behind all appearances and I never lose the awareness of God.

O Portia, in your mastery,
I feel transforming chemistry.
In your light of reality,
I find the golden alchemy.

**O Portia, opportunity,
I am beyond duality.
I focus now internally,
with you I grow eternally.**

7. The material universe is not set apart from God and the rest of God's creation. The material universe is not separated from God or from the spiritual realm by some impenetrable barrier. This universe is an extension of the spiritual realm, it is an extension of God.

O Portia, in the cosmic stream,
I am awake from human dream.
Removing now the ego's beam,
I earn my place on cosmic team.

**O Portia, opportunity,
I am beyond duality.
I focus now internally,
with you I grow eternally.**

8. I am transcending the illusion that I am separated from my Creator. My Creator is right here with me. My Creator is omnipresent within its creation, and therefore I can never be separated from my Creator.

O Portia, you come from afar,
you are a cosmic avatar.
So infinite your repertoire,
you are for earth a guiding star.

O Portia, opportunity,
I am beyond duality.
I focus now internally,
with you I grow eternally.

9. Mother Mary, I am willing to let you enter my being. I merge my Being with your own being. Take me by the hand and show me the deeper reality behind your words, the reality that cannot be expressed in words because they are far too linear.

O Portia, I am confident,
I am a cosmic instrument.
I came to earth from heaven sent,
to help bring forward her ascent.

O Portia, opportunity,
I am beyond duality.
I focus now internally,
with you I grow eternally.

2. I accept my spiritual heritage

1. I can only be separated from my Creator in my own mind because the mind creates the sense of separation. This sense of separation is nothing but an illusion, a mirage projected unto the screen of life by a certain part of my consciousness.

O Portia, in your own retreat,
with Mother's Love you do me greet.
As all my tests I now complete,
old patterns I no more repeat.

O Portia, opportunity,
I am beyond duality.
I focus now internally,
with you I grow eternally.

2. All self-conscious beings were created out of the Being of the Creator itself. I am part of a hierarchy of spiritual beings that form the Chain of Being, reaching to the Creator itself.

O Portia, Justice is your name,
upholding Cosmic Honor Flame,
No longer will I play the game,
of seeking to remain the same.

O Portia, opportunity,
I am beyond duality.
I focus now internally,
with you I grow eternally.

3. I accept my true origin and my true identity. I am experiencing that life has a greater purpose. I am part of a grand scheme that is aimed at creating the kingdom of God right here on earth, thereby turning this planet into a world so beautiful that it will fulfill my deepest dreams, my deepest longings.

O Portia, in the cosmic flow,
one with you, I ever grow.
I am the chalice here below,
of cosmic justice you bestow.

**O Portia, opportunity,
I am beyond duality.
I focus now internally,
with you I grow eternally.**

4. I see that life is worth living, that life has a greater purpose, and there is a greater purpose for creating abundance. I am not here to fulfill temporary human desires.

O Portia, cosmic balance bring,
eternal hope, my heart does sing.
Protected by your Mother's wing,
I feel at one with everything.

**O Portia, opportunity,
I am beyond duality.
I focus now internally,
with you I grow eternally.**

5. I am here to express the fullness of my greater identity, my divine individuality. I am here to serve as a co-creator with God who can bring the light of God, the perfection of God, the harmony of God, the qualities of God into this world.

O Portia, bring the Mother Light,
to set all free from darkest night.
Your Love Flame shines forever bright,
with Saint Germain now hold me tight.

O Portia, opportunity,
I am beyond duality.
I focus now internally,
with you I grow eternally.

6. I am here to be the light of the world and to turn this world into a kingdom of light, the light that consumes the darkness that is currently covering the land.

O Portia, in your mastery,
I feel transforming chemistry.
In your light of reality,
I find the golden alchemy.

O Portia, opportunity,
I am beyond duality.
I focus now internally,
with you I grow eternally.

7. My consciousness, my mind, is the open door for bringing more of God's light, more of the high-frequency spiritual light, into the lower vibrations of the material universe.

O Portia, in the cosmic stream,
I am awake from human dream.
Removing now the ego's beam,
I earn my place on cosmic team.

O Portia, opportunity,
I am beyond duality.
I focus now internally,
with you I grow eternally.

8. I am expanding the connection with my I AM Presence. I am bringing more light into this world, raising the total amount of light that is available for creating form.

> O Portia, you come from afar,
> you are a cosmic avatar.
> So infinite your repertoire,
> you are for earth a guiding star.

> **O Portia, opportunity,**
> **I am beyond duality.**
> **I focus now internally,**
> **with you I grow eternally.**

9. I am directing the light from my I AM Presence, using it to create forms that express more of God's abundance. Abundance is manifest as a physical reality.

> O Portia, I am confident,
> I am a cosmic instrument.
> I came to earth from heaven sent,
> to help bring forward her ascent.

> **O Portia, opportunity,**
> **I am beyond duality.**
> **I focus now internally,**
> **with you I grow eternally.**

3. I invoke spiritual light

1. The master key to abundance is that everything on earth is created from spiritual light that is lowered in vibration until it vibrates within the spectrum of frequencies that make up the material universe.

> O Portia, in your own retreat,
> with Mother's Love you do me greet.
> As all my tests I now complete,
> old patterns I no more repeat.

> **O Portia, opportunity,**
> **I am beyond duality.**
> **I focus now internally,**
> **with you I grow eternally.**

2. My mind can lower the vibration of spiritual light to the material frequency spectrum. Once the light is lowered in vibration, my mind can impose an image upon it that creates a certain form.

> O Portia, Justice is your name,
> upholding Cosmic Honor Flame,
> No longer will I play the game,
> of seeking to remain the same.

> **O Portia, opportunity,**
> **I am beyond duality.**
> **I focus now internally,**
> **with you I grow eternally.**

3. I am reaching into the spiritual realm, establishing a connection to my I AM Presence and serving as the open door for bringing spiritual light into the frequency spectrum of the material universe.

> O Portia, in the cosmic flow,
> one with you, I ever grow.
> I am the chalice here below,
> of cosmic justice you bestow.

> **O Portia, opportunity,**
> **I am beyond duality.**
> **I focus now internally,**
> **with you I grow eternally.**

4. I am transcending the programming which says there is only a certain amount of abundance in this world and that I live in a world that is defined by lack and limitations.

> O Portia, cosmic balance bring,
> eternal hope, my heart does sing.
> Protected by your Mother's wing,
> I feel at one with everything.

> **O Portia, opportunity,**
> **I am beyond duality.**
> **I focus now internally,**
> **with you I grow eternally.**

5. I am part of the effort whereby we are reaching beyond the material universe, establishing a connection to our I AM Presences and bringing forth the ideas and the understanding that will give birth to new inventions and new technology.

O Portia, bring the Mother Light,
to set all free from darkest night.
Your Love Flame shines forever bright,
with Saint Germain now hold me tight.

O Portia, opportunity,
I am beyond duality.
I focus now internally,
with you I grow eternally.

6. I am part of the effort whereby we are expanding the amount of abundance currently found on earth. We are multiplying our creative talents, multiplying our understanding of the laws of God.

O Portia, in your mastery,
I feel transforming chemistry.
In your light of reality,
I find the golden alchemy.

O Portia, opportunity,
I am beyond duality.
I focus now internally,
with you I grow eternally.

7. We are transcending our current level of awareness and truly becoming co-creators with God, who can create abundance out of what today seems worthless.

O Portia, in the cosmic stream,
I am awake from human dream.
Removing now the ego's beam,
I earn my place on cosmic team.

O Portia, opportunity,
I am beyond duality.
I focus now internally,
with you I grow eternally.

8. Everything I see around me, even physical matter, is made from spiritual light. The amount of resources and abundance found on earth is in direct proportion to the amount of spiritual light that has been brought into the material frequency spectrum.

O Portia, you come from afar,
you are a cosmic avatar.
So infinite your repertoire,
you are for earth a guiding star.

O Portia, opportunity,
I am beyond duality.
I focus now internally,
with you I grow eternally.

9. Matter did not appear out of nowhere. It is a product of the Mother Light being lowered in vibration until it reaches the frequency spectrum of physical matter.

O Portia, I am confident,
I am a cosmic instrument.
I came to earth from heaven sent,
to help bring forward her ascent.

**O Portia, opportunity,
I am beyond duality.
I focus now internally,
with you I grow eternally.**

4. I accept unlimited abundance

1. There is not a fixed amount of matter. God's co-creators are bringing more light into the material frequency spectrum and expanding the amount of natural resources on this planet.

O Portia, in your own retreat,
with Mother's Love you do me greet.
As all my tests I now complete,
old patterns I no more repeat.

**O Portia, opportunity,
I am beyond duality.
I focus now internally,
with you I grow eternally.**

2. Abundance is not a fixed quantity. We are bringing forth more abundance by making more efficient use of natural resources. We are bringing more spiritual light into the material realm and thereby increasing the amount of resources and abundance available on earth.

O Portia, Justice is your name,
upholding Cosmic Honor Flame,
No longer will I play the game,
of seeking to remain the same.

O Portia, opportunity,
I am beyond duality.
I focus now internally,
with you I grow eternally.

3. I have, right within myself, right within my own consciousness, the ability to reach into the spiritual realm, to connect to my I AM Presence, and to bring spiritual light into the material world.

O Portia, in the cosmic flow,
one with you, I ever grow.
I am the chalice here below,
of cosmic justice you bestow.

O Portia, opportunity,
I am beyond duality.
I focus now internally,
with you I grow eternally.

4. I am increasing the amount of abundance manifest in my life, and I do this without taking that abundance from any other part of life.

O Portia, cosmic balance bring,
eternal hope, my heart does sing.
Protected by your Mother's wing,
I feel at one with everything.

O Portia, opportunity,
I am beyond duality.
I focus now internally,
with you I grow eternally.

5. I am transcending the consciousness of lack. I am stepping into the consciousness of true abundance. I am helping remove lack and suffering from earth by bringing more spiritual light into this world.

O Portia, bring the Mother Light,
to set all free from darkest night.
Your Love Flame shines forever bright,
with Saint Germain now hold me tight.

O Portia, opportunity,
I am beyond duality.
I focus now internally,
with you I grow eternally.

6. My mind is the open door for God's light to stream into this world. I am increasing the amount of spiritual light flowing through my consciousness. I am increasing the amount of abundance that is available to me in the material world.

O Portia, in your mastery,
I feel transforming chemistry.
In your light of reality,
I find the golden alchemy.

O Portia, opportunity,
I am beyond duality.
I focus now internally,
with you I grow eternally.

7. There is no limit to the amount of abundance I can manifest in my life.

O Portia, in the cosmic stream,
I am awake from human dream.
Removing now the ego's beam,
I earn my place on cosmic team.

O Portia, opportunity,
I am beyond duality.
I focus now internally,
with you I grow eternally.

8. My mind forms a pipeline between my conscious awareness
and my I AM Presence. I am increasing the size of the pipeline,
whereby God is giving me more spiritual energy that is increasing my creative powers.

O Portia, you come from afar,
you are a cosmic avatar.
So infinite your repertoire,
you are for earth a guiding star.

O Portia, opportunity,
I am beyond duality.
I focus now internally,
with you I grow eternally.

9. God is unlimited. God does not have a finite amount of light
that is available for his co-creators. God has an infinite supply of
light, and I am multiplying my creative abilities.

O Portia, I am confident,
I am a cosmic instrument.
I came to earth from heaven sent,
to help bring forward her ascent.

O Portia, opportunity,
I am beyond duality.
I focus now internally,
with you I grow eternally.

Sealing

In the name of the Divine Mother, I call to Portia and Mother Mary for the sealing of myself and all people in my circle of influence in the creative flow of the Divine Mother, the River of Life. I call for the multiplication of my calls by all representatives of the Divine Mother, so that we form the perfect figure-eight flow of "As Above, so below." Thus, I accept that this is fully manifest, because the mouth of the Lord, the Divine Mother that I AM, has spoken it. Amen.

11 | SECRET LESSONS BEHIND
THE HUMAN STRUGGLE

My beloved heart, I ask you to take a step back and look at the history of human interactions on earth. I ask you to consider how human beings have treated each other throughout known history. I ask you to look for one word that would characterize human interactions. I am sure you can come up with several words that are very descriptive, but I think you will agree with me that the one word that more than anything describes how human beings have interacted is the word "struggle."

Human interactions have been characterized by a struggle between individuals and between groups of people, even between humankind and Mother Nature. Human beings have had a tendency to see themselves, even to identify themselves, as being in opposition to other people or even in opposition to the planet upon which they live and upon which they depend for their survival. You have a struggle for control over land, for control over material possessions and for control over other human beings. I now ask you to consider what is the very cause of this struggle, the ongoing human power struggle that has caused untold suffering throughout known history, and even more so in the history that is not currently known to scientists.

The one cause behind the human struggle is the belief that there is not enough for everyone. There is not enough land, there are not enough resources, there is not enough food, there is not enough power. From this comes the sense that if I want more of something, then I must take it from someone else, I must take it by force. I earlier gave you the image that if every human being had a magic lamp and could have all desires fulfilled by the genie in the lamp, there would be no conflicts upon earth. If all people could have their desires fulfilled without taking from anyone else, the human power struggle would come to an end. Even the sense of struggle would dissipate and vanish as the morning dew vanishes before the rising sun.

Ah my beloved, do you see the tremendous importance of this concept? Consider how much suffering has been caused by the human power struggle. Consider the tremendous impact it could have on this planet if at least a critical mass of human beings could be helped to overcome this sense of struggle, to overcome the sense of lack that causes the struggle, and thereby accept that they can have the abundant life without taking it from other people or without taking it by force from Mother Nature.

God has built a safety mechanism into the Ma-ter Light itself. This safety mechanism is the contracting force that seeks to return all form to formlessness, that seeks to return the Ma-ter Light to its ground state. I will now explain to you exactly what happens when people seek to take something by force. This is a principle that has been described in virtually every religion. In the Bible you find the concept that as a man sows, so shall he also reap (Galatians 6:7). You find Jesus' teachings about doing unto others what you would have them do unto you (Matthew 7:12). You will find similar concepts in every religion, and these ideas describe the most important principle for how the material universe works. In order to describe this in a very succinct way, one might say that God has created a universe that works like a mirror. Whatever you send out into the space-time continuum, will be returned to you by the cosmic mirror.

The universe is made from the Ma-ter Light, and as I have said, the Ma-ter Light has the potential to take on any form but it cannot take on form by itself. The Ma-ter Light obediently takes on form when it is acted upon by a self-aware mind. The Ma-ter Light will take on whatever form is held as a mental image in that self-aware mind. Whatever you hold in your mind, determines the image you project unto the Ma-ter Light, and thus it determines what form the Ma-ter Light will take on in the material frequency spectrum. If you hold on to the mental image that life is a struggle, then surely the universe will mirror back to you circumstances that reflect the belief that life is a struggle. *It is the sense of struggle that creates the struggle.*

The Law of Free Will does not exist alone. God has not created a universe in which you can do whatever you want. The Law of Free Will exists in a polarity with what scientists have called the law of action and reaction. This law mandates that even though you have the right to project any image upon the Ma-ter Light, you will have to experience the form into which you trap a portion of the Ma-ter Light. When you create something, you will inevitably experience your own creation in the form of your physical circumstances. This is not only just, but it is also one way for you to learn how to better use your creative abilities.

Imagine a universe in which you could do whatever you wanted and never reap the consequences of your actions. How would you possibly learn from this? Consider certain children who have grown up with parents who sought to protect them from the consequences of their choices. Such children quickly become spoiled and think they can get away with anything. They act out more and more because the child has a desire for the parent to set limits for its behavior. This desire truly springs from your drive to learn your lessons in life because you know that if there are no consequences, there is no learning.

You also have a strong desire to learn your lessons in life. Although your outer mind might rebel against God's law that you will reap what you sow, your inner being is grateful for the fact that the Law of Cause and Effect mandates that you experience what you create. Your inner being knows that this is the way to quickly learn how to use your creative powers in a way that teaches you how to create the best possible life experience for yourself.

I hope to help you see that no matter how difficult your circumstances are right now, there is a lesson hiding behind them. The lesson is that you have created your circumstances in the past by forming a mental image and projecting it upon the Ma-ter Light. This means that you are not forever trapped in circumstances beyond your control. You can, at any moment, choose to change the mental images in your mind and thereby project a better image unto the Ma-ter Light. When you learn about the cycles of how God's energy flows through the levels of the material universe, as I will teach you later, you will see that it is only a matter of time before your outer situation begins to reflect the new images you hold in your mind.

The essence of my teaching is that if you currently feel trapped in undesirable circumstances, you are not truly trapped. The sense of being trapped, the sense of struggle, exists only in the human mind. When you come to a greater understanding of how the universe works and a greater understanding of your own creative powers, you will see that God has given you the power to change absolutely any circumstance, any limitation. You can go beyond that limitation and manifest the abundant life right here in this world. Although you may think you are trapped by circumstances beyond your control, you are never truly trapped. There is always something you can do to improve your situation. No matter what the outer circumstances might be, you always have the option to take control over your inner circumstances, over the way you respond to the outer situation. When you recognize that your outer circumstances are nothing but a reflection of your inner circumstances from the past, you will know that by changing the mental images in your mind, you will inevitably change what is reflected back to you by the cosmic mirror.

***

The human struggle has been going on for untold millennia. The struggle for material possessions, power or control is born from the sense that there is not enough abundance in the physical world. The material abundance found in this world is not a fixed quantity. The material abundance is like the tip of an iceberg, and I am sure you know that an iceberg has only ten percent of its mass above the surface of the water. Most of the iceberg is invisible to the human eye and, likewise, the material substance that you can detect with your physical senses is only a small part of a larger whole. All matter is truly made from vibrating energy and thus the material abundance is only the visible part of the total abundance in this world. The total amount of abundance in the material frequency spectrum is not confined to the physical matter that you can detect with your senses. The total amount of abundance available to human beings is dependent on the amount of energy that has been brought into the energy system of planet earth.

Physical matter is made from energy and physical energy is truly created from invisible spiritual energy that has been captured into a particular form. Physical matter is energy that has been lowered in vibration until it vibrates within a certain spectrum of frequencies. Physical matter is a substance that can be manipulated by your physical body. Physical matter is simply an expression of, an extension of, the finer energies that cannot be detected by your physical senses but that can nevertheless be given form by your mind.

Take a new look at the human power struggle. Human beings are not competing exclusively for material wealth or material possessions. Much of the struggle between human beings is not over material substance, it is about something non-material, something that cannot be detected by the physical senses or digested by the body but nevertheless has value to human beings. What is that something, that non-material substance, over which human beings are fighting? Could it possibly be the finer energies that cannot be detected by the senses but are still part of the energy system of earth? These energies are so necessary for a human being to feel nurtured, abundant, complete or secure. You have heard the saying that man does not live from bread alone, and is it not proof that human beings have many needs that are not material and cannot be fulfilled by material possessions?

In many cases, the human power struggle is aimed at giving people a feeling. So many people seek to accumulate money, yet if you look at the world and the richest people, you will see that many of them have accumulated such huge sums of money that they could not possibly spend the money for the rest of their lives. Any human being has finite needs when it comes to material possessions. There are only so many things you can buy, so many things you can do, so much food you can eat. There will come a point when a person has accumulated enough money to fulfill all of his or her material needs for the rest of the natural life span. You see so many people who are not able to stop their quest for money in order to spend the rest of their lives enjoying the money they already have. They are driven to continue accumulating more and more money, even though the effort of accumulating and defending the money prevents them from enjoying their lives. What are these people seeking, what are they struggling to attain? They are struggling to attain a feeling, and that feeling is more important to them than the money or what enjoyment the money can buy. They are struggling to achieve a feeling of security or perhaps a feeling of power, control or superiority.

For a very long time I have been a keen student of human psychology. As an ascended being I have the ability to look beyond all surface appearances that confuse human beings and make it impossible for them to understand what goes on at the subconscious levels of the psyche. The eyes of an ascended being can penetrate all of the smokescreens that fool human beings. I see that behind the outer need for security is an underlying need. That need is what we might call the need for wholeness.

This is a need that is built into the very design of your being, and it is another safety mechanism designed by God. Its purpose is to prevent free will from causing co-creators to be lost in the consciousness of separation. God does not want you to be trapped in an endless spiral of reaping the consequences of your former choices, having those consequences determine your present choices—which creates more consequences that you cannot escape. When God designed your lifestream, it was designed to always seek wholeness, just as the Ma-ter Light was designed to always seek the equilibrium of its ground state. God has not created the lack or the suffering on earth; it was created through the collective consciousness of humankind after people lost the direct connection to their spiritual selves, their I AM Presences. When that connection was lost, the lifestream experienced a sense of incompleteness, a sense of being unwhole, of being alone—even a sense of being abandoned. This gave the lifestream a desire to reestablish its former wholeness, its former completeness. When you look at the cornucopia of human desires, you will never be able to understand the true drive in human psychology unless you look beyond outer appearances.

Human beings do not really have a desire to accumulate more than a certain amount of material possessions. Human beings do not have a desire to experience more than a certain amount of bodily pleasures. A lifestream has a certain desire to experience life in the material universe. Such desires can be fulfilled by a finite amount of experiences or a finite amount of possessions. What creates the insatiable drive for more possessions, more pleasures, more power or any of the other things that human beings desire, is actually the lifestream's underlying desire for wholeness. Because co-creators do not see the true nature of this desire and the true aim of the desire, they seek to fill the desire by the things they *do* see, the things they *do* experience. Because lifestreams have forgotten their spiritual origin and have forgotten their purpose for coming to earth, they do not understand their true desires. Because co-creators do not see that they have descended into a lower state of consciousness in which they have lost their former wholeness, their former holiness as spiritual beings who are sons and daughters of God, they do not understand that the true desire of their beings is to regain their wholeness. Since they do not see their spiritual selves, they do not understand that the drive they feel is a drive for wholeness, a drive that can only be satisfied by reestablishing the connection to their spiritual selves. Instead of seeking first the kingdom of God and his righteousness, whereby all other things shall be added unto them as Jesus promised (Matthew 6:33), they seek to fill their desire through the things they can see in this world. They seek to build *outer* security rather than *inner* wholeness.

Many people seek to reestablish their inner wholeness by accumulating material possessions, thereby building a sense of material security. Some people seek security by gaining power over others, which they think will make them feel whole. Behind the drive for any outer possessions or experiences is the drive to accumulate energy. When the lifestream has the correct connection to the I AM Presence, it feels a constant flow of spiritual energy streaming through all levels of its being directly from the I AM Presence. It is this flow of spiritual energy that gives the lifestream the sense of being whole, of being one with the flow of the River of Life that is God's creation. The lifestream feels it is part of the All of God instead of being alone and unwhole. Even though the co-creator does not consciously realize what is happening, it has an inner drive for obtaining energy. It knows that the key to reestablishing its wholeness is energy. Because it does not understand its true origin and identity, it again thinks that it must take energy from this world and use it to reestablish its wholeness.

The energies found in this world are of a lower frequency than the energies in the spiritual realm. No matter how much material energy you accumulate, your lifestream will not feel whole. Trying to reestablish your inner wholeness by accumulating material possessions or material energies is as impossible as trying to fill a black hole. It simply cannot be done, and thus the lifestream is engaged in an impossible quest until it raises its understanding and stops attempting the impossible. The only thing that can reestablish your sense of wholeness is to reopen the direct, conscious connection to your I AM Presence. You will then feel the high-frequency spiritual energies flow from your I AM Presence through all levels of your lower being. You will know that you are in the flow of the River of Life, and only by being in this flow will you feel whole and complete within yourself. You will know that you need nothing from outside yourself because you have the River of Life flowing within your own being.

***

Let me return to the image of the magic lamp. If you had a magic lamp and if all you had to do was rub it and a genie would jump out and fulfill your every desire, would you feel that life on earth was a struggle? Would you bother to compete with other people over a finite amount of material possessions? Would you bother to seek to take energy from others if you had access to an inexhaustible supply within yourself? Would you not rather rub your lamp and command the genie to fulfill your desires by giving you the necessary energy, even the energy that has taken on the appearance of physical matter?

Everything I have explained to you up until this point has had the purpose of showing you that you do indeed have a magic lamp. Instead of seeking to work out your living by the sweat of your brow (Genesis 3:19), through taking it by force from other people or from Mother nature, you have the alternative of going within and reestablishing the connection to your I AM Presence. By seeking first the kingdom of God, the kingdom that Jesus told you is within, you will have access to the unlimited abundance of God rather than the limited abundance of this world. Your I AM Presence is an extension of your Creator, and your I AM Presence has access to the infinite energy of your Creator that is freely available in the spiritual realm. Your I AM Presence will give you all the spiritual energy that is needed to fulfill all of your true desires in this material world. Your I AM Presence will even give you spiritual energy that your mind can capture into a form that becomes material substance.

For you to receive this energy, you must reestablish and expand the conduit, the pipeline, so that your outer being, your conscious mind, becomes the open door whereby the light of God, the Sun of your I AM Presence, can shine into this world and dispel the darkness that currently gives you a sense of lack, of emptiness, a sense of being unwhole, perhaps even unworthy. My beloved, if you can fully absorb and accept this teaching, you have the potential to turn your life around completely and to set yourself on a course that *can* and *will* lead you to the ultimate fulfillment you seek, namely the inner sense of wholeness that comes from knowing what Jesus expressed when he said: "I and my Father are one" (John 10:30).

***

You might have realized already that what people seek is not material possessions but an inner feeling. You might have seen that feeling as happiness, fulfillment or perhaps even as peace of mind. What you really seek is wholeness and that wholeness is available to you at any moment. In order to find and establish that wholeness, you must reverse the direction of your attention. I know very well that you have grown up in a society that programs you to believe that if you have a need, if you have a desire, then you must find something outside yourself in order to fill that desire. You have grown up in a consumer culture that programs you to seek some product or some service in order to fill your desires. The very essence of this consumer culture is that someone wants to sell you something. Behind that is a deeper desire to control you through your needs. The very essence of this culture is to actually promote the belief that this world is a world of lack and that you do not have enough within yourself to be whole and fulfilled. You need to exchange something with someone else, and through that need, other people or institutions can influence you, perhaps even control you. It was when Jesus said that the kingdom of God is within you that the prince of this world and his henchmen in the established religion decided to kill him. They did not want Jesus to continue to preach the one secret that the forces of this world do not want you to know. That secret is the eternal fact that the true key to the fulfillment of your desires, the true key to experiencing God's abundant life, is to stop looking for that abundance outside yourself. In order to find abundance, to find wholeness, you must go inside yourself, you must enter the kingdom of God within you and thereby discover the true key to the abundant life, which is your I AM Presence and the spiritual light radiating through that Sun of your being.

When you realize this truth, you become spiritually self-sufficient, and therefore you no longer need anything from any source outside yourself. You no longer need anything from any other human being or any human institution, organization or business. You are truly independent in a spiritual way. I am not hereby saying that you will not need or want to interact with other human beings. I am saying that your interactions with other people will take on an entirely new goal and purpose. Instead of interacting with others based on a sense of lack, you will now interact with people based on a sense of inner abundance. Instead of seeking to take something from others by force, your will seek to give to others. This does not mean that you will never receive anything from other human beings because you will often allow God to fulfill your needs through others. In so doing, you are not coming from a state of lack that causes you to feel deprived or to feel that other people owe you something. You will not fear that others will not cooperate, and you will not be willing to use force to get other people to give you what you think you cannot be whole without.

You have understood the principle that it is the Father's good pleasure to give you the kingdom and that he will give it to you freely if you are willing to receive it freely – meaning without fear or fear-based expectations or attachments – and then to freely share what you have freely received (Matthew 10:8). When a group of people are in this state of consciousness, they will give to each other, and in so doing they will multiply their talents beyond what any of them could achieve alone. This will bring even more of God's abundance into their society whereby life becomes an upward spiral of increasing abundance for everyone.

Oh my beloved, this is the true potential for human society, namely that human beings come together in multiplying their individual talents and pooling them together so that the whole becomes more than the sum of its parts. When people give self-lessly and receive selflessly, they reestablish the right connection to God. God will truly multiply their talents, will truly make them rulers over many things and bring even more abundance into this world. A society can enter an upward spiral that brings about a golden age of peace, prosperity and abundance for all members of that society. This has been manifest in past civilizations, and some civilizations were able to maintain such a golden age for a very long period of time before people finally started to descend into a lower state of consciousness.

***

Let me now explain to you the choice you have to make, the choice concerning what you will make the goal for the rest of your life. All of the physical matter that is available to human beings on earth is created from finer energies. The physical matter is simply the tip of the iceberg of the total amount of energy that is available within the material frequency spectrum. Much of that energy is not available as physical energy, such as heat or electricity. It is available as what we might call psychic energy, meaning mental and emotional energy. The total amount of material abundance that is available in this world depends not only on the physical matter but on the total amount of energy that is available within the material frequency spectrum, which is what some scientists call the space-time continuum.

Even physical matter is energy that has been captured into a certain matrix. It is an expression of the Ma-ter Light, which has been captured into a certain form because a self-aware mind has imposed an image on that Ma-ter Light. Before the Ma-ter Light was lowered in vibration and became physical matter, it was first lowered into the frequency spectrum that I have called psychic energy. Before that, the Ma-ter Light vibrated at the higher frequencies of the spiritual realm.

The abundance that is available to human beings in the material world is in direct proportion to the total amount of energy that is available in the entire energy system of earth. This includes frequencies that are higher than those of physical matter yet not as high as the frequencies in the spiritual realm. This energy can be manifest as physical matter, as material energy, such as electricity or sunlight, or it can be manifest as psychic energy that cannot be detected by the senses but can be felt in the form of emotional and mental energy, feelings and thoughts. Scientists have told you that everything is energy, which means that nothing exists that is not energy. You know very well that you have feelings and you have thoughts. Both your feelings and your thoughts must be forms of energy according to the definition of science. Even though you cannot physically detect psychic energy, you know it exists because you experience it as a reality in your feelings and in your thoughts. It is possible for you to go within your heart and know with an inner knowing that in order to have abundance, it is not enough to use your physical body. You also need to use your mind and use it to gather psychic energy, learning how to turn that energy into the material substance you desire. This brings us to the crucial point where I can explain to you the choice you are facing. Here are the two options available to you. In order to manifest greater abundance in your life, you can take the approach chosen by most people on this planet. You can seek to accumulate a greater amount of material substance and psychic energy from the pool of energy that is already available in the material frequency spectrum. You can seek to accumulate by taking abundance from a finite amount of energy and matter.

The consequence of taking this approach is that you must accumulate energy and material possessions through force. In many cases you must do this by taking it either from other people or from Mother Nature, and both might not give it to you without a fight. This will set up a struggle between you and other people or between you and nature. You will have to work out your living by the sweat of your brow. You will have to use force to accumulate wealth and you will have to use continued force to defend it from the forces seeking to take it away from you.

If everyone is seeking to accumulate abundance from the same finite amount, if everyone is seeking to get a bigger piece of the same pie, there will be a constant struggle to attain and maintain your abundance. The safety mechanism built into the Ma-ter Light will seek to return all energy to its ground state, and this too will create a force that will seek to take away what you have taken through force. When you seek to take through force, you set yourself up in conflict with all other people who take the same approach and with Mother Nature herself.

I am sure you can see the limitations of this approach. I am sure you can see in your heart that even if you did manage to accumulate great material wealth, this would not be a permanent state of abundance, and therefore it would not be true abundance. You would not truly have the abundant life by taking this approach.

The second approach you can take is to completely purify your mind from the sense of lack that causes you to believe that the only way to accumulate abundance is through force and through a struggle. You can choose to follow the example set by Jesus and other spiritual teachers of going into the kingdom of God within you, attaining a state of oneness with your I AM Presence, with your spiritual Father, and then allowing God's light to stream into your being and into your world, manifesting God's abundance in your life.

***

If you do take the second approach, you are not competing to accumulate wealth from a finite amount. You are not competing for a bigger piece of the one pie. You are opening a connection to God's infinite abundance and you are allowing God the pleasure of giving you his kingdom by expanding the pie. There are no limitations in the spiritual realm, and thus there is no limit to the amount of spiritual energy that your I AM Presence can let flow through your being. The only limitation is how much spiritual energy you are able to receive through your outer mind.

This is the concept that gave birth to the legend of the Holy Grail. The Holy Grail is said to be a chalice, a cup, but truly the Holy Grail is a symbol for a chalice that can hold God's abundance in the form of spiritual light. The true meaning of this legend is that your mind, your being, is meant to become the chalice that can hold the spiritual light from your I AM Presence. God will not allow his pearls to be cast before swine (Matthew 7:6). God will not allow his abundance to be buried in the ground (Matthew 25:18) or to fall on barren ground (Matthew 13:5). God will not give you abundance until you have proven that you can be faithful over a few things (Matthew 25:21), until you have proven that your lower being has become a chalice that will make wise use of that abundance so that you will be a wise steward over what God has given you.

You have two options. You can seek to manifest the abundant life by taking it from the finite amount of energy that is available in the material frequency spectrum. Or you can seek to receive abundance directly from the infinite amount that is available in the spiritual realm. If you choose the first option, you will do nothing to increase the amount of abundance that is available on earth. You can accumulate personal abundance only by taking material substance or psychic energy from others. If you choose the second option, you will not only receive abundance for yourself, you will bring more abundance into this world, and thereby you will increase the amount of energy that is available to all people. In pursuing your personal abundance, you will also increase the abundance of the whole, and this is the true meaning of multiplying your talents, namely that you increase the total amount of abundance in this world.

What you are truly doing is increasing the total amount of light in the material world, and thereby you are making a personal contribution to turning this world into the kingdom of God. This is your true reason for being. You were designed to serve as a co-creator with God by bringing spiritual light into the material frequency spectrum, using it to displace darkness by creating perfectly beautiful and balanced forms that are an expression of the laws and the perfection of God. It is when you fulfill this intended role that God will make you ruler over many things because you have been faithful over a few things, over a finite amount of spiritual light. It is when you fulfill this role that you will hear the words spoken about Jesus: "This is my beloved son (or daughter) in whom I am well pleased" (Matthew 3:17).

***

Let me now give you a truth that should cause you to pause and that should make it easier for you to choose between the two options—if you have not already made your choice. I have referred to some of the many gurus in the world who claim they can teach you how to quickly and easily accumulate all the money you want. I have referred to some of them as false gurus, and I will now explain why they are false teachers.

Your mind, meaning your conscious and subconscious mind, has a built-in ability to impose an image upon the Ma-ter Light, causing that light to take on the form defined by the image. Through the power of your thoughts, you impose a mental image upon the light that has been lowered into the material frequency spectrum. Through the power of your emotions, you give motion and direction to that energy, and this is what causes it to be lowered into the frequency spectrum of physical matter so that it becomes a manifest reality in your life.

Jesus had attained a very high degree of mastery over matter itself. Jesus had the ability to heal the sick, even to the point of changing the molecular and atomic structure of a person's body so that diseased cells were instantly healed and made whole. Jesus had the ability to turn water into wine and to multiply the loaves and fishes. This is an ability that is built into your mind. Most people on earth are not anywhere close to having the mastery over matter demonstrated by Jesus. All people on earth have the ability to attain this mastery, which is why Jesus said that those who believe on him shall do the works that he did (John 14:12).

There are two ways to attain this mastery. There is a low road and there is a high road. The mastery demonstrated by Jesus was clearly the high road because Jesus recognized that he could, of his own self, do nothing but that it was the Father, the I AM Presence, within him who was doing the work. When you recognize your I AM Presence as the true source, as the true doer in your life, you realign yourself with the laws of God and with the creative intent of God. God's design for this universe is to create a platform where all of God's co-creators, all self-aware beings, can live in harmony with each other and with the whole. When you use your creative powers to the fullest, you are bringing more abundance into this world, and thus you are magnifying the whole without taking it from someone else.

It is possible that you can use the powers that are built into your mind to manipulate God's energy and accumulate abundance for yourself without increasing the total amount of abundance in this world. You are then using the power of your mind to draw unto yourself more energy and more physical abundance from the supply that is already available in the energy system of earth. In so doing, you must of necessity take it from other parts of life, and you are depriving those parts of life and the whole of life of that energy.

A substantial number of people on this planet have attained a very high degree of mastery in terms of drawing energy and material wealth unto themselves by taking it through force, by taking it from the finite amount of abundance available in the material world. They are doing this with absolutely no consideration for how their actions affect other people or Mother earth. These lifestreams have completely abandoned all considerations for the whole or for God's creative intent. They see themselves as being separated from God and they see themselves as being apart from the Body of God. They believe they belong to an elite who has the right to do whatever they want, no matter how it affects other parts of life. They believe it is their right to enslave other people or make them the serfs who toil on the earth to produce wealth for the elite. If you look at history, you will see the existence of this elite and how, in every culture and in every civilization known to man, a small elite has managed to control the general population and make them work to give the elite excessive amounts of material wealth, power, pleasure, privilege and energy.

My purpose for telling you this is twofold. If you are to manifest God's abundant life, you must free yourself from the mindset of this elite. You must come apart and be a separate and chosen people, and I will explain this in greater detail later. For now, the most important purpose for my teaching is to make you aware that this elite, this power elite, has attained a certain ability to attract psychic energy and material wealth to themselves. They have done this by using the power built into the human mind in order to take energy from other parts of life. Needless to say, this is a violation of God's law, and thus it is a misuse of your creative powers. It is important for you to understand that it is indeed possible to misuse your creative powers. You need to understand this because only by doing so can you avoid falling for the promises made by the self-appointed prosperity gurus who promise you that by following them, you can accumulate wealth through shortcuts.

I earlier said that most of the get-rich-quick schemes simply do not work, and this is true. There are people who have discovered ways to manipulate psychic energy and matter through the power of the mind whereby they are able to accumulate great amounts of wealth, often by influencing other people. Most of these people use this ability to continue to accumulate wealth, but a few have set themselves up as gurus, claiming that they can teach you how to accumulate wealth in the same way they have done so. My beloved heart, do you see the subtlety here? These people point not only to themselves but also to some of the richest and most successful people in the world as proof that their system works. Some of their systems *do* indeed work, although it will take a long time for most people to learn how to manipulate energy—and thus this is not a get-rich-quick scheme. It is indeed possible to accumulate wealth by using the power built into your mind. If you only measure success by the amount of wealth a person has accumulated, you might easily be trapped into thinking that you should follow the example of the richest people on earth. You might easily believe the promises made by these success gurus who will tell you how to take abundance through force.

It is possible for you to learn how to use the power of your mind to accumulate wealth through force, to accumulate abundance by taking it from others, by manipulating the system. I will always respect the Law of Free Will. If you truly have a need to experience what it feels like to take abundance through force and thereby be trapped in an endless spiral of seeking to accumulate more wealth and seeking to defend it, then who am I to stop you from having that experience. I want to make absolutely sure that I have explained to you the consequences of accumulating wealth in this way. I have already told you that the Law of Free Will is in polarity with the Law of Cause and Effect. When you seek to accumulate wealth through force, you will indeed set in motion causes that will come back to you as effects that will seek to take away from you what you seek to possess through force.

The Ma-ter Light itself has a built-in mechanism that reduces all form to nothingness by returning the Ma-ter Light to its ground state. It is possible to use the power of your mind to force the Ma-ter Light to take on a certain form. When you do so, you create an imbalance in the Ma-ter Light because you create a form that is not based on the creative principles used by God. In creating this imbalance, the Law of Cause and Effect, the law of action and reaction, will automatically create an opposing force as strong as the force you generated. For each action whereby you seek to take wealth by force, the universe generates a reaction that seeks to take away that wealth. The purpose is that the earth can be returned to balance and the Ma-ter Light can be returned to its ground state. By using force, you can maintain your unbalanced form for a time, but doing so requires a constant struggle on your part, a struggle that will take away attention and energy from other activities. For some people this struggle prevents them from enjoying their wealth, or perhaps it swallows up their lives completely. Obviously, it also prevents them from growing spiritually.

If you desire to experience this sense of struggle, God has given you the right to create this experience in your life. You can continue to experience the struggle for a very long period of time. It is my hope that this course will inspire you to see that you truly do not desire to be trapped on this treadmill of action and reaction, that you truly do not desire to be swallowed up by this ongoing human power struggle. It is my hope that you will see that there is far greater joy in plunging yourself into the River of Life, reestablishing your connection to your I AM Presence and allowing the sunlight of your Presence to shine through your being. There is far greater joy in participating in God's original plan for this universe, becoming a co-creator with God and thereby allowing the power of God within you to manifest the permanent abundant life. There is far greater joy in receiving the abundant life directly from Above instead of taking it from other parts of life through force. There is far greater joy in seeking abundance vertically than horizontally.

I hope I have inspired you to go deeply within your heart and consider the two options I have presented to you. Do you want to spend the rest of your life in a struggle for a finite amount of abundance? Or do you want to redirect your life so that you can be part of the River of Life that brings more abundance into this world? If you choose the first option, I can do nothing more for you and this course will teach you nothing of value. If you choose the second option, I will teach you how to reestablish and expand the connection to your I AM Presence. I will show you how to open the floodgates that let the River of Life flow through your being and manifest true abundance, the abundance that cannot be taken away by the forces of this world. When you have made your choice to accept the abundant life from Above, then join me as I give you the next chapter.

12 | I INVOKE SPIRITUAL WHOLENESS

In the name I AM THAT I AM, Jesus Christ, I call to all representatives of the Divine Mother, especially the Goddess of Liberty and Mother Mary, to help me seek the spiritual independence that turns my mind into the Holy Grail. Help me transcend all blocks to my ability to manifest abundance, including...

[Make personal calls.]

1. I transcend the human struggle

1. I am transcending the consciousness behind the struggle between individuals and between groups of people, even between humankind and Mother Nature.

> O Liberty now set me free
> from devil's curse of poverty.
> I blame not Mother for my lack,
> O Blessed Mother, take me back.

O Cosmic Mother Liberty,
conduct Abundance Symphony.
My highest service I now see,
abundance is now real for me.

2. I no longer see myself, I no longer identify myself, as being in opposition to other people or in opposition to the planet upon which I live.

O Liberty, from distant shore,
I come with longing to be More.
I see abundance is a flow,
abundance consciousness I grow.

O Cosmic Mother Liberty,
conduct Abundance Symphony.
My highest service I now see,
abundance is now real for me.

3. I am transcending the consciousness behind the ongoing human power struggle, namely the belief that there is not enough for everyone, that if I want more of something, then I must take it from someone else.

O Liberty, expose the lie,
that limitations can me tie.
The Ma-ter light is not my foe,
true opulence it does bestow.

O Cosmic Mother Liberty,
conduct Abundance Symphony.
My highest service I now see,
abundance is now real for me.

4. I am accepting that I am having the abundant life without taking it from other people or without taking it by force from Mother Nature.

O Liberty, expose the plot,
projected by the fallen lot.
O Cosmic Mother, I now see,
that Mother's not my enemy.

**O Cosmic Mother Liberty,
conduct Abundance Symphony.
My highest service I now see,
abundance is now real for me.**

5. God has created a universe that works like a mirror. Whatever I send into the space-time continuum, will be returned to me by the cosmic mirror.

O Liberty, with opened eyes,
I now reject the devil's lies.
I now embrace the Mother realm,
for I see Father at the helm.

**O Cosmic Mother Liberty,
conduct Abundance Symphony.
My highest service I now see,
abundance is now real for me.**

6. The Ma-ter Light obediently takes on form when it is acted upon by my mind. The Ma-ter Light will take on whatever form is held as a mental image in my mind.

O Liberty, a chalice pure,
my lower bodies are for sure.
Release through me your symphony,
your gift of Cosmic Liberty.

O Cosmic Mother Liberty,
conduct Abundance Symphony.
My highest service I now see,
abundance is now real for me.

7. Whatever I hold in my mind determines the image I am projecting unto the Ma-ter Light, and thus it determines what form
the Ma-ter Light will take on in the material frequency spectrum.

O Liberty, the open door,
I am for Symphony of More.
In chakras mine light you release,
the flow of love shall never cease.

O Cosmic Mother Liberty,
conduct Abundance Symphony.
My highest service I now see,
abundance is now real for me.

8. It is the sense of struggle that creates the struggle, and I am –
right now and consciously – choosing to completely surrender
the sense of struggle.

O Liberty, release the flow,
of opulence that you bestow.
For I am willing to receive,
the Golden Fleece that you now weave.

**O Cosmic Mother Liberty,
conduct Abundance Symphony.
My highest service I now see,
abundance is now real for me.**

9. When I create something, I will inevitably experience my own creation in the form of physical circumstances. This is not only just, but it is also one way for me to learn how to better use my creative abilities.

O Liberty, release the cure,
to free the tired and the poor.
The huddled masses are set free,
by loving Song of Liberty.

**O Cosmic Mother Liberty,
conduct Abundance Symphony.
My highest service I now see,
abundance is now real for me.**

2. I transcend my outer circumstances

1. My ego rebels against God's law that I will reap what I sow. Yet I am connected to my inner being, and I am grateful for the fact that the law of cause and effect mandates that I experience what I create.

O Liberty now set me free
from devil's curse of poverty.
I blame not Mother for my lack,
O Blessed Mother, take me back.

O Cosmic Mother Liberty,
conduct Abundance Symphony.
My highest service I now see,
abundance is now real for me.

2. I know this is the way to quickly learn how to use my creative powers. I am learning how to create the best possible life experience for myself.

O Liberty, from distant shore,
I come with longing to be More.
I see abundance is a flow,
abundance consciousness I grow.

O Cosmic Mother Liberty,
conduct Abundance Symphony.
My highest service I now see,
abundance is now real for me.

3. No matter how difficult my circumstances are right now, there is a lesson hiding behind them. I have created my circumstances in the past by forming a mental image and projecting it upon the Ma-ter Light.

O Liberty, expose the lie,
that limitations can me tie.
The Ma-ter light is not my foe,
true opulence it does bestow.

O Cosmic Mother Liberty,
conduct Abundance Symphony.
My highest service I now see,
abundance is now real for me.

4. I am not forever trapped in circumstances beyond my control. I am changing the mental images in my mind and projecting a better image unto the Ma-ter Light. It is only a matter of time before my outer situation begins to reflect the new images I hold in my mind.

O Liberty, expose the plot,
projected by the fallen lot.
O Cosmic Mother, I now see,
that Mother's not my enemy.

**O Cosmic Mother Liberty,
conduct Abundance Symphony.
My highest service I now see,
abundance is now real for me.**

5. The sense of being trapped, the sense of struggle, exists only in the human mind. God has given me the power to change absolutely any circumstance, to go beyond limitations and manifest the abundant life right here in this world.

O Liberty, with opened eyes,
I now reject the devil's lies.
I now embrace the Mother realm,
for I see Father at the helm.

**O Cosmic Mother Liberty,
conduct Abundance Symphony.
My highest service I now see,
abundance is now real for me.**

6. There is always something I can do to improve my situation. No matter what the outer circumstances might be, I always have the option to take control over my inner circumstances, over the way I respond to the outer situation.

> O Liberty, a chalice pure,
> my lower bodies are for sure.
> Release through me your symphony,
> your gift of Cosmic Liberty.

> **O Cosmic Mother Liberty,**
> **conduct Abundance Symphony.**
> **My highest service I now see,**
> **abundance is now real for me.**

7. My outer circumstances are nothing but a reflection of my inner circumstances from the past. I am changing the mental images in my mind, and thereby I will inevitably change what is reflected back to me by the cosmic mirror.

> O Liberty, the open door,
> I am for Symphony of More.
> In chakras mine light you release,
> the flow of love shall never cease.

> **O Cosmic Mother Liberty,**
> **conduct Abundance Symphony.**
> **My highest service I now see,**
> **abundance is now real for me.**

8. The human struggle is really a struggle for a feeling of security, and that feeling is a result of energy beyond the material spectrum.

O Liberty, release the flow,
of opulence that you bestow.
For I am willing to receive,
the Golden Fleece that you now weave.

**O Cosmic Mother Liberty,
conduct Abundance Symphony.
My highest service I now see,
abundance is now real for me.**

9. Behind the outer need for security is an underlying need for wholeness. My lifestream is designed to seek wholeness.

O Liberty, release the cure,
to free the tired and the poor.
The huddled masses are set free,
by loving Song of Liberty.

**O Cosmic Mother Liberty,
conduct Abundance Symphony.
My highest service I now see,
abundance is now real for me.**

3. I transcend human desires

1. What creates the insatiable drive for more possessions, more pleasures, more power or any of the other things this world offers, is my underlying desire for wholeness.

O Liberty now set me free
from devil's curse of poverty.
I blame not Mother for my lack,
O Blessed Mother, take me back.

O Cosmic Mother Liberty,
conduct Abundance Symphony.
My highest service I now see,
abundance is now real for me.

2. My true desire is to regain my wholeness, and it can only be
satisfied by reestablishing the connection to my I AM Presence.
I desire inner wholeness more than outer security.

O Liberty, from distant shore,
I come with longing to be More.
I see abundance is a flow,
abundance consciousness I grow.

O Cosmic Mother Liberty,
conduct Abundance Symphony.
My highest service I now see,
abundance is now real for me.

3. I am reestablishing my connection to my I AM Presence. I
am experiencing a constant flow of spiritual energy streaming
through all levels of my being directly from the I AM Presence.

O Liberty, expose the lie,
that limitations can me tie.
The Ma-ter light is not my foe,
true opulence it does bestow.

O Cosmic Mother Liberty,
conduct Abundance Symphony.
My highest service I now see,
abundance is now real for me.

4. This flow of spiritual energy gives me the sense of being whole, of being one with the flow of the River of Life. I am part of the All of God instead of being alone and unwhole.

O Liberty, expose the plot,
projected by the fallen lot.
O Cosmic Mother, I now see,
that Mother's not my enemy.

O Cosmic Mother Liberty,
conduct Abundance Symphony.
My highest service I now see,
abundance is now real for me.

5. I need nothing from outside myself because I have the River of Life flowing from within my own being.

O Liberty, with opened eyes,
I now reject the devil's lies.
I now embrace the Mother realm,
for I see Father at the helm.

O Cosmic Mother Liberty,
conduct Abundance Symphony.
My highest service I now see,
abundance is now real for me.

6. Instead of seeking to take by force from other people or from Mother Nature, I am going within and reestablishing the connection to my I AM Presence. I am seeking first the kingdom of God, the kingdom that is within me.

> O Liberty, a chalice pure,
> my lower bodies are for sure.
> Release through me your symphony,
> your gift of Cosmic Liberty.

> **O Cosmic Mother Liberty,**
> **conduct Abundance Symphony.**
> **My highest service I now see,**
> **abundance is now real for me.**

7. My I AM Presence is an extension of my Creator, and my I AM Presence has access to the infinite energy of my Creator that is freely available in the spiritual realm.

> O Liberty, the open door,
> I am for Symphony of More.
> In chakras mine light you release,
> the flow of love shall never cease.

> **O Cosmic Mother Liberty,**
> **conduct Abundance Symphony.**
> **My highest service I now see,**
> **abundance is now real for me.**

8. My I AM Presence is giving me the spiritual energy that is needed to fulfill all of my true desires in this material world.

O Liberty, release the flow,
of opulence that you bestow.
For I am willing to receive,
the Golden Fleece that you now weave.

O Cosmic Mother Liberty,
conduct Abundance Symphony.
My highest service I now see,
abundance is now real for me.

9. My conscious mind is the open door whereby the light of God, the Sun of my I AM Presence, can shine into this world and dispel the darkness that currently gives me a sense of lack, of being unwhole and unworthy.

O Liberty, release the cure,
to free the tired and the poor.
The huddled masses are set free,
by loving Song of Liberty.

O Cosmic Mother Liberty,
conduct Abundance Symphony.
My highest service I now see,
abundance is now real for me.

4. My life goal is spiritual independence

1. I am completely turning my life around and setting myself on a course that will lead to the ultimate fulfillment I seek, namely the inner sense of wholeness that comes from knowing that: "I and my Father are one."

O Liberty now set me free
from devil's curse of poverty.
I blame not Mother for my lack,
O Blessed Mother, take me back.

**O Cosmic Mother Liberty,
conduct Abundance Symphony.
My highest service I now see,
abundance is now real for me.**

2. I have grown up in a society that programs me to believe that
if I have a need or desire, I must find something outside myself
in order to fill it. This programming springs from a desire to
control me through my needs.

O Liberty, from distant shore,
I come with longing to be More.
I see abundance is a flow,
abundance consciousness I grow.

**O Cosmic Mother Liberty,
conduct Abundance Symphony.
My highest service I now see,
abundance is now real for me.**

3. The secret of life is that the true key to the fulfillment of my
desires, the true key to experiencing God's abundant life, is to
stop looking for that abundance outside myself. To find abundance, to find wholeness, I am looking inside myself.

O Liberty, expose the lie,
that limitations can me tie.
The Ma-ter light is not my foe,
true opulence it does bestow.

**O Cosmic Mother Liberty,
conduct Abundance Symphony.
My highest service I now see,
abundance is now real for me.**

4. I am spiritually self-sufficient, and therefore I no longer need anything from any source outside myself. I no longer need anything from any other human being or any human institution, organization or business. I am truly independent in a spiritual way.

O Liberty, expose the plot,
projected by the fallen lot.
O Cosmic Mother, I now see,
that Mother's not my enemy.

**O Cosmic Mother Liberty,
conduct Abundance Symphony.
My highest service I now see,
abundance is now real for me.**

5. My interactions with other people are based on a sense of inner abundance. Instead of seeking to take something from others by force, I seek to give to others.

O Liberty, with opened eyes,
I now reject the devil's lies.
I now embrace the Mother realm,
for I see Father at the helm.

**O Cosmic Mother Liberty,
conduct Abundance Symphony.
My highest service I now see,
abundance is now real for me.**

6. It is the Father's good pleasure to give me the kingdom. He gives it to me freely because I am receiving it freely. I am freely sharing what I have freely received.

O Liberty, a chalice pure,
my lower bodies are for sure.
Release through me your symphony,
your gift of Cosmic Liberty.

**O Cosmic Mother Liberty,
conduct Abundance Symphony.
My highest service I now see,
abundance is now real for me.**

7. I am working together with others and we are multiplying our individual talents and pooling them together so that the whole becomes more than the sum of its parts. We give selflessly and receive selflessly, reestablishing the right connection to God.

O Liberty, the open door,
I am for Symphony of More.
In chakras mine light you release,
the flow of love shall never cease.

O Cosmic Mother Liberty,
conduct Abundance Symphony.
My highest service I now see,
abundance is now real for me.

8. I am opening a connection to God's infinite abundance. I am allowing God the pleasure of giving me his kingdom by expanding the total amount of energy on earth. There is no limit to the amount of spiritual energy that my I AM Presence can let flow through my being.

O Liberty, release the flow,
of opulence that you bestow.
For I am willing to receive,
the Golden Fleece that you now weave.

O Cosmic Mother Liberty,
conduct Abundance Symphony.
My highest service I now see,
abundance is now real for me.

9. I am the Holy Grail. My mind is the chalice for the spiritual light from my I AM Presence. I am making wise use of my abundance. I am allowing God's light to stream into my being and world, manifesting God's abundance in my life.

O Liberty, release the cure,
to free the tired and the poor.
The huddled masses are set free,
by loving Song of Liberty.

O Cosmic Mother Liberty,
conduct Abundance Symphony.
My highest service I now see,
abundance is now real for me.

Sealing

In the name of the Divine Mother, I call to Liberty and Mother Mary for the sealing of myself and all people in my circle of influence in the creative flow of the Divine Mother, the River of Life. I call for the multiplication of my calls by all representatives of the Divine Mother, so that we form the perfect figure-eight flow of "As Above, so below." Thus, I accept that this is fully manifest, because the mouth of the Lord, the Divine Mother that I AM, has spoken it. Amen.

13 | AWAKENING FROM THE COLLECTIVE ILLUSION

I would like to pull together some of the thoughts I have given you in the previous keys so that I may present a more coherent picture of what it will take for you to manifest the abundant life. I have explained the true meaning of the statement that it is the Father's good pleasure to give you the kingdom, namely that you were designed to be a co-creator with God. You were designed to constantly receive the abundant life from Above. You would receive that abundant life in the form of a constant stream of spiritual energy, flowing through your I AM Presence into your conscious mind. This flow of energy could then be directed by you into manifesting the abundant life in this world. By doing so, you would fulfill your role as a co-creator with God and multiply the energy and creative abilities given to you by God. You can then take dominion, first over yourself and then over the material universe whereby you will help bring God's kingdom into manifestation on earth.

The reason you do not currently have the abundant life manifest is that you have forgotten your original role. You have lost your true sense of identity as a co-creator with God. Instead, you have come to accept a false identity, a pseudo identity, as a mortal human being who is separated from God. You might even have come to believe that there is no God, that there is no spiritual realm, that there is no I AM Presence and that you are all alone in a hostile world, surrounded by people who are trying to take from you what you believe is rightfully yours.

Most of the people who are engaged in conflicts are trapped in a self-centered or egotistical state of consciousness. People are so focused on themselves that they have no awareness left over for considering the bigger picture. They have no awareness left over for considering how their actions affect other people or even for considering the higher awareness that they are part of the Body of God on earth and that everything they do affects the whole. They are also so focused on life in the material universe that they have no attention left over for considering that there is a spiritual realm and that they might receive abundance directly from Above rather than taking it by force in this world.

If you are to manifest the abundant life and overcome the sense of struggle that traps so many people in an ongoing conflict over limited resources, you have to transcend this egotistical, materialistic state of consciousness. You have to rise above it and reclaim your true identity as a son or daughter of God who is worthy to be a co-creator with God. You are fully capable of co-creating the abundant life right here on earth. This higher state of consciousness is a consciousness that is based on oneness with your source rather than separation from God. This is the oneness that Jesus described when he said: "I and my Father are one" (John 10:30). He truly meant: "I and my I AM Presence are one." The consciousness demonstrated by Jesus is the sense of identity that is based on the reality of who you are rather than the false image of who you are not. Although we might call this state of consciousness by many names, I would like to call it personal Christhood or the Christ consciousness. It was the role of Jesus to come to earth and demonstrate this state of consciousness.

***

Before we go on to consider exactly how to manifest the Christ consciousness, I would like to describe in further detail what the Christ consciousness actually means. The material universe is made from the finer energies of the spiritual realm that have been lowered in frequency and have taken on a certain form. The true measure of the abundance that is available to human beings on earth is the amount of spiritual energy that has been lowered in vibration and now vibrates within the material frequency spectrum. Some of that energy has been lowered into the frequency spectrum of physical matter whereas some of it exists as psychic energy. Some of it is manifest as material abundance whereas some of it is *potential* abundance that can become manifest as material abundance through the power of people's minds.

The ultimate key to increasing the abundance on earth, so that all people can share in the abundant life, is to bring more spiritual energy into the material frequency spectrum. Only a person who has achieved Christ consciousness is capable of bringing energy from the spiritual realm into the material realm. Only a person with the Christ consciousness can be the open door for God's light to stream into this world, and that is why Jesus could say about himself: "I am the way the truth and the life" (John 14:6), "I am the door" (John 10:9) and: "As long as I am in the world, I am the light of the world" (John 9:5). Any person who achieves Christ consciousness, can say the same. Every person has the potential to achieve Christ consciousness. Let us now consider the options for manifesting abundance that are open to those who have *not* achieved the Christ consciousness. If people believe in the materialistic philosophy that there is no God, or if they believe in the orthodox idol worship of Jesus as the exception rather than as the example, they do not have the option of increasing the total amount of energy available in the matter realm. They can increase their abundance only by taking from the amount of material substance and psychic energy that is already available in the energy system of earth.

We can set up a scale that illustrates how close people are to Christ consciousness or how far below it they have descended. Let us begin by considering the cave man and the state of consciousness represented by the cave man. In the cave man you see a being who is completely identified with the physical body and with the lower instincts of that body. The cave man barely deserves the label of "man," for he is acting more like an intelligent animal than a human being. The cave man does not have a high enough level of awareness to imagine that he could change his environment. He is therefore living as an animal and adapting to the environment, scratching out a living by taking what he needs from Mother Nature. This he does by taking everything through force, by killing animals or gathering whatever food is available.

When he comes in conflict with other cave dwellers, his only response is to defend what he believes is his by using violence. There is no negotiation, no set of laws or agreements between different tribes or nations in order to divide the territory and avoid confrontation. As soon as the cave man is provoked, his animal instincts flare up and he responds with the flight or fight syndrome that is so typical in animals. If he cannot get away, he will turn on you and fight you. What scientists currently consider the beginning of the evolutionary chain of humankind represents the absolute low point when it comes to Christ consciousness. The cave man stage was not the beginning of humankind. It was a low point to which human beings had descended by misusing their creative abilities. The cave man represents the lowest state of awareness, in terms of man's creative abilities, known to the modern world.

Since the cave man stage there has been a gradual upward trend, a rise in the awareness of how to use your creative abilities to change your environment and even manipulate energy. One great leap forward came when people learned how to use fire and to preserve and control the fire as a tool. Another major leap came when people learned to build their own houses rather than rely on natural caves. Still another leap came when people learned agriculture, and therefore they could use the land to produce more food than was available through hunting. The rise in civilization that we have seen over the past 2,000 years also represents a rise in awareness about how the universe works. People have become increasingly able to change their environment instead of passively adapting to it. Much of this has been focused on learning how to use material substance and the laws of nature, and thus it has been focused on gathering abundance from the supply that is already available in the frequency spectrum of physical matter.

Over the past century, you have seen an increased awareness about finer energies, including the scientific understanding that matter is a form of energy. You have also seen a rise in people's understanding of the spiritual side of life, which has led to a greater awareness of the fact that your mind has a major influence on every aspect of your life, as evidenced in the self-help field. Humankind has now moved into a phase where people are no longer confined to manifesting abundance from physical matter. People have started, although the official understanding is yet primitive, to manifest abundance by using the power of their minds. Many people are still focused on using the mind to discover deeper laws of nature that allow them to make better use of matter. An increasing number of people are beginning to explore the mind's potential for taking dominion over matter, thereby converting psychic energy into material substance by lowering its vibration and making it take on physical form.

When it comes to the growth in human consciousness, one aspect is the growth in awareness, in understanding, of how the world works. As you increase this awareness, you become better at using the laws of nature to your advantage. You can then begin to actively change your environment so that it can fulfill your needs with less effort on your part. As you can see today in human society, this increase in awareness is not without pitfalls. It does not necessarily lead to the abundant life or to a permanent state of happiness and peace of mind. The indiscriminate use of humankind's greater awareness can create problems that have the potential to threaten the long-term survival of the human race. An increase in awareness is not the same as Christ consciousness. An increase in awareness is part of attaining Christ consciousness, but it is not the full Christ consciousness.

Increased awareness of how to manipulate the laws of nature – without an increased sense of oneness with God and all life – can take you away from the Christ consciousness. The increased awareness about the material world will not automatically produce Christ consciousness. It can provide the foundation for a person's ascent to the Christ consciousness, but there is no guarantee that this ascent will occur. The increase in awareness of people's creative abilities can become a trap if it is not balanced by an increase in the love of the heart. The increase in awareness takes place in the mind, yet the mind is not the faculty that gives human beings the ability to love one another and live in peace. People simply become better at taking things through force whereas the real key to abundance is to go beyond force and know that it is the Father's good pleasure to give you the kingdom. You can attain everything you need through love rather than force.

This brings us to the other aspect of Christ consciousness, the real key to Christ consciousness, which is a shift away from an approach to life that is based on lack and fear into an approach that is based on abundance and love. The cave man represented an evolutionary low point in terms of both the mind's awareness of the world and the heart's ability to love beyond the self. Since then, humankind has increased both the mind's capacity to understand the world and the heart's capacity for love. Unfortunately, the heart has not been expanded as quickly as the mind. You now see people who have the ability to create new technology but not the ability to use it wisely—including the ability to choose to not always do what is technically possible.

***

All human conflicts spring from the consciousness of lack. The overriding feeling in this state of mind is the feeling of fear. This can be the fear that there is not enough for everyone and so if I do not take something, someone else will. Or if I do not defend what I have, then someone will take it away from me.

In this frame of mind you live in a world where you are surrounded by threats. This constant fear of loss inevitably leads to selfishness, and it blocks the ability to think about the long-term consequences of one's actions, to think about other people or to think about the whole. We now see that Christ consciousness has two main characteristics:

- An increased awareness about your creative abilities. This includes greater awareness of the laws of nature that guide the unfoldment of the material universe and

the greater laws of God that provide a framework within
which the laws of nature work.

•   An increased awareness that you are not an individual who is separated from the whole of God's creation
or from your source. No human is an island, and in
order for you to be truly happy, you need to understand
that you can only be completely fulfilled when you see
yourself as one with God and with the Body of God on
earth.

When you look at yourself as an isolated individual, you
automatically descend into a consciousness of fear, separation
and lack. If you increase the mind's awareness of the laws of
nature without overcoming your fear, you will not be able to
turn your new awareness into a more abundant life. You will
still be gripped by fear, and your awareness will simply give you
more powerful means for taking abundance from others. Your
increase in awareness does not increase the abundance in this
world, it only increases the tension and violence in this world.

You can transcend this debilitating fear only by realizing that
you are part of a larger whole, that you are an individualization
of God. Only when you fully realize and accept that you are a
part of God's creation, will you believe that it is God's pleasure
to give you the kingdom and that you don't need to live in lack or
take everything by force. When you have this sense of identity,
this sense of oneness with all life and oneness with your Creator,
you automatically experience the perfect love, the unconditional
love, that God has for you as an extension of himself. This is
the perfect love that will cast out all fear in your being. When
you overcome fear, your approach to life will be based on love.
You can follow Jesus' command to love God with all your heart,

soul and mind and to love your neighbor as yourself (Matthew 22:37).

What is the key to experiencing this love? Ah, is there not a double meaning in these words of Jesus? Could we not interpret the words: "Love your neighbor as yourself" to mean that you should not simply love your neighbor the same way you love yourself. Could we not consider that there might be an even deeper meaning, namely that you love your neighbor as yourself because you realize that your neighbor *is* yourself. You realize that you and your neighbor are both part of the same Body of God and you both came from the same source. You realize with Jesus: "Inasmuch as ye have done it unto the least of these my brethren, ye have done it unto me" (Matthew 25:40).

In order to fully love God with all your heart mind and soul, you need to recognize that God is not apart from you, that God is a part of you because you are a part of God. You are an individualization of God, and therefore you love God as yourself because you realize that God *is* your real self, your real identity. This gives rise to the state of oneness with God, in which you no longer think that the outer self, the sense of identity based on separation from God, is the doer. Instead, you realize that it is the higher self, the I AM Presence within you, who is the doer, who is the first cause, who is the source of all good and perfect gifts.

These ideas are truly the missing link that can allow you to evolve out of the consciousness of selfishness and egotism and evolve into the Christ consciousness. This is the missing link that can allow you to rise from the level of an intelligent animal to the level of a true spiritual being, a true co-creator with God. This is as big of a leap as the fabled leap between monkeys and human beings, for which science has found no missing link—because the missing link is a leap in consciousness.

***

Let us now return to the idea that human beings can descend far below the level of the Christ consciousness. When you descend to the very lowest level, you are truly functioning as an animal, adapting to a given environment and taking by force whatever abundance is available in that environment. Your consciousness is completely focused on yourself and your own survival and desires. Your consciousness is completely focused on the material universe, which means that you see only visible matter and the conditions in nature as the means for the fulfillment of your desires. You do not have the ability to imagine that something unseen, something from a higher realm, might fulfill your desires. You cannot imagine that you might get what you want through a higher power than physical force.

As you grow in awareness, you learn that behind the phenomena you can observe with your senses is a set of guiding principles, or laws of nature. When you begin to know these laws, you can use them to fulfill your desires with less work. You can even get to the point where you can fulfill your needs without using force, without taking it from other people or without forcefully taking it from Mother Nature. Some cultures have proven that they can live in perfect harmony with their environment, always using renewable resources and therefore maintaining a culture for thousands of years without raping the environment and destroying its capacity to support them.

Such harmony with nature requires an awareness of the whole that cannot come from the mind but only from the heart. What you see in Western society today is that the increase in the awareness of the laws of nature has a dark side. It is quite possible that people can use the laws of nature to gain a temporary advantage that has long-term consequences that prove destructive either for themselves or for future generations.

Modern technology has created pollution that has long-term consequences for the environment and even for human genes. It was only a few decades ago that humankind became aware that certain chemicals used to kill annoying insects took a long time to break down and would therefore enter the food chain, eventually ending up in the human body with many negative consequences as a result. Even today, you see an increased awareness concerning how the pollution created by modern technology can have long-term effects on the global climate, possibly even creating devastating climatic conditions.

Technology based on an understanding of nature but without the development of the heart can indeed give people a temporary advantage, yet in the long run it decreases the amount of material wealth available on this planet. This kind of technology is a force-based technology. People have learned how to manipulate the laws of nature, but they do so from a state of lack and fear, which causes them to attempt to take heaven by force (Matthew 11:12). Because they are using their creative abilities in an unbalanced manner, the Ma-ter Light creates an opposite reaction that eventually takes away the security they are trying to build through force.

This is a clear proof that if the increase in people's awareness of the laws of nature is not balanced with an increase in the heart's capacity for love of something beyond the self, then you will not transcend the state of consciousness based on fear that leads to the use of force. You will increase your power to use force, and Mother Nature will reflect your actions back to you in the form of an opposite reaction. The more powerful your unbalanced action, the more powerful the reaction from Mother Nature in the form of so-called natural disasters. This is precisely what you are seeing as the result of humankind's misuse of technology. You now see that if the increase in awareness is not coupled with an increase in love and a sense of oneness with all

life, then humankind does not come closer to actually manifesting Christ consciousness. Humankind increases its destructive
powers, and thereby people increase the reaction from Mother
Nature, from the Ma-ter Light itself.

***

As devastating as the unbalanced use of technology can be
in the realm of physical matter, there are far more devastating
effects of an unbalanced growth in awareness. At the lowest stage
in the evolution of human consciousness, you have people who
are only aware of the material realm, meaning that they see only
physical matter as a resource for the fulfillment of their desires.
If they cannot detect something with their senses, it seems to
have no value or even existence to them. These people can only
acquire abundance from the energy that is already manifest as
physical matter, which of course limits their potential to accumulate abundance. They have to take what is already physically
manifest, and therefore they automatically set themselves up in
competition with all other people at the same level of awareness.

When you rise from this low level of consciousness, you
become aware that there is more to abundance than meets the
eye. Many people already have a certain awareness of the importance of invisible energy. Many see the value of using a higher
understanding to create abundance from what others consider
worthless. Most people do not have a clear, conscious understanding of psychic energy, they do not even have the basic
understanding I have given you in previous chapters. Some have
learned to subconsciously manipulate psychic energy through
the power of their minds. Many of these people have a purely
intellectual understanding of the fact that matter is made from
energy and that their minds have the power to manipulate energy.
These people truly do not have the development of the heart,

they simply have a greater intellectual awareness of the material universe and the energies that are part of this universe. They know that the material universe is more than physical matter and that the key to accumulating greater amounts of abundance is to learn how to manipulate psychic energy through the mind.

Unfortunately, this increased awareness of the mind's abilities can be attained without having an increase in the heart's awareness of the whole. People can learn how to manipulate psychic energy without increasing their love for God or for their fellow man. They can learn how to manipulate energy while they are still completely self-centered and egotistical. Once again, let us look at the two components that are necessary for the manifestation of Christ consciousness:

• An increased awareness of your creative abilities. This starts as greater knowledge of the laws of nature whereby you can accumulate abundance by making better use of physical matter. The next step is to learn how to use the mind to make use of psychic energy as the foundation for generating material abundance.

• An increased awareness of yourself as part of a larger whole and a love for that whole as yourself. You can then use your creative abilities in harmony with the laws of God so that by increasing your personal abundance, you are increasing the total amount of abundance. You are not taking from others but adding to the sum of abundance available on earth. This culminates in the ability to bring spiritual energy into the material frequency spectrum and this is the ultimate source of abundance.

Only when the evolution of consciousness incorporates both elements, will you be able to evolve out of selfishness and avoid falling into the trap of using your greater creative abilities in a selfish manner. There are certain people on this earth who have attained a very high degree of ability to manipulate psychic energy. They have attained the ability to manipulate other people. Your thoughts and feelings are forms of energy. If a person has attained mastery in terms of manipulating mental and emotional energy, such a person can actually manipulate your thoughts and feelings. The person can control you through your mental and emotional bodies. If you want an obvious example of a person with this ability, consider how Adolph Hitler was able to manipulate a large part of the German population into becoming mindless robots in his scheme for power and control.

There are many people in today's world who have this ability, and some of them have learned to use it behind the scenes so that they are not recognized by the public. Some of them even use this ability in such a way that they are seen as celebrities. These are people who have learned how to make use of the psychic energy that has been brought into the material frequency spectrum but has not yet been lowered into the frequency spectrum of physical matter. This energy still exists as a potential to take on physical form but the actual form has not yet been determined. When a person learns how to manipulate this energy, that person can attain some mastery over how the energy is manifest as form. This can allow such a person to accumulate great material wealth, which is partly done by manipulating other people into doing the actual work that produces the wealth yet concentrates it in the hands of the person who is pulling the strings behind the scene. These are people who have attained a high degree of mental mastery over matter, a mastery of mind over matter, yet they have not attained the corresponding degree of mastery of the heart. They do not see themselves as one with God or as one with their fellow man. They see themselves as being apart from God, often as being in opposition to God. They think they can do whatever they want without suffering the consequences, and some of them even believe they are so powerful that they can manipulate God's laws so that they do not reap what they have sown. Some even have an agenda of openly rebelling against God's law and creating a world in which God is not found. They are attempting to use the power of their minds to control all other people on this planet in order to prove that this world is a sphere where God does not exist and where an intelligent Creator is not needed. This is a clear demonstration of what I told you earlier, namely that when people do not have the absolute guiding rod of knowing the law that God has put in their inward parts, they think they become a law unto themselves. They use the relative, dualistic mind to set up their own rules for what is good and evil, and in their blindness and arrogance, they think their own relative law has replaced God's absolute law.

It is possible to learn how to use the power of the mind to manipulate psychic energy without having the expanded heart that allows you to use energy in a way that benefits the whole. You can manipulate energy to fulfill your self-centered needs and desires without considering what consequences this has for the Body of God on earth or for Mother Nature. These are the kind of people that Jesus was talking about when he said: "If therefore the light that is in thee be darkness, how great is that darkness," (Matthew 6:23) and: "The kingdom of heaven suffereth violence and the violent take it by force" (Matthew 11:12). If you have learned how to use psychic energy for selfish purposes, then you are turning that energy into darkness. The amount of darkness will be as great as the amount of light you are misqualifying through your fear-based attempt to take by force what God would give you freely—if you had been willing to transcend your sense of separation from God.

***

The increase in awareness of your creative abilities is a part of attaining Christ consciousness. If that awareness is confined to the mind and is not balanced by the growth of the heart, then it is possible that people can pervert their creative abilities and use them for selfish purposes. When you attain the balanced Christ consciousness, where the increase in the awareness of your creativity is balanced by the love of the heart, you will use your creative abilities only in harmony with the laws of God. You will not seek to fulfill self-centered, egotistical desires because you will realize that you are not a separate individual. You are part of God and thus part of the Body of God. What is best for you is what is also best for the whole. When you overcome the self-centered consciousness of fear, you will realize that there is no conflict between your true personal desires and what is good for the whole of the Body of God on earth. You are part of the whole, so only by magnifying the whole can you be truly fulfilled.

It is indeed possible to fulfill your personal desires in a way that increases the total amount of abundance in this world and therefore magnifies the whole. When you do not have the increase in the love of the heart – which gives you the sense of oneness with the whole – you can become trapped in the mind. You then begin to believe in the false idea that you have a right to exercise your mental powers without considering the whole. When you have the full Christ consciousness, you have the full awareness of yourself as an extension of God. You have the perfect balance between your personal desires and what is good for all other people. You also know how to fulfill your personal desires in a way that is in harmony with the laws of God—laws that are designed to ensure the highest good for the whole. This balance is achieved through the mind of Christ so what is the mind that allows you to manipulate energy without considering the whole? What is the mind that allows you to use God's energy to create forms that are out of alignment with the laws of God? Is it not the mind of anti-christ? Is not the very consciousness of anti-christ the mindset that allows a person to manipulate energy yet does not give that person the love of the heart to use energy in harmony with the laws of God?

Some of the false gurus in the prosperity field have discovered ways to manipulate psychic energy, thereby using it to manipulate other people or even manipulate physical matter so that they can attract abundance to themselves. If such people do not have the increased awareness of the heart, they are actually attracting abundance through the mind of anti-christ. They are using the power of their minds to manipulate energy in a way that is completely out of harmony with the laws of God, the most important of which is the Law of Love that creates harmony between the individual and the whole.

It is important for you to consider this topic, even though I am aware that for some people this will seem like an unpleasant topic that might generate some fear. There is no need to fear the forces of anti-christ when you have the awareness of how they work. Only that which is unknown is to be feared because if you do not understand how certain forces are seeking to manipulate you, how can you defend yourself from them? When you see through the mindset of anti-christ, you can avoid being manipulated or tempted by people who are trapped in this mindset. You can rebuke the devil, as Jesus did when he was tempted after his stay in the wilderness (Matthew 4:1). Only by rebuking the mindset of anti-christ, that has pervaded almost every aspect of life on this planet, can you free yourself from this mindset.

How can you hope to attain the Christ consciousness if you do not free yourself from the mindset of anti-christ? This simply cannot be done. As Jesus said, you cannot serve two masters (Matthew 6:24). You cannot serve God and mammon, you cannot serve God through the consciousness of Christ – that seeks what is best for all – and at the same time serve mammon – meaning the consciousness of selfishness – through the mind of anti-christ.

You must choose this day whom you will serve (Joshua 24:15), whether you will serve the consciousness of life, namely the consciousness of Christ, or the consciousness of death, which is the consciousness of anti-christ. I say, as did Moses: "Choose life—Choose the consciousness of Christ that is the doorway to eternal life, the eternal life of oneness with your source and oneness with all life." (Deuteronomy 30:19)

You can continue, for the rest of your life, to increase your awareness of psychic energy and how to manipulate that energy into creating material abundance for yourself. As long as you are trapped in the consciousness of anti-christ, you are trapped in the consciousness of duality. All of your actions will be out of harmony with the laws of God. That which is out of harmony with the laws of God creates an unbalanced impulse, which means that the Ma-ter Light itself will create an opposing impulse in order to maintain balance in the universe.

It is truly possible for you to use the consciousness of anti-christ to temporarily gather to yourself material abundance or power on this earth. The material universe is designed with a certain delay factor, which means that it is possible for a self-aware being to misuse its creative powers and to create forms that are out of alignment with the laws of God. Because of the delay factor built into the material universe, such unbalanced forms will not instantly self-destruct. They can exist for some time, and therefore it is possible for you to use the mind of anti-christ to create material abundance that might last you for the rest of this lifetime. The Bible is correct when it states that as you sow, so will you reap (Galatians 6:7). The Bible is also true when it states that there is life after the death of the physical body (Matthew 16:28). This means that if you do not reap what

you have sown while your physical body is alive,
your lifestream will reap what you have sown in the fu

***

If you have grown up in a traditional Christian culture, you
have been programmed to believe that you have only one lifetime here on earth. This is a false idea that entered the Christian
religion because of influence from people who were trapped in
the consciousness of anti-christ. The consciousness of anti-christ
sees the individual self as separated from the whole, and thus the
consciousness of anti-christ is the source of all selfishness. The
more a person becomes trapped in the consciousness of anti-
christ, the more selfish the person becomes, and the ultimate
example is the consciousness of the cave man. When you are
self-centered, you cannot see beyond your immediate desires,
and thus you cannot accept the idea that your actions have consequences that you cannot escape. An extremely self-centered
person cannot accept the truth that you will surely reap in a
future lifetime what you sow in this lifetime. That is precisely
why the truth about reincarnation was taken out of orthodox
Christianity, as Jesus explains in more detail in his book [*The
Mystical Teachings of Jesus*]

Even orthodox Christianity teaches that the soul survives
the death of the physical body. Mainstream Christianity cannot
explain the fact that some children are born with crippling diseases while others are born perfectly healthy. According to orthodox doctrines, there is no logical explanation for this observable
fact. This has caused many Christians to reason that God must
be an unfair God who punishes innocent children, seemingly for
no reason. The reality is that God does not punish anyone. God
has simply set up a universe that acts as a mirror, and thus the
universe reflects back to you whatever you send out. When you

your creative abilities in a way that is out of harmony with e laws of God, you create an unbalanced action. In order to maintain balance in the universe, the cosmic mirror creates an opposite reaction. This reaction will not instantaneously cancel out your action. There is a delay factor built into the universe, and the purpose is to give you greater opportunity to learn.

If there was no delay, many of your actions would generate a return that would instantly kill you. Because of the delay, you can make a mistake without instantly annihilating yourself and missing the opportunity to learn. You have some time between the mistake and the return current from the universe. You can grow in awareness so that when the reaction comes back to you, you have transcended the consciousness that caused the original action. If you do rise above that state of consciousness, God has the option of setting aside or reducing the reaction from the universe so that you can continue the opportunity to grow in your present lifetime without having it interrupted by your actions from a former lifetime. This makes perfect sense when you realize that God's only desire is for you to grow by constantly transcending your state of consciousness, your sense of identity. God is not the angry and punishing God he is portrayed to be by so many religions.

The conditions you experience in this lifetime are not God's punishment and they are not the results of a game of chance. They are the effects of causes you have set in motion in previous lifetimes through the choices you made in those lifetimes. Your current situation was not created by God; it was created by your own self, and thus you are reaping now what you have sown in the past. If you do not realize that what you are experiencing in this lifetime is the effect of causes you set in motion in the past, how can you overcome the sense that you are a victim of forces beyond your control? You are meant to be a co-creator with God. If you are to experience abundance in your life, you cannot passively wait for God to drop that abundance in your lap. You must take an active role and realign yourself with the laws of God, with your I AM Presence, so that you can become the open door for the light of your I AM Presence to stream into your world and manifest abundance.

Most people in today's world, whether they have been brought up in an orthodox religion or materialistic science, have been programmed to believe that they are victims of forces beyond their control. They are either victims of an angry and judgmental God or victims of the laws of nature that are beyond human control. As long as you are in this state of consciousness and believe you are the helpless victim of forces beyond control, how could you possibly become a co-creator and manifest abundance in your life through your own efforts? All you can do is to take the passive approach and hope that some miracle will manifest abundance in your life.

This mindset is precisely what makes so many people vulnerable to the false gurus that promise a get-rich-quick scheme. When you think that your only option for bringing about abundance is to find a shortcut that will bring abundance through some indescribable miracle, you are easily swayed by the empty promises of those who claim they have discovered such a shortcut. You will be easy prey for those who claim they can teach you how to use your mind to attract abundance. They will not teach you about the long-term consequences or tell you that their system works through the mind of anti-christ.

***

My aim with this course is to offer you a true and scientific path to lasting abundance. It is not my goal to show you a shortcut to some temporary abundance. It is my goal to show you the true path to the abundant life that can be maintained indefinitely as long as you stay in the Christ consciousness. That is why it is necessary for me to expose the fallacy of not only the false gurus but of the entire mindset of anti-christ that prevents you from fulfilling your rightful role. Your true role is to be a conscious co-creator who can reach into the spiritual realm and bring more spiritual energy into the material frequency spectrum. This is the only way to increase the total amount of abundance available on earth, and it simply cannot be done through the mind of anti-christ. People with this mindset cannot reach into the spiritual realm. When you are trapped in the consciousness of separation that causes you to deny your oneness with God, how could you possibly establish a connection to your I AM Presence and become the open door for the light of God? This cannot be done, and thus the mind of anti-christ can never reach beyond the material frequency spectrum. It is forever condemned to taking abundance from this world, thus having to take it by force.

We might say that God has built another safety mechanism into the design of the universe. The ultimate creative power is to bring spiritual energy into the material frequency spectrum. This simply cannot be done by a mind that is trapped in selfishness and therefore likely to use such energy for egotistical purposes. Such a mind can manipulate psychic energy but does not have access to spiritual energy. Only a mind that has overcome selfishness, through a sense of oneness with God and with the Body of God, has access to God's infinite abundance.

Even those who have attained a high degree of mastery over psychic energy still have not attained the ability to reach into the spiritual realm and draw down more of God's energy. They have attained the mastery that allows them to accumulate abundance by drawing on the greater resource of psychic energy, energy that is beyond physical matter yet below spiritual energy. Such people can manifest more abundance than you could ever manifest only by working at the level of physical matter. Do not be fooled into thinking that such people have true spiritual mastery or that they have the Christ consciousness. While their achievements might seem impressive from an outer viewpoint, they are like nothing in the light of God's truth. That is why Jesus warned against the false prophets (Matthew 7:15) who would come in his name, some of them being able to show signs and wonders, yet under the surface they are like ravening wolves because they have no love in their hearts.

Such people have done nothing to increase the total amount of abundance in this world. They have simply learned how to manipulate the psychic energy that is already in the material frequency spectrum. They can do this only through force, which means that they either take psychic energy from other people or that they use psychic energy to manipulate other people into doing the physical work and then turning the fruits of their labor over to the power elite. This is why the true power struggle on earth is a struggle for energy, including psychic energy.

Once again, you have two ways to manifest abundance. You can indeed follow the false gurus and use the mindset of anti-christ to generate a temporary material abundance for yourself. You might be able to accumulate great wealth over the course of this lifetime by doing so. My beloved, I am simply telling you the truth here—I am being completely honest with you. Some of the false gurus out there are indeed telling you a truth when they say that they have discovered a system whereby you can manifest abundance through the power of the mind. One might say that they are not false gurus in the lower sense that they are making a false promise. They are telling you that they have a system that will enable you to manifest wealth, and that claim is true. They are not telling you about the long-term consequences of doing this. They are *not* telling you that if you follow their system, you will bind yourself to the consciousness of anti-christ, and you will inevitably reap what you have sown, either in this lifetime or in a future lifetime. I am here to tell you that there is an alternative whereby you can manifest abundance without being trapped by the consciousness of anti-christ. This is the true key—not simply to temporary material abundance, but to the permanent abundant life, the eternal life. This is the true key that leads you out of death, the consciousness of death, and into the eternal life of the Christ consciousness. When you achieve that state of oneness, which is the kingdom of God, all else will indeed be added unto you (Matthew 6:33).

My beloved, I assume that if you are studying this course, you already know in your heart that you have no desire to learn how to manipulate psychic energy through the consciousness of anti-christ. You know very well that you want to come home to your Father's kingdom, and therefore you are not looking for shortcuts. It is with great love that I reach out to you and offer you my hand so that I can lead you to a greater understanding of what it will take to overcome the consciousness of anti-christ and manifest the consciousness of Christ. In the next chapters I will explain how you can follow the call of Paul to: "Let this mind be in you, which was also in Christ Jesus" (Philippians 2:5).

14 | I INVOKE MASTERY OVER MATTER

In the name I AM THAT I AM, Jesus Christ, I call to all representatives of the Divine Mother, especially Venus and Mother Mary, to help me transcend the mindset of anti-christ and attain the Christ consciousness that gives me mastery over matter. Help me transcend all blocks to my ability to manifest abundance, including…

[Make personal calls.]

1. I acknowledge my Christ potential

1. I am fully capable of co-creating the abundant life right here on earth. I am in oneness with my source rather than separated from God. I and my I AM Presence are one.

O Venus, show me how to serve,
your cosmic beauty I observe.
What love from Venus you now bring,
our planets do in tandem sing.

O Venus, service so divine,
you are for earth a cosmic sign.
Your selfless service is now mine,
a life in service I define.

2. The state of consciousness demonstrated by Jesus is the sense of identity that is based on the reality of who I am rather than the false image of who I am not. I accept my potential to manifest personal Christhood.

O Venus, your love is the key,
the hardened hearts on earth are free.
Embracing future bright and bold,
our planet's story is retold.

O Venus, service so divine,
you are for earth a cosmic sign.
Your selfless service is now mine,
a life in service I define.

3. I am part of the movement to explore the mind's potential for taking dominion over matter. I am learning to convert psychic energy into material substance by lowering its vibration and making it take on physical form.

O Venus, loving Mother mine,
my heart your love does now refine.
I am the open door for love,
descending like a Holy Dove.

O Venus, service so divine,
you are for earth a cosmic sign.
Your selfless service is now mine,
a life in service I define.

4. The real key to abundance is to go beyond force. I know that it is the Father's good pleasure to give me the kingdom. I am attaining everything I need through love rather than force.

O Venus, play the secret note,
that is for hatred antidote.
All poisoned hearts you gently heal,
as love's true story you reveal.

O Venus, service so divine,
you are for earth a cosmic sign.
Your selfless service is now mine,
a life in service I define.

5. I am shifting away from an approach to life that is based on lack and fear into an approach that is based on abundance and love.

O Venus, love fills every need,
for truly, love is God's first seed.
O let it blossom, let it grow,
sweep earth into your loving flow.

O Venus, service so divine,
you are for earth a cosmic sign.
Your selfless service is now mine,
a life in service I define.

6. I am increasing my awareness of my creative abilities. I know the laws of nature and the greater laws of God that provide a framework within which the laws of nature work.

> O Venus, music of the spheres,
> heard by those who God reveres.
> Our voices now as one we raise,
> singing in adoring praise.

> **O Venus, service so divine,**
> **you are for earth a cosmic sign.**
> **Your selfless service is now mine,**
> **a life in service I define.**

7. I see myself as one with God and with the Body of God on earth. I am part of a larger whole, I am an individualization of God.

> O Venus, we are joining ranks,
> Sanat Kumara we give thanks.
> Our planet has received new life,
> to lift her out of war and strife.

> **O Venus, service so divine,**
> **you are for earth a cosmic sign.**
> **Your selfless service is now mine,**
> **a life in service I define.**

8. I fully realize and accept that I am a part of God's creation. I know it is God's pleasure to give me the kingdom and that I don't need to live in lack or take everything by force.

O Venus, your sweet melody,
consumes veil of duality.
Absorbed in tones of Cosmic Love,
all conflict we now rise above.

O Venus, service so divine,
you are for earth a cosmic sign.
Your selfless service is now mine,
a life in service I define.

9. I am experiencing the perfect love, the unconditional love,
that God has for me as an extension of itself. This is the perfect
love that is casting out all fear in my being. My approach to life
is based on love.

O Venus, shining Morning Star,
a cosmic herald, that you are.
The earth set free by sacred sound,
our planet is now heaven-bound.

O Venus, service so divine,
you are for earth a cosmic sign.
Your selfless service is now mine,
a life in service I define.

2. I am part of the Body of God

1. I am loving God with all my heart, soul and mind and loving
my neighbor as myself. I see that my neighbor *is* myself. My
neighbor and I are part of the same Body of God and we came
from the same source.

O Venus, show me how to serve,
your cosmic beauty I observe.
What love from Venus you now bring,
our planets do in tandem sing.

**O Venus, service so divine,
you are for earth a cosmic sign.
Your selfless service is now mine,
a life in service I define.**

2. God is not apart from me. God is a part of me because I am a part of God. I am an individualization of God. I love God as myself because God *is* my real self, my real identity.

O Venus, your love is the key,
the hardened hearts on earth are free.
Embracing future bright and bold,
our planet's story is retold.

**O Venus, service so divine,
you are for earth a cosmic sign.
Your selfless service is now mine,
a life in service I define.**

3. The outer self, the sense of identity based on separation from God, is *not* the doer. My I AM Presence within me, is the doer. It is the first cause, the source of all good and perfect gifts.

O Venus, loving Mother mine,
my heart your love does now refine.
I am the open door for love,
descending like a Holy Dove.

O Venus, service so divine,
you are for earth a cosmic sign.
Your selfless service is now mine,
a life in service I define.

4. I am using the laws of nature to fulfill my desires with less work. I am fulfilling my needs without using force, without taking it from other people or without forcefully taking it from Mother Nature.

O Venus, play the secret note,
that is for hatred antidote.
All poisoned hearts you gently heal,
as love's true story you reveal.

O Venus, service so divine,
you are for earth a cosmic sign.
Your selfless service is now mine,
a life in service I define.

5. I am attaining mental mastery over matter, mastery of mind over matter. I am attaining the corresponding degree of mastery of the heart. I am one with God and one with my fellow man.

O Venus, love fills every need,
for truly, love is God's first seed.
O let it blossom, let it grow,
sweep earth into your loving flow.

O Venus, service so divine,
you are for earth a cosmic sign.
Your selfless service is now mine,
a life in service I define.

6. I am attaining the full awareness of myself as an extension of God. I have the perfect balance between my personal desires and what is good for all other people.

> O Venus, music of the spheres,
> heard by those who God reveres.
> Our voices now as one we raise,
> singing in adoring praise.

> **O Venus, service so divine,**
> **you are for earth a cosmic sign.**
> **Your selfless service is now mine,**
> **a life in service I define.**

7. I am fulfilling my personal desires in a way that is in harmony with the laws of God—laws that are designed to ensure the highest good for the whole.

> O Venus, we are joining ranks,
> Sanat Kumara we give thanks.
> Our planet has received new life,
> to lift her out of war and strife.

> **O Venus, service so divine,**
> **you are for earth a cosmic sign.**
> **Your selfless service is now mine,**
> **a life in service I define.**

8. I am using the power of my mind to manipulate energy in a way that is in complete harmony with the laws of God, the most important of which is the Law of Love that creates harmony between the individual and the whole.

O Venus, your sweet melody,
consumes veil of duality.
Absorbed in tones of Cosmic Love,
all conflict we now rise above.

O Venus, service so divine,
you are for earth a cosmic sign.
Your selfless service is now mine,
a life in service I define.

9. I am transcending the mindset of anti-christ. I am rebuking
the devil and rejecting the temptation to use my mind's abilities
for selfish purposes.

O Venus, shining Morning Star,
a cosmic herald, that you are.
The earth set free by sacred sound,
our planet is now heaven-bound.

O Venus, service so divine,
you are for earth a cosmic sign.
Your selfless service is now mine,
a life in service I define.

3. I have power over my situation

1. The mindset of anti-christ is irrelevant to me. I am serving
God through the consciousness of Christ.

O Venus, show me how to serve,
your cosmic beauty I observe.
What love from Venus you now bring,
our planets do in tandem sing.

**O Venus, service so divine,
you are for earth a cosmic sign.
Your selfless service is now mine,
a life in service I define.**

2. I choose life. I choose the consciousness of Christ that is
the doorway to eternal life, the eternal life of oneness with my
source and oneness with all life.

O Venus, your love is the key,
the hardened hearts on earth are free.
Embracing future bright and bold,
our planet's story is retold.

**O Venus, service so divine,
you are for earth a cosmic sign.
Your selfless service is now mine,
a life in service I define.**

3. I am seeing beyond my immediate desires. I accept that my
actions have consequences that I cannot escape. I will reap in a
future lifetime what I sow in this lifetime.

O Venus, loving Mother mine,
my heart your love does now refine.
I am the open door for love,
descending like a Holy Dove.

**O Venus, service so divine,
you are for earth a cosmic sign.
Your selfless service is now mine,
a life in service I define.**

4. I accept the reality of reincarnation, which means God is a fair God who does not punish anyone. My circumstances in this life are the results of choices I made in past lives.

O Venus, play the secret note,
that is for hatred antidote.
All poisoned hearts you gently heal,
as love's true story you reveal.

**O Venus, service so divine,
you are for earth a cosmic sign.
Your selfless service is now mine,
a life in service I define.**

5. I am learning from my past choices and transcending the consciousness that caused me to make those choices. I am calling forth the opportunity to grow in my present lifetime without having it interrupted by my actions from a former lifetime.

O Venus, love fills every need,
for truly, love is God's first seed.
O let it blossom, let it grow,
sweep earth into your loving flow.

**O Venus, service so divine,
you are for earth a cosmic sign.
Your selfless service is now mine,
a life in service I define.**

6. God's only desire is for me to grow by constantly transcending my state of consciousness, my sense of identity.

> O Venus, music of the spheres,
> heard by those who God reveres.
> Our voices now as one we raise,
> singing in adoring praise.

> **O Venus, service so divine,**
> **you are for earth a cosmic sign.**
> **Your selfless service is now mine,**
> **a life in service I define.**

7. The conditions I experience in this lifetime are not God's punishment and they are not the results of a game of chance. They are the effects of causes I have set in motion in previous lifetimes through the choices I made in those lifetimes.

> O Venus, we are joining ranks,
> Sanat Kumara we give thanks.
> Our planet has received new life,
> to lift her out of war and strife.

> **O Venus, service so divine,**
> **you are for earth a cosmic sign.**
> **Your selfless service is now mine,**
> **a life in service I define.**

8. My current situation was not created by God; it was created by my own self. I am reaping now what I have sown in the past. I am transcending the sense that I am a victim of forces beyond my control.

O Venus, your sweet melody,
consumes veil of duality.
Absorbed in tones of Cosmic Love,
all conflict we now rise above.

**O Venus, service so divine,
you are for earth a cosmic sign.
Your selfless service is now mine,
a life in service I define.**

9. I am taking an active role and realigning myself with the laws of God, with my I AM Presence. I am the open door for the light of my I AM Presence to stream into my world and manifest abundance.

O Venus, shining Morning Star,
a cosmic herald, that you are.
The earth set free by sacred sound,
our planet is now heaven-bound.

**O Venus, service so divine,
you are for earth a cosmic sign.
Your selfless service is now mine,
a life in service I define.**

4. I am in oneness

1. I am walking a true and scientific path to lasting abundance. I am walking the true path to the abundant life that can be maintained indefinitely as long as I stay in the Christ consciousness.

O Venus, show me how to serve,
your cosmic beauty I observe.
What love from Venus you now bring,
our planets do in tandem sing.

**O Venus, service so divine,
you are for earth a cosmic sign.
Your selfless service is now mine,
a life in service I define.**

2. I am a conscious co-creator, reaching into the spiritual realm
and bringing more spiritual energy into the material frequency
spectrum. I am increasing the total amount of abundance available on earth through the mind of Christ.

O Venus, your love is the key,
the hardened hearts on earth are free.
Embracing future bright and bold,
our planet's story is retold.

**O Venus, service so divine,
you are for earth a cosmic sign.
Your selfless service is now mine,
a life in service I define.**

3. The ultimate creative power is to bring spiritual energy into
the material frequency spectrum. This cannot be done by a mind
that is trapped in selfishness.

O Venus, loving Mother mine,
my heart your love does now refine.
I am the open door for love,
descending like a Holy Dove.

O Venus, service so divine,
you are for earth a cosmic sign.
Your selfless service is now mine,
a life in service I define.

4. I am transcending selfishness through a sense of oneness with
God and with the Body of God. I have access to God's infinite
abundance.

O Venus, play the secret note,
that is for hatred antidote.
All poisoned hearts you gently heal,
as love's true story you reveal.

O Venus, service so divine,
you are for earth a cosmic sign.
Your selfless service is now mine,
a life in service I define.

5. I am reaching into the spiritual realm and drawing down more
of God's energy. I am manifesting more abundance than I could
ever manifest only by working at the level of physical matter.

O Venus, love fills every need,
for truly, love is God's first seed.
O let it blossom, let it grow,
sweep earth into your loving flow.

O Venus, service so divine,
you are for earth a cosmic sign.
Your selfless service is now mine,
a life in service I define.

6. I am attaining spiritual mastery and the Christ consciousness. I am manifesting abundance without being trapped by the consciousness of anti-christ.

> O Venus, music of the spheres,
> heard by those who God reveres.
> Our voices now as one we raise,
> singing in adoring praise.

> **O Venus, service so divine,**
> **you are for earth a cosmic sign.**
> **Your selfless service is now mine,**
> **a life in service I define.**

7. I am manifesting not only material abundance. I am manifesting the permanent abundant life, the eternal life.

> O Venus, we are joining ranks,
> Sanat Kumara we give thanks.
> Our planet has received new life,
> to lift her out of war and strife.

> **O Venus, service so divine,**
> **you are for earth a cosmic sign.**
> **Your selfless service is now mine,**
> **a life in service I define.**

8. I am walking out of death, the consciousness of death, and into the eternal life of the Christ consciousness. I am reaching for the kingdom of God, and I know all else will indeed be added unto me.

O Venus, your sweet melody,
consumes veil of duality.
Absorbed in tones of Cosmic Love,
all conflict we now rise above.

O Venus, service so divine,
you are for earth a cosmic sign.
Your selfless service is now mine,
a life in service I define.

9. I want to come home to my Father's kingdom, and I am not
looking for shortcuts. I am willing to let this mind be in me,
which was and is also in Christ Jesus.

O Venus, shining Morning Star,
a cosmic herald, that you are.
The earth set free by sacred sound,
our planet is now heaven-bound.

O Venus, service so divine,
you are for earth a cosmic sign.
Your selfless service is now mine,
a life in service I define.

Sealing

In the name of the Divine Mother, I call to Venus and Mother Mary for the sealing of myself and all people in my circle of influence in the creative flow of the Divine Mother, the River of Life. I call for the multiplication of my calls by all representatives of the Divine Mother, so that we form the perfect figure-eight flow of "As Above, so below." Thus, I accept that this is fully manifest, because the mouth of the Lord, the Divine Mother that I AM, has spoken it. Amen.

15 | ATTAINING A BALANCED STATE OF CONSCIOUSNESS

Let me speak about the essence of the Christ consciousness. When your Creator decided to create individualizations of itself, a certain dilemma came into being. That dilemma is how to balance the relationship between an individualization of the whole and the whole itself so that the individual does not feel separated from the whole or acts in ways that diminish, rather than magnify, the whole.

Your Creator has a state of consciousness that is all-encompassing. Everything in the world of form is contained within the consciousness of your Creator—because your Creator has created everything out of its own substance, Being and consciousness. Likewise, everything created by self-aware co-creators – individualizations of the Creator – was created out of God's Being. Your Creator is in everything that was ever created, and thus your Creator has an awareness of being the All and being in all. It is not entirely correct to say that the Creator creates form. It would be more correct to say that the Creator manifests itself as a certain form. The Creator takes on a certain form and clothes itself in limitations without losing its

Allness. Once a form is brought into existence, that form exists precisely because it has certain characteristics that set it apart from:

- The Allness of God, in which there is no form.

- The void, in which there is only darkness and thus no form.

- Other forms in the world of form.

The very essence of a given form is that it is defined by individual characteristics that set it apart, that differentiate it. If that form did not have any characteristics, it would still be within the Allness, and thus it would not exist as a distinct form. When the Creator manifests itself as a self-aware being, that being must of necessity have individual characteristics. If the being had no individuality, it would not exist as a distinct being, it would still be undifferentiated from the Allness of God's Being. When it comes to inanimate forms or beings that do not have self-awareness (such as animals), the existence of individual characteristics do not pose a problem because differentiation from the All can never lead to separation from the All.

When it comes to self-aware beings, a potential problem, a sort of enigma, comes into being. A self-aware being can exist only because it has awareness; it is conscious of its own existence. The very core of your identity is your awareness that you exist as a distinct being with individual characteristics and the potential to express those characteristics through your creative powers. This is precisely what you were designed to do, namely to express your individuality and thereby co-create the kingdom of God wherever you are, including on planet earth.

You were also designed to express your individuality as part of the All and as part of the Body of God, the family of co-creators that exist in the world of form. You were *not* designed to express your creativity as if you existed in a vacuum. You were designed to express your individuality in a way that enhances the whole of which you are a part—and from which you can never be apart.

You can function as a co-creator with God only because you have imagination and free will. The way you express your imagination and free will is an expression of your self-awareness. The way you see yourself is what determines how you use your imagination to envision forms that are not yet manifest. It also determines how you use your will to decide which forms to manifest or which forms you can and cannot manifest. As long as your sense of self-awareness is in alignment with God's reality, namely that you are part of the All and part of the Body of God on earth, your individual expression will be in alignment with the whole.

The very fact that you have unlimited imagination means that you can envision a sense of self-awareness as being apart from the All of God and as being separated from, even in competition with, other self-aware beings. The fact that you have unrestricted free will means that you can choose to accept such a limited self-image as real, and thereby you can create a new self-image that is based on separation rather than the original sense of oneness with which you were created.

This possibility is an inevitable aspect of giving you free will and imagination. It is *not* inevitable that you should choose to use your creative abilities to generate such a limited self-image. God did everything possible to make it easy for you to maintain a correct self-image and to build upon that image to become more than you were created to be—rather than to create a false self-image that makes you less than you were created to be.

***

The essential question is how a self-aware being can avoid acting as if it is separated from God, as if it is apart from God, or acting as if it is the only self-aware being in the universe or the only being that matters. I am sure you can see this dilemma. God created a great number of self-aware beings that are meant to act as co-creators. None of these self-aware beings were created as an island. No being was created to exist alone or independently of God or of others. No being was created to be the favorite son who could act as a king, with all other self-aware beings the mere servants of that one. Truly, as the Bible says: "God is no respecter of persons" (Acts 10:34). The Creator loves all of its co-creators with an infinite love. When love is infinite and unconditional, there can be no comparisons and thus there are no favorite sons or daughters. All are loved with the same love because all are of equal value and equal importance in the eyes of the Creator. How can it be otherwise when every self-aware being is created out of the substance of the Creator and thus is the Creator manifesting itself as that individualized being?

Once the Creator has given a self-aware being imagination and free will, it becomes possible that the co-creator can separate itself from the whole and begin to act as if it is apart from others, even more important than others. In the act of separating itself from the whole, the self-aware being partakes of the "fruit of the knowledge of good and evil" (Genesis 2:17), which truly means relative good and evil. In this consciousness of duality, comparisons are possible and thus a co-creator can build a self-image as being better than or more valuable than others. The being might build the desire to rule over others and to control the whole rather than working to magnify the whole.

If a co-creator accepts this dualistic self-image as reality, the co-creator will begin to act as if it *is* reality. A co-creator can gradually become so focused on this self-created "reality" that it forgets its true identity. The co-creator – who was designed to always retain its awareness of itself as an individualization of God – can lose that state of oneness, can lose that state of Grace, and thereby fall into a limited sense of identity as a separate being that is apart from God and apart from the Body of God.

This is a possibility that comes into existence the very moment God creates beings who have self-awareness, imagination and free will. God has no desire to see any of his sons and daughters become lost in a lesser sense of identity. It is the Father's good pleasure to give you the kingdom, but you can receive that kingdom only when you see yourself as a son or daughter of God who is capable of and worthy to receive that kingdom. If you become trapped in a lower sense of identity in which you see yourself as apart from the whole – and therefore think you are either unworthy to receive God's abundance or entitled to all of it – you cannot receive the fullness of the kingdom. This is not what God wants to see happen so how can this possibly be avoided? In reality, it can never be ruled out as a possibility. The only way to take away the possibility that you could become trapped in a lower state of identity is to take away your imagination and free will. If you do not have the ability to imagine a limited state of identity and if you do not have the will to accept it as real, then you cannot become lost. If you do not have these creative faculties, you cannot serve as a co-creator with God and therefore you cannot become more. You cannot serve in expanding the intensity of God's light in order to fill up the void with light. Becoming more and filling up the void is the very purpose for existence.

***

The question God faces is how to make it as safe as possible for you to exercise your creativity, meaning that you can do so without forgetting your origin, your source. While this problem has no absolute solution – because you always have free will – it does have a solution that is absolute in the sense that you can never lose the potential to reclaim your true identity. God has designed an ingenious way to make it possible for you to always come back to his kingdom, no matter how far from it you have moved in consciousness.

The one Creator started the creative process by generating two complementary forces. In the religion of Taoism, these forces have been called the Yin and the Yang, but I like to call them the expanding force of the Father and the contracting force of the Mother. These two forces may seem to be opposites, but that is not an unconditional truth. Although they seemingly have opposite directions, they are actually complementary forces. They do not cancel out each other, they only balance each other. It is when the forces are perfectly balanced that a sustainable form is created.

What does it mean that something is sustainable? The key is to understand the very purpose of creation, namely to expand God's light, to expand God's kingdom, in order to fill the void. Constant growth, constant self-transcendence is the goal. The role of the expanding force is to drive creation in an outward, expanding direction so that it never stands still. It never becomes confined to a particular form but always grows towards becoming more.

In order to create anything out of the singularity of the Creator, there must be an outgoing force. If the outgoing force was the only force, creation would simply be a continuous explosion in which no distinct form is possible. The contracting force of the Mother balances the expanding force of the Father, and when there is balance, it is possible to create a form that can be sustained. These two basic forces of creation provide the foundation for the creation of form. The essential key to a successful creation is the correct balance between the two basic forces. If the expanding force becomes too strong, all form is blown apart. If the contracting force becomes too strong, growth comes to a halt, and eventually all forms will collapse upon themselves and the Ma-ter Light will return to its ground state. There must be something that can maintain the correct balance between the two forces and ensure a creation that is sustainable without ever standing still. Sustainability does not mean stillstand; it means constant self-transcendence. Why so? Because the very definition of life is something that is growing, something that is constantly in the process of transcending itself, something that is always becoming more of God in manifestation and can thus replace the darkness that is in the void.

Neither the expanding nor the contracting force can create form in themselves. The expanding force will always expand, and the contracting force will always contract, and either way all form, all structure, is obliterated. In order for a form to be created, that form must first exist as a potential, as a mental image. This image must balance the two forces so that the form can be sustained in a dynamic state whereby the form is not static but a platform for further growth. The contracting force of the Mother is built into the Ma-ter Light. We might compare this to an ocean that is calm and without waves. The expanding force of the Father is like the wind that blows upon the ocean and stirs up the waves. These waves in the infinite ocean of light are what appear as distinct forms. The Ma-ter Light has the potential to take on any form, and some of those forms can cancel out each other, as waves on the ocean can cancel out each other. What determines how specific forms are brought into existence? The characteristics of a specific form must exist as a potential before that form is imposed upon the Ma-ter Light. The expanding force of the Father must have a matrix to flow into so that it can stir the Ma-ter Light to take on a particular form rather than an indiscriminate explosion. Neither the expanding force nor the contracting force can create such a mental image and use it to direct the expanding force unto the Mother Light. Such an image can be held only in a self-aware mind, a mind that has the imagination to envision an image and the will to impose it upon the Ma-ter Light. Such a mind must also have self-awareness, making it aware of its existence and of its ability to use the basic forces of creation. The Creator has such a mind, but the Creator did not want to create everything by itself. The Creator decided to manifest itself as individual beings who can act as co-creators. These beings have the mental capacity to envision an image of a form that is not yet manifest, and they can then project that image upon the Ma-ter Light. As the expanding force of the Father flows into the matrix, the Ma-ter Light takes on the corresponding form. What gives co-creators this ability? It is the fact that they are created from, that they are individualizations of, another aspect of God, another extension of the Creator, namely what the Bible calls the Word or the only begotten Son of the Father, full of grace and truth (John 1:14).

***

Many Christians have come to believe that Jesus Christ was the only begotten Son of God or that he was God from the very beginning. This is an idea that is not unconditionally true. As Every self-aware being that was ever created is a son or daughter of God. Everything that was ever created came out of the Being and consciousness of God, and therefore, from a certain viewpoint it was God from the very beginning. The moment an individualized form or being comes into existence, it takes on distinct characteristics, and thus it is no longer the All of God.

This is equally true for Jesus Christ as it is for you. Jesus came out of the All of God, and he was and is a son of God. You too came out of the All and you too are a son or daughter of God. Jesus even affirmed his equality with all life in the statement: "Inasmuch as ye have done it unto the least of these my brethren, ye have done it unto me" (Matthew 25:40).

If you have grown up in the idolatry promoted by orthodox Christianity, you might consider my statements to be blasphemous. Jesus never set himself apart from others, nor did he set himself at the same level as God. Why do you think he said: "Why callest thou me good, there is none good but one, that is, God" (Matthew 19:17). Jesus considers the orthodox doctrine that he was the only begotten Son of God to be the worst form of blasphemy and a mockery of his entire mission. By creating these doctrines, Jesus has been set apart from all other people, and thus he has become an idol rather than an example. It is not to Jesus' liking that so many Christians dance around this golden calf, rather than acknowledging the fact that Jesus came to show them their true potential for reclaiming their divine inheritance. The real difference between you and Jesus is that he recognized and accepted his origin as a son of God whereas you have not yet done so. You do have the potential to reclaim your true identity by following the example set by Jesus and letting this mind be in you, which was also in Christ Jesus (Philippians 2:5).

What was the mind that was in Jesus? It was the Christ mind, the true begotten Son of the Father, meaning the Creator. This state of consciousness is a universal mind, a universal sense of awareness, generated by God the Creator to serve the specific function of being a mediator between itself and all individualized extensions of itself, namely God's co-creators. The purpose of the Christ mind is to ensure that no co-creator can ever permanently lose his or her true identity or the awareness of God's laws. The Christ mind serves to ensure that all form is created according to the laws of God and that a form which is out of alignment with these laws cannot exist indefinitely.

When God created you, he gave you a unique individuality. This is your creative potential, and as you exercise your creative powers, you will naturally express your individuality in everything you create. Your individuality is God's gift to you, and as you let your light shine, your individuality becomes manifest as your gift to the world. Your God-given individuality is truly beautiful and magnificent beyond what most people can accept with their current sense of identity. As Jesus said: "Ye are Gods" (John 10:34), meaning that you are designed with a beauty and perfection far beyond the level of human identity and awareness. You were created to be infinitely more than you can currently accept, and this God-given individuality can never be lost because it is permanently recorded in the Universal Christ Mind. The only begotten Son of the Father is the keeper of your true individuality, and thus the Christ mind is also the key to regaining that identity. The Christ mind is the only key to your salvation because salvation means that you overcome the limited sense of identity that springs from the mind of anti-christ, the mind of separation from your source. In order to have eternal life, you must reclaim the identity that springs from the mind of Christ, the mind of oneness with your source.

The Christ mind also serves to guide your creative efforts and ensure that they will always be in alignment with the laws of God and that there will be harmony between you and the Body of God. No self-aware being can access the pure light of God without going through the Christ consciousness. As Jesus said: "I am the way, the truth, and the life: no man cometh unto the Father, but by me" (John 14:6). The Christ consciousness knows the laws of God, and thus it has an absolute standard for judging whether the form envisioned by a co-creator is in harmony with those laws (unconditional good) or out of harmony with those laws (evil). In order to create any form, a co-creator must envision the form and then allow the power of God to flow through it, whereby it is imposed upon the Ma-ter Light. Your power to create form depends on the intensity and force of the light driving your creative efforts. The ultimate creative force is the expanding light of the Father, and when you create with this light, you have maximum creative powers. As Jesus said: "With men it is impossible, but not with God: for with God all things are possible" (Mark 10:27). In order to access God's power, you must have the Christ consciousness and your envisioned form must be in harmony with the laws of God. When you are embodied as a human being, your lower mind must become the open door for a stream of energy that flows from your I AM Presence. It is this spiritual energy that becomes the driving force behind your creative efforts. As Jesus said: "I can of mine own self do nothing" (John 5:30) and: "But the Father that dwelleth in me, he doeth the works (John 14:10).

When you envision a mental image based on the Christ mind, it will always be in perfect harmony with the laws of God and with the creative intent of God. As an individual, you are not the fullness of the Universal Christ Mind, but that mind has been individualized for you. As Jesus said: "Take, eat: this is my body, which is broken for you: this do in remembrance of me (1Corinthians, 11:24). Through this individualized Christ mind, you can create in perfect harmony with the laws of God, and thus your creation will have maximum power. That is why Jesus – through the Christ mind – had the power to override natural law and perform what people saw as miracles. In reality, Jesus was making use of a higher law that supersedes the laws of nature as they are currently understood by science.

When you follow this process of using the mind of the Son to access the creative power of the Father and to define the form that is projected upon the light of the Mother, your creation will magnify the whole. The Universal Christ Mind will permanently record your good deeds so that they can never be lost. This is what Jesus called your treasure laid up in heaven: "But lay up for yourselves treasures in heaven where neither moth nor rust doth corrupt, and where thieves do not break through nor steal (Matthew 6:20).

Because you have free will, you can chose to envision a form that is out of harmony with the laws of God and you can will to manifest that form. In order to manifest an imperfect form, you cannot use the pure light of God. Your only option is to use the lesser light, namely the psychic energy that has already been brought into the material frequency spectrum. You can still create by using this light so the false gurus are correct when they say it is possible to hoard great wealth by using the power of the mind. This creation will never be as powerful as what is created through the Christ mind. Because it is created by using the mind of anti-christ, you will inevitably reap what you have sown: "For they have sown the wind, and they shall reap the whirlwind (Hosea 8:7).

***

God wanted to make sure that your experimentation with your creative powers would become an upward spiral whereby you would grow in self-awareness and grow in the awareness that the self is one with the All. Anything you do in harmony with God's laws is permanently recorded in the Christ mind. This becomes your attainment, your momentum, that you can use as a solid foundation – as the rock of Christ – for expanding your creative powers and your self-awareness. While this treasure can never be lost, you can use your imagination and free will to separate yourself from it, even to the point of forgetting all about it and your true identity. When that happens, you obviously cannot build upon the foundation of your past actions, and you are, so to speak, forced to start over from scratch. Because your past good deeds cannot be permanently lost, your treasure is always there waiting for you. At any moment, you can decide to stop the downward spiral of separating yourself from your Self. You can start walking the spiritual path that will empower you to reclaim your true identity. When you do so, you can once again access your treasure in heaven and use it as a foundation to further expand your creative powers and self-awareness. Your true identity – the identity built on the mind of Christ – can never be lost. The false identity – the identity of separation built on the mind of anti-christ – is indeed mortal and can therefore be lost. It *must* be lost in order for you to reclaim your true identity.

When God created this world of form, God defined certain guiding principles that would ensure that this system of worlds could grow in a sustainable manner, could grow without being blown apart or contracting into nothingness. God designed these principles to make sure that the expanding force of the Father would not become so strong that it would blow apart the universe in a giant explosion. At the same time, God created laws to ensure that the contracting force of the Mother would not stop the expansion of the light that is meant to fill the void, which would start a contracting cycle that would return all created forms to the nothingness from which they started.

Within the framework of the creative principles defined by God, there is unlimited freedom to create form. As a co-creator with God, your creativity is not limited by the laws of God. God's laws are not a restriction of your creative freedom. They serve as a framework, as guiding principles, so that you can exercise your creative abilities without destroying yourself or other co-creators. God's laws are set up to ensure that you can exercise your creativity in a way that magnifies the whole by expanding and intensifying the light of God. Think back to how I described the creative process. When God creates a new sphere in the void, that sphere is not completely filled with God's light. Self-aware co-creators are then sent into that sphere in order to multiply their talents and take dominion, thereby filling the sphere with light. It can then serve as a foundation for an expansion into the next sphere. The key is to realize that filling a sphere with light does not mean that it is filled with undifferentiated light. A sphere becomes filled with forms that are in alignment with God's laws but express the creativity of the co-creators who inhabit that sphere.

You are meant to express your God-given individuality in creating forms that will manifest God's kingdom where you are. You truly have unlimited creativity and your efforts are in no way wasted. They will become a part of the permanent kingdom of God that appears when a sphere reaches a certain intensity of light. When that happens, there is so little darkness left that it cannot obscure the underlying reality that everything is created from God's Being, from the pure light of God. There is no longer any danger that self-aware beings can be trapped in a sense of separation from God. How could they, when they are surrounded by forms that radiate the light of God and express the harmony of God's laws?

Because there is not yet enough light in the material universe – at least not on earth – it is not possible to perceive – at least not with the physical senses – that everything is made from the light of God. It is not possible to directly see God as the underlying cause, as the first cause, behind all appearances. That is why it is possible for a self-aware being to become trapped in the consciousness of separation, thinking it is separated from God's abundance. When the intensity of the light is raised on this planet, it will become possible to see the spiritual light radiating through all forms—the forms that will be in harmony with God's laws. The kingdom of God will be established on earth and this planet can become a star that radiates the Light of Freedom, freedom from the consciousness of death.

It is the very design of your being to be the open door for the light of God to be expanded in this world. When the light of God is expanded, you will magnify all of life through your creative efforts. There is no conflict between you, as an individual, and other individuals. Your creative efforts expand the light and thereby the amount of abundance available in this world. You are serving to magnify all other parts of this world, including all other co-creators. In so doing, you are also magnifying your true self, which is the entire Body of God, unified through the body and blood – the consciousness – of Christ.

I know these ideas can seem abstract and difficult to grasp with your outer mind. I remind you that there is great value in stretching the mind. I would also remind you that what you cannot grasp with the mind, you can always grasp with the heart. It is not my purpose with this course to give you only intellectual understanding. It is my purpose to help you come closer to Christ consciousness, which means that I aim to expand both your understanding and your heart's capacity for love. I give you many concepts that can be difficult to grasp with the mind – the horizontal, linear way of looking at life that is characteristic of the mind – yet these concepts can be grasped by the spherical, vertical, nonlinear way of the heart.

***

Let me now give you a further description of the Christ mind. The Christ mind is truly an extension of the mind of God. Its purpose is to serve as the connecting link between the Creator and its self-aware co-creators. The Christ mind has a specific focus, a specific purpose, namely to empower the individual to maintain and expand its sense of identity as part of the All, as connected to the All—until the individual, self-aware being grows in self-awareness and realizes that the Self *is* the All. This does not mean that the individual loses its individuality. It means that the individual realizes that it is the All of the Creator, manifest as, focused through, that individuality. The individual, self-aware being no longer looks at the world and looks at life from the limited viewpoint of its individual awareness. It looks at life from the expanded viewpoint of the consciousness of the Creator, shining through the individuality.

As an illustration of this, imagine that you have grown up in a room with no windows. The room has a door with a peephole through which the light of the sun can shine. You can never see the totality of the sun; you see only one small, individual ray of the sun. If you had grown up in such a room, your view of the sun would be determined by your vantage point. You might believe there is no sun or that the individual light ray exists on its own. Once you open the door and step out into the bright sunshine, you will gain an expanded awareness of the sun and its real power. You will now realize that the sun is far more powerful than the small ray of light in the room. You will realize that the ray of light did indeed come from the sun and could not have existed without the sun. Yet the sun is still seen as far away.

Now imagine that you travel to the very center of the sun and view the solar system from there. You would no longer be limited by your first impression of the sun, namely the small ray of light shining through the door. You would now experience the totality of the sun, yet you would not lose the awareness of the individual light ray. You would be aware that the individual light ray was truly an extension of the sun itself. It was actually the sun shining through that little hole in the door, manifesting itself as an individual ray of light. There is no real separation between the source and the individual ray of light. The only limitation is the size of the hole through which the light is shining.

If you expand the connection to your I AM Presence, there is no limit to how much light can shine through your being.

When God created you as an individual being, you were not given the full awareness of the sun, meaning the All of God's consciousness. You were created as an individual being with an individual ray of light shining through your consciousness. In your limited state of consciousness, it was natural that you would see yourself as an individual being, distinct from the All of God. You did not yet have enough self-awareness to identify yourself as one with the Allness of God, as an extension of the All of God.

If one was to describe this in linear terms, which as I have mentioned before does not give an accurate image of God's reality, one would say that you were created as an individual, yet you had an awareness that you were created by God. You saw yourself as an individual being connected to a remote God. Your connection to God was not outside yourself; it was located inside yourself in the form of your I AM Presence. You saw yourself as a planet, orbiting the sun of your I AM Presence and therefore held in a stable orbit by the gravitational force of your I AM Presence. Although you had a clear awareness of your I AM Presence, you were not yet able to see that your I AM Presence was an extension of, an individualization of, the Creator. You had the concept of God as a remote Being beyond your direct experience.

You were created with a limited awareness that was focused on your individual form. You thought of yourself as having been created by God and sent into this world. You are meant to expand your awareness until you realize that the Creator is not apart from its creation. God is the All in All, and thus you are not created by a remote God and sent into a world where God is not found. God is right here with you, and thus the concept that you were created by God is too limited, too linear. In reality, you are God manifesting itself as your individual being. You are God expressing itself as your individual being. That is why Jesus said that the kingdom of God is within you (Luke 17:21). The process of awakening to your true identity has several phases:

- You start by seeing the sun of your I AM Presence as the source of your life.

- You realize that the light shining through your I AM Presence is the light, the power, of the Creator.

- You realize that the Creator is everywhere within creation and thus the light of God can potentially shine from any point within creation.

- This finally leads to the recognition that the light is not coming from a remote source but is coming from within your Self. You have then become a self-sufficient Being who is radiating God's light from within yourself, as the sun is radiating light from within itself.

After you were created as an individual lifestream, you descended into the denser energies of the material universe. What allowed you to have and maintain the conscious awareness of your I AM Presence after this descent was and is the Christ consciousness, the only begotten Son of the Father. This consciousness is what the Bible calls the Word, and as the Bible says, everything was created out of the Son of God, out of the Christ consciousness, and it was defined through the Word. Everything ever created by a self-aware co-creator has come out of the Christ consciousness, meaning that the Christ consciousness is within every created form. Without him, without both God the Father and God the Son, was not anything made that was made (John 1:3). You can never lose your potential to regain the Christ consciousness. No matter how far you descend in consciousness, you always have the potential to reclaim your connection to God and your true identity. You can never be separated from the Christ consciousness because it is within everything, even the imperfect forms that are out of harmony with God's laws. That is why Jesus said that even the stones would cry out in defense of the Christ (Luke 19:40). One function of the Christ consciousness is to make sure that a co-creator can never be completely lost in the creation, can never be so far removed from God that there is no possibility of coming back home. You can never move away from the Christ consciousness, and thus the sense of separation will always be an illusion that exists only in your mind. You can, at any time, start walking the path that leads you to replace that illusion with the truth that will make you free (John 8:32).

***

The original design of God for your lifestream is that you start out as an individual being with a limited self-awareness. You start out as an individual who is connected to God but nevertheless distinct from (but not separated from) the All of God. There is a difference between having a connection to the All of God as opposed to being separated from that All by an impenetrable barrier. In the first case, you can expand the connection and eventually attain the self-awareness of being one with the All. In the second case, you have no option for ever becoming one with the All.

As you exercise your creative abilities, as you use your imagination and free will, you will gradually grow in self-awareness. You will also grow in awareness of how the universe works and how God's laws work. God has put his laws in your inward parts, meaning that your conscious self can know those laws through the Christ mind. When your lifestream started its journey in the material universe, you did not have a conscious awareness of God's laws. Your outer mind, the reasoning mind, did not have an understanding of God's laws. How could you follow God's laws? You could do so by using the intuitive faculties of the heart whereby you could tune in to the Universal Christ Mind and follow the laws without having a conscious awareness of how exactly they work. As you exercise your creative faculties, you will gradually expand your awareness of God's laws. You will build your conscious understanding of why the laws work the way they do, why following the laws is in your own best interest and how the laws balance your individual creative efforts with the good of the whole.

As you grow in self-awareness, you gradually become able to look beyond your individual sense of self. You not only tune in to the greater awareness of God's laws, you also begin to expand your awareness of the Body of God, meaning other co-creators. You begin to see beyond your personal desires and realize that co-creators did not come to this planet just to fulfill their individual desires. There is a divine plan for the growth of earth, and it has the perfect harmony between the individual and the collective good. By realigning yourself with the divine plan for the Body of God, you will find the greater fulfillment of seeing how your individual efforts fit into and enhance the greater plan for the earth and for humankind. This will give you a far greater sense of fulfillment than any individual effort can give you.

As you gain a greater understanding and respect for other people, you expand your ability to love your neighbor as yourself. Your relationships will then be based on love and abundance rather than fear and want. As you gain a greater appreciation for God's laws and God's creation, you gradually begin to love God with all your heart, soul and mind (Luke 10:27). As you continue to co-create with God and to expand your self-awareness, you gradually begin to realize that your true self is your I AM Presence, which is an individualization of your Creator. You then begin to realize, as did Jesus, that: "I and my Father are one" (John 10:30). You being to realize that your Father has worked hitherto (John 5:17) by creating the world of form as a platform for your creative expression. You must work by multiplying your talents and taking dominion over your own sense of self. When you have taken dominion over self, you can take dominion over the planet upon which you live and help turn that planet into the kingdom of God, a sphere that is filled with God's light and perfection, thus replacing the darkness that covers the land.

***

The essence of the Christ consciousness can be captured in one word, and that word is "balance." The Christ consciousness balances the expanding force of the Father and the contracting force of the Mother whereby sustainable forms are created, forms that are in perfect harmony with the laws of God. The Christ consciousness balances the relationship between the individual co-creator and the Body of God so that there is perfect harmony between the individual and the whole. The Christ consciousness empowers the individual co-creator to follow the laws of God and thereby exercise its creative abilities in a way that magnifies all of creation and has no negative effects on any part of life. The Christ consciousness balances the relationship between the individual co-creator and the Creator so that a co-creator can never be completely lost in the world of created forms.

Any form that is defined by and through the Christ consciousness is a perfect form. It is a form that is in perfect harmony with the laws of God and with the creative intent of

God—which is that all co-creators should grow in harmony with each other so that all life becomes more. It is through the Christ consciousness that you can follow the call of Jesus: "Be ye therefore perfect, even as your Father in heaven – your I AM Presence – is perfect" (Matthew 5:48).

The perfection that I am talking about is not the kind of perfection envisioned by most people. Many people believe in the dualistic idea, the idolatrous idea, that if something is perfect, it could never change. The entire purpose for the creation of this universe is to create a sphere in the void and to gradually fill it with the light of God until it can be expanded and fill up a greater portion of the void. The very purpose for creation, the purpose of life, is constant growth, constant expansion, constant self-transcendence.

The world of form came into being because God has a desire to be more. This desire to be more is the driving force behind all creation and is built into all creation. The traditional idea of heaven as a static place in which angels sit on pink clouds playing harps for all eternity is completely out of touch with God's vibrant, dynamic reality. Heaven is a far more dynamic place than earth because all Beings in heaven are constantly working on expanding God's light for the purpose of becoming more of God, more of the All.

The drive to be more is also built into the Christ consciousness, and thus the Christ mind drives individual co-creators to constantly exercise their creative abilities and expand their self-awareness. The Christ consciousness drives you to become more, to expand your self-awareness, until you attain the full God consciousness and know that you are an individualization of the All, that you are not separated from God. Instead, you are God manifesting itself through your individual sense of self.

The perfection that I am talking about is not static, it is not a graven image. It is dynamic, it is ever-growing, always becoming more of the perfection of God. I have told you before that the contracting force of the Mother is built into the Ma-ter Light itself. This contracting force will always seek to return the Ma-ter Light to its ground state, in which no form is manifest. One might say that the contracting force is constantly seeking to break down any form. It is not God's intent that all forms should be broken down and become nothing so that the efforts of the co-creators would be nullified. It is God's intent that no form should ever stand still, no form should become permanent. God wants forms to remain dynamic, meaning that any form is a foundation for further growth. Even a perfect form is meant to be transcended and used as a foundation for manifesting an even higher form.

The Christ consciousness empowers the co-creator to design a form that is in perfect harmony with God's creative intent. No form will ever be permanent because the contracting force of the Mother will break down anything that stands still, anything that becomes a closed system, as the second law of thermodynamics says. What is the key to making sure your creative efforts are not broken down? It is to remain in the Christ consciousness whereby you never want to stand still or to maintain a certain form. You are constantly creating new and better forms, thus remaining in the River of Life, the ever-flowing creative force that *is* God the Creator.

When you are in the flow of life, you have no attachments to a particular form. You have no desire to see that form remain permanent, you only desire to use it as a springboard for expanding your creativity. You never expect that you can create something that will become permanent. You never think that when a form is replaced by a higher form, your creative efforts were wasted. You realize that your creative efforts are never wasted—as long as you remain in the flow of the River of Life. You are focused on the process of creation rather than on the result of creation—a particular form. You are focused on the journey rather than the destination because you realize that life is a never-ending journey.

***

As an illustration of this, consider a grain of wheat that is put into the ground. It might seem like the grain is lost in the ground, but after a time it sprouts. The sprout is beautiful, yet what farmer would want the sprout to remain as it is? As the sprout grows into a plant, the exact form of the sprout is lost, yet the creative effort of the plant is not lost; it is simply transformed into a new stage, a new form. The plant is beautiful with its green leaves, but it is eventually turned into a stalk with seeds and it turns yellow. The green plant is lost, but the creative efforts of the plant are not lost. When the wheat is harvested, the plant is lost, yet some of the grain becomes the seed for next year's harvest and some of it is used as nourishment for human beings who serve as co-creators on earth with the potential to magnify God's creation. The purpose for the creative effort that drives one grain of wheat to sprout and grow is not to produce the sprout, the green plant or the mature plant and maintain that form forever. The purpose of the creative force is to drive the process of life itself, a process that is constantly expanding and magnifying the whole of God's creation.

As a co-creator, you are not designed to become attached to any form you have created, no matter how beautiful it might be or how much effort it took to produce it. You are meant to be part of the River of Life whereby you constantly use one form as the springboard for an even greater creative accomplishment. This is what you are designed to do, and it is only by being in the flow of life that you will feel truly fulfilled and alive. This consciousness of constant self-transcendence is the consciousness of life. The attachment to a particular form and the attempt to preserve that form is the consciousness of death, the consciousness of anti-christ. The consciousness of anti-christ is what causes self-aware beings to become attached to a limited sense of self and refuse to transcend it. They set themselves outside of the flow of life, and the contracting force of the Mother will immediately begin to break down what they seek to hold on to, what they seek to possess.

This is the deeper meaning behind Jesus' statement: "For whosoever will save his life shall lose it: and whosoever will lose his life for my sake shall find it" (Matthew 16:25). If you seek to hold on to a limited sense of identity and refuse to transcend it, the contracting force of the Mother will inevitably take from you that sense of life. If you are willing to lose the static sense of life – the graven image – in order to transcend that stage and attain a greater sense of self, you are in the Christ consciousness. Through that Christ consciousness, through that constant self-transcendence, you will be in the flow of life that is never-ending and thus has eternal life.

The only true form of eternal life is not a static state but a dynamic state of constant self-transcendence. Because you have self-awareness, imagination and free will, you are who you think you are. God has given you the right to create any sense of identity you like, even the sense that you are a mortal sinner. God has *not* given you the right to remain in that sense of identity forever because that would mean that you would be left behind by the flow of God's creation. Why would a loving God want you to remain stuck in a limited sense of identity that prevents you from having the abundant life? If you seek to retain a limited sense of identity, you will inevitably lose it. If you are willing to grow, you will never lose your sense of self. You can never preserve a particular sense of identity, but you can preserve the ongoing sense of identity that is independent of any created form. This is your true identity that is beyond anything in this world. The Creator is beyond its creation. Likewise, a co-creator is beyond his or her creation, even beyond the world of form. You were created as an extension of the Creator, and thus you are more than any form you might have created in this world. You are more than any sense of identity you might have created after you disconnected yourself from your I AM Presence and came to see yourself as a separate being. God allows you to separate yourself from him, but because God's love for you is unconditional, God does not accept any conditions that would keep you separated from him forever. God will not allow any condition to cause you to become permanently trapped in the state of separation that will always be less than the fullness of the abundant life.

***

My beloved, let me once again give you a concept that can be difficult to grasp with the linear mind but that can be grasped with the heart. The material universe can be compared to a movie theater. As you know, there are three basic elements that allow you to watch a movie. One is the screen upon which the movie is projected, another is the filmstrip in the projector and the third is the light coming from the light bulb in the projector. The light bulb in the projector can be compared to the expanding force of the Father, which is the driving force behind the creation of any form. This is the spiritual light streaming through your I AM Presence. The screen compares to the Ma-ter Light, which will reflect any form that is projected upon it by the projector. The filmstrip compares to the consciousness of a co-creator.

Now imagine that you go into a movie theater to watch a movie and the first picture of the movie keeps repeating over and over. Even though there is a filmstrip in the projector and the filmstrip is moving, every image on the filmstrip is the same. Obviously, this would not make a movie; it would make a static picture that would quickly become boring. What makes the movie is that every single picture on the filmstrip is a little bit different from the proceeding picture, and this is what gives you the illusion that you are watching a moving picture, even though you are actually watching a collection of still frames. The individual still pictures are simply being projected unto the screen in such rapid succession that your eyes are fooled into thinking it is a continuous movie.

Life in the material universe is much like a movie. The outer situation you are facing right now is the result of choices you have made in the past and choices you make in the present. Your outer situation is the result of a mental image that you are holding in your mind and projecting unto the screen of life. In the film projector, a new image is displayed many times a second. Your outer situation is a result of the fact that, many times every second, your mind is projecting an image unto the Ma-ter Light. At any moment, you have the opportunity to change the image you project upon the Ma-ter Light. If you do not change the image, if you take unto yourself a graven image, you will keep projecting the same image and that is why it will seem like your life is never changing. This is why you run into the same problem over and over again and why your life can seem like a never-ending struggle. If you are currently in a situation that causes you pain and suffering, the reason is that you are projecting a limited, an imperfect, image unto the screen of life. You are projecting an image that was not created from the Christ consciousness and is therefore out of alignment with the laws of God, the very laws that are designed to give you the abundant life. If your situation remains the same, if it seems like you are boxed in by limitations that you cannot get beyond, the reason is that you are projecting the same image unto the screen of life over and over again. The only possible solution, the only possible way for you to improve your situation, is that you must change the image in your mind. You must get out of the state of spiritual paralysis that causes your mind – your imagination, free will and sense of identity – to be stuck on the same graven image, thereby violating the second commandment (Exodus 20:4). You must turn the images in your mind into a moving picture so that your life becomes a movie that gradually progresses towards the happy ending.

Albert Einstein defined insanity as the process in which you keep doing the same thing, yet you expect different results. In this context, it means that you keep projecting the same mental image, yet you somehow expect that one day the screen will display a different picture. Einstein was one of the greatest scientists of all time because he had understood the essence of the laws of nature. He had understood what I said earlier, namely that the universe is a mirror. If you keep projecting the same image into the cosmic mirror, the universe will inevitably keep reflecting the same outer situation back to you. If you want to change your outer situation, you must begin by changing your inner situation. If you want to change what is projected unto the screen of life, you must change the image on the filmstrip in your mind. If you want to improve your life, you must make sure that the image in your mind is defined through the consciousness of Christ and not through the consciousness of anti-christ.

***

We can learn one more thing from the analogy of a movie theater. The driving force in the film projector is the expanding force of the Father. I have earlier compared this to a stream of spiritual light that flows through your I AM Presence and then through your mind. Your mind imposes a mental image upon that light, and it is this image that is projected unto the movie screen as the outer situation you experience on earth. The driving force behind your existence is the light of God. If you turn off the light bulb in the film projector, what will happen? The movie theater will become dark. If you lose your connection to your I AM Presence, then your mind will be cut off from its original source of light. If you reduce the size of that connection, it is like dimming the light in the movie projector.

This does not mean that you will instantly self-destruct or that you can no longer create form. It does mean that you can no longer project images unto the screen of life by using the pure light of God from your I AM Presence. You are now forced to project images unto the screen of life by using the psychic energy that has already been brought into the material frequency spectrum. This light has a lower vibration, and therefore it does not have the same power as the pure light from your I AM presence. It will take more energy and more effort to project images unto the screen of life by using light of a lower vibration. This will limit your creative abilities, and it will turn your life into a struggle.

The driving force behind your creative efforts is a stream of energy flowing through your mind, as the light flows through the film projector. When you have some degree of Christ consciousness, you can receive the high-frequency light directly from your I AM Presence. The only limitation to your creative power is the size of the pipeline connecting your outer sense of self to your I AM Presence. When you have this pure light flowing through you, your creation is effortless because it is the light that does the work. You realize the truth in Jesus' statement: "I can of my own self do nothing" (John 5:30).

When you descend below the level of the Christ consciousness, you must gather psychic energy from this realm before you can create anything. If you do not understand the process of gathering psychic energy and using it to create form, your creative powers are reduced further, and you must now accumulate abundance exclusively by working with physical matter. In either case, you will have to take energy from a finite supply, which often means that you will have to compete with others for that energy. You have to take what you need through force, and this inevitably traps you in a treadmill of action and reaction, force and counter-force.

This struggle will continue until you reestablish the connection to your I AM Presence, and this connection is the essence of the Christ consciousness. When you overcome the sense of separation and reestablish a sense of oneness with your source, your life is no longer a struggle. The power of God's light can now flow unhindered through your mind, and thus your Father can work hitherto and you work (John 5:17). As Jesus said: "With God all things are possible" (Matthew 19:26), and thus all sense of struggle is behind you. You can then say with Jesus: "For my yoke is easy, and my burden is light" (Matthew 11:30).

Keep in mind that even when you are connected to your I AM Presence, you cannot stand still, you cannot create a form and expect it to exist indefinitely. The purpose of life, the very definition of life, is constant self-transcendence. You must continually update and improve the mental images in your mind. When you do so, when you prove yourself to be faithful over a few things, God will make you ruler over more light that will allow you to create even greater abundance and even more beautiful and perfect forms.

When you are functioning at the level of the Christ consciousness – or rather *because* you are functioning at the level of the Christ consciousness – you are not in a static state. You are constantly growing, constantly self-transcending. You are perfect even as your Father in heaven is perfect (Matthew 5:48) because you are constantly becoming more as God is constantly becoming more through *you*.

***

Because God has given you unrestricted free will and unlimited imagination, it is possible that you can use your imagination to envision forms that are not in alignment with the laws of God. It is possible that you can build a sense of self that is not a reflection of the original design for your lifestream. Instead of seeing yourself as a son or daughter of God, you can begin to see yourself as a being who is separated from God, perhaps even a being who has been abandoned by God or has been forcefully cast out of paradise. You might even build the image that you are in opposition to God and that you hate everything God stands for, including God's laws that you see as a restriction of your creative freedom.

When you use your will power to accept such a limited self-awareness as real, perhaps even as the only possible reality, you can gradually put yourself in a state of consciousness in which you are no longer able to define mental images based on the Christ consciousness. All of the mental images held in your mind are defined through the consciousness of anti-christ, the consciousness of separation from God and separation from the whole. This will cause your mental images to become more and more self-centered, to become more and more egotistical. You then lose your awareness of the whole and you lose your concern for how your actions affect other people. This can become a downward spiral that gradually takes you far below your true creative potential, your true divine potential.

There truly is no definite limit to how far a self-aware being can descend below the level of the Christ consciousness. God has given you unrestricted free will and unlimited imagination.

The only limitation is that God has not given you forever to experiment with the consciousness of anti-christ. The very moment you partake of the fruit of the knowledge of good and evil, you lose the immortal life of the Christ consciousness. You now become subject to the lower laws of mortality, of which the second law of thermodynamics is just one. When you descend below the level of the Christ consciousness, you are no longer in the eternal flow of the River of Life. You become subject to the laws of time and space, and these laws will limit you to a specific location in space and they will limit you to a specific location in time. Space and time are by definition limited concepts, and as you cannot be everywhere in space, you cannot exist forever in time. The limited sense of self that is a result of you partaking of the mind of anti-christ cannot exist forever. There must come a day when you must choose whom you will serve, when you must choose whether you are willing to return to the consciousness of Christ and the eternal life of the Christ consciousness, or whether you will continue to limit your sense of identity to the consciousness of anti-christ that must inevitably die. This is indeed the judgment day spoken of in the Bible (Matthew 10:15). If you do refuse to grow towards the Christ consciousness, if you refuse to transcend your limited sense of self, then your opportunity to experiment with the consciousness of anti-christ will indeed come to an end in what the Bible calls the second death (Revelation 2:11).

The original design for your lifestream can never be lost. That design is forever preserved in the mind of Christ, the Universal Christ Mind. Your potential to be saved – to be redeemed, to return to your former estate, to return to Grace, to return to Paradise – cannot be lost. No matter what you have done in this world, no matter how far you have descended below the level of the Christ consciousness, you have the potential to turn around and start the upward journey that will bring you back to the

Christ consciousness. One function of the Christ consciousness is to hold what we might call the immaculate concept. This is the image that was held in the mind of your Creator when your lifestream was first conceived in the mind of God. This is the concept that defines your individuality, the individual gifts that your Creator gave you when you were first conceived. These characteristics are there, sealed in the Christ consciousness. If you are willing to transcend the limited sense of self that you currently have, you can uncover that immaculate concept. You can restore your sense of self, your sense of identity, by once again becoming one with that immaculate concept. You are who you think you are so if you can envision and accept the immaculate concept, you will *be* the immaculate being that God created.

Planet earth was originally created in a higher state of perfection than what is currently manifest. Human beings have taken this planet far below its original perfection, yet that original design still exists as an immaculate concept in the Christ mind. There is a very real potential that a critical mass of human beings can raise their consciousness to the level of the Christ and thereby serve as the open doors for bringing the immaculate concept back into physical manifestation. The current conditions on earth are nothing more than a movie projected unto the screen of life through the collective consciousness of humankind. Most people on this planet currently believe in the illusion that no other image is possible or realistic. If only a small number of people refuse to believe this illusion and realign their vision of the earth with the immaculate concept, the Ma-ter Light will rejoice in outpicturing this immaculate concept rather than the current concept that is so heavily influenced by the mind of anti-christ.

If you feel that the teachings I give in this course stir something deep within your heart, it is likely that you descended into your present embodiment precisely because you wanted to become one of the Christed ones who can help lift the earth out of its current limitations and bring it into a golden age in which all people share in the abundant life. I will talk more about this idea in coming chapters, [See Volume 2 and 3] yet as our next step we need to gain a greater understanding of how self-aware beings descended into the limited sense of self that is based on the consciousness of anti-christ. By understanding how you lost the grace of the Christ consciousness, you will also uncover the key to regaining that state of Grace.

16 | I INVOKE MY HIGHEST IDENTITY

In the name I AM THAT I AM, Jesus Christ, I call to all representatives of the Divine Mother, especially Omega and Mother Mary, to help me rediscover my reason for coming to earth so I can express my individuality through the balance of the Christ mind. Help me transcend all blocks to my ability to manifest abundance, including...

[Make personal calls.]

1. I transcend separation from my Source

1. I now consciously surrender any self-image as being better than or more valuable than others. I surrender the image of being worse than or less valuable than others. I surrender the desire to rule over others and to control the whole. I am working to magnify the whole.

Omega, I now meditate,
upon your throne in cosmic gate.
I'm born out of the figure-eight,
that Alpha and you co-create.

O Song of Life, you vitalize,
all hearts you truly synchronize.
O Sacred Sound, you alchemize,
turn earth into a paradise.

2. I am designed with a beauty and perfection far beyond the level
of human identity and awareness. I was created to be infinitely
more than I can currently accept, and this God-given individuality can never be lost because it is permanently recorded in the
Universal Christ Mind.

Omega, in your sacred space,
my cosmic parents I embrace.
I see that it is such a grace,
that I take part in cosmic race.

O Song of Life, you vitalize,
all hearts you truly synchronize.
O Sacred Sound, you alchemize,
turn earth into a paradise.

3. The Christ mind is the keeper of my true individuality, and it
is the key to regaining my true identity. I am overcoming the limited sense of identity that springs from the mind of anti-christ.
I reclaim the identity that springs from the mind of Christ, the
mind of oneness with my source.

Omega in the Central Sun,
you show me life is cosmic fun.
And thus a victory is won,
my homeward journey has begun.

**O Song of Life, you vitalize,
all hearts you truly synchronize.
O Sacred Sound, you alchemize,
turn earth into a paradise.**

4. The Christ mind guides my creative efforts and they are always in alignment with the laws of God. There is harmony between me and the Body of God. Through my individualized Christ mind, I am creating in perfect harmony with the laws of God, and my creation has maximum power.

Omega, femininity
is doorway to infinity.
With you I have affinity,
to know my own divinity.

**O Song of Life, you vitalize,
all hearts you truly synchronize.
O Sacred Sound, you alchemize,
turn earth into a paradise.**

5. I am the All of the Creator, manifest as, focused through, my individuality. I no longer look at life from the limited viewpoint of my individual awareness. I look at life from the expanded viewpoint of the consciousness of the Creator, shining through my individuality.

Omega, in your cosmic flow,
my plan divine I clearly know.
My heart is now a lamp aglow,
as love on all I do bestow.

**O Song of Life, you vitalize,
all hearts you truly synchronize.
O Sacred Sound, you alchemize,
turn earth into a paradise.**

6. God is right here with me. I am God manifesting itself as my individual being. I am God expressing myself as my individual being. That is why the kingdom of God is within me.

Omega, cosmic Mother Flame,
this is the light from which I came.
As I take part in cosmic game,
Christ victory I do proclaim.

**O Song of Life, you vitalize,
all hearts you truly synchronize.
O Sacred Sound, you alchemize,
turn earth into a paradise.**

7. I see beyond my personal desires. I did not come to this planet just to fulfill my individual desires. There is a divine plan for the growth of earth, and I am realigning myself with it. I am experiencing greater fulfillment by seeing how my individual efforts fit into and enhance the greater plan for the earth.

Omega, I now comprehend,
why I did to earth descend.
And thus I fully do intend,
to help this planet to ascend.

**O Song of Life, you vitalize,
all hearts you truly synchronize.
O Sacred Sound, you alchemize,
turn earth into a paradise.**

8. The essence of the Christ consciousness is balance. The Christ consciousness balances the expanding force of the Father and the contracting force of the Mother. It balances the relationship between my individuality and the Body of God.

Omega, I do now aspire,
to join the ranks of cosmic choir.
My heart burns with a Christic fire,
that is this planet's sanctifier.

**O Song of Life, you vitalize,
all hearts you truly synchronize.
O Sacred Sound, you alchemize,
turn earth into a paradise.**

9. Any form that is defined by and through the Christ consciousness is a perfect form. It is a form that is in perfect harmony with the laws of God and with the creative intent of God—which is that all co-creators grow in harmony with each other so that all life becomes more.

Omega, my heart is ablaze,
my life is in an upward phase.
Come teach me now the secret phrase,
so that I can this planet raise.

O Song of Life, you vitalize,
all hearts you truly synchronize.
O Sacred Sound, you alchemize,
turn earth into a paradise.

2. I am constantly co-creating

1. Through the Christ mind, I am exercising my creative abilities
and expanding my self-awareness. I am becoming more until I
attain the full God consciousness and know that I am an individualization of the All, that I am one with God. I am God manifesting itself through my individual sense of self.

Omega, I now meditate,
upon your throne in cosmic gate.
I'm born out of the figure-eight,
that Alpha and you co-create.

O Song of Life, you vitalize,
all hearts you truly synchronize.
O Sacred Sound, you alchemize,
turn earth into a paradise.

2. God wants forms to remain dynamic, meaning that any form is a foundation for further growth. I am in the Christ consciousness, and I never want to stand still or to maintain a certain form. I am constantly creating new and better forms, remaining in the River of Life, the ever-flowing creative force that is God the Creator.

Omega, in your sacred space,
my cosmic parents I embrace.
I see that it is such a grace,
that I take part in cosmic race.

**O Song of Life, you vitalize,
all hearts you truly synchronize.
O Sacred Sound, you alchemize,
turn earth into a paradise.**

3. I am in the flow of life, and I have no attachments to a particular form. I have no desire to see any form remain permanent, I only desire to use it as a springboard for expanding my creativity.

Omega in the Central Sun,
you show me life is cosmic fun.
And thus a victory is won,
my homeward journey has begun.

**O Song of Life, you vitalize,
all hearts you truly synchronize.
O Sacred Sound, you alchemize,
turn earth into a paradise.**

4. I am focused on the process of creation rather than on the result of creation. I am focused on the journey rather than the destination because I realize that life is a never-ending journey.

Omega, femininity
is doorway to infinity.
With you I have affinity,
to know my own divinity.

**O Song of Life, you vitalize,
all hearts you truly synchronize.
O Sacred Sound, you alchemize,
turn earth into a paradise.**

5. I am part of the River of Life, and I am constantly using one form as the springboard for an even greater creative accomplishment. By being in the flow of life, I feel truly fulfilled and alive.

Omega, in your cosmic flow,
my plan divine I clearly know.
My heart is now a lamp aglow,
as love on all I do bestow.

**O Song of Life, you vitalize,
all hearts you truly synchronize.
O Sacred Sound, you alchemize,
turn earth into a paradise.**

6. The consciousness of constant self-transcendence is the consciousness of life. The attachment to a particular form and the attempt to preserve that form is the consciousness of death, the consciousness of anti-christ.

Omega, cosmic Mother Flame,
this is the light from which I came.
As I take part in cosmic game,
Christ victory I do proclaim.

**O Song of Life, you vitalize,
all hearts you truly synchronize.
O Sacred Sound, you alchemize,
turn earth into a paradise.**

7. I am willing to lose the static sense of life in order to transcend
that stage and attain a greater sense of self. Through the Christ
consciousness, through constant self-transcendence, I am in the
flow of life that is never-ending, and thus I have eternal life.

Omega, I now comprehend,
why I did to earth descend.
And thus I fully do intend,
to help this planet to ascend.

**O Song of Life, you vitalize,
all hearts you truly synchronize.
O Sacred Sound, you alchemize,
turn earth into a paradise.**

8. Because I have self-awareness, imagination and free will, I am
who I think I am. God has given me the right to create any sense
of identity I like, but God has not given me the right to remain
in that sense of identity forever.

Omega, I do now aspire,
to join the ranks of cosmic choir.
My heart burns with a Christic fire,
that is this planet's sanctifier.

O Song of Life, you vitalize,
all hearts you truly synchronize.
O Sacred Sound, you alchemize,
turn earth into a paradise.

9. I am willing to grow. I am losing a particular sense of identity, but I am preserving the ongoing sense of identity that is independent of any created form. This is my true identity that is beyond anything in this world.

Omega, my heart is ablaze,
my life is in an upward phase.
Come teach me now the secret phrase,
so that I can this planet raise.

O Song of Life, you vitalize,
all hearts you truly synchronize.
O Sacred Sound, you alchemize,
turn earth into a paradise.

3. I am more than any self in this world

1. The Creator is beyond its creation. As a co-creator, I am beyond my creation, even beyond the world of form. I am an extension of the Creator, and thus I am more than any form I might have created in this world. I am more than any sense of identity I have created out of separation.

Omega, I now meditate,
upon your throne in cosmic gate.
I'm born out of the figure-eight,
that Alpha and you co-create.

**O Song of Life, you vitalize,
all hearts you truly synchronize.
O Sacred Sound, you alchemize,
turn earth into a paradise.**

2. God's love for me is unconditional, and God does not accept any conditions that would keep me separated from him forever. God will not allow any condition to cause me to become permanently trapped in the state of separation that will always be less than the fullness of the abundant life.

Omega, in your sacred space,
my cosmic parents I embrace.
I see that it is such a grace,
that I take part in cosmic race.

**O Song of Life, you vitalize,
all hearts you truly synchronize.
O Sacred Sound, you alchemize,
turn earth into a paradise.**

3. My outer situation is the result of choices I have made in the past and choices I make in the present. My outer situation is the result of a mental image that I am holding in my mind and projecting unto the screen of life.

Omega in the Central Sun,
you show me life is cosmic fun.
And thus a victory is won,
my homeward journey has begun.

**O Song of Life, you vitalize,
all hearts you truly synchronize.
O Sacred Sound, you alchemize,
turn earth into a paradise.**

4. My outer situation is the result of my mind projecting an image unto the Ma-ter Light. At any moment, I have the opportunity to change the image I project upon the Ma-ter Light. The only possible way for me to improve my situation is that I must change the image in my mind.

Omega, femininity
is doorway to infinity.
With you I have affinity,
to know my own divinity.

**O Song of Life, you vitalize,
all hearts you truly synchronize.
O Sacred Sound, you alchemize,
turn earth into a paradise.**

5. I am transcending the state of spiritual paralysis that causes my mind – my imagination, free will and sense of identity – to be stuck on the same graven image. I am turning the images in my mind into a moving picture, and I am constantly transcending my mental images.

Omega, in your cosmic flow,
my plan divine I clearly know.
My heart is now a lamp aglow,
as love on all I do bestow.

**O Song of Life, you vitalize,
all hearts you truly synchronize.
O Sacred Sound, you alchemize,
turn earth into a paradise.**

6. Through the Christ consciousness, I am receiving high-frequency light directly from my I AM Presence. This pure light makes it possible for me to transcend any limitation I face. My creation is effortless because it is the light that does the work.

Omega, cosmic Mother Flame,
this is the light from which I came.
As I take part in cosmic game,
Christ victory I do proclaim.

**O Song of Life, you vitalize,
all hearts you truly synchronize.
O Sacred Sound, you alchemize,
turn earth into a paradise.**

7. I am reestablishing the connection to my I AM Presence, and this connection is the essence of the Christ consciousness. I am overcoming the sense of separation and reestablishing a sense of oneness with my source. My life is no longer a struggle.

Omega, I now comprehend,
why I did to earth descend.
And thus I fully do intend,
to help this planet to ascend.

**O Song of Life, you vitalize,
all hearts you truly synchronize.
O Sacred Sound, you alchemize,
turn earth into a paradise.**

8. The power of God's light is flowing unhindered through my mind, and thus my Father can work hitherto and I work. With God all things are possible and I say with Jesus: "My yoke is easy, and my burden is light."

Omega, I do now aspire,
to join the ranks of cosmic choir.
My heart burns with a Christic fire,
that is this planet's sanctifier.

**O Song of Life, you vitalize,
all hearts you truly synchronize.
O Sacred Sound, you alchemize,
turn earth into a paradise.**

9. The purpose of life, the very definition of life, is constant self-transcendence. I am continually updating and improving the mental images in my mind. I am faithful over a few things, and God will make me ruler over more light that will allow me to create even greater abundance and even more beautiful and perfect forms.

Omega, my heart is ablaze,
my life is in an upward phase.
Come teach me now the secret phrase,
so that I can this planet raise.

O Song of Life, you vitalize,
all hearts you truly synchronize.
O Sacred Sound, you alchemize,
turn earth into a paradise.

4. I know why I came to earth

1. In the Christ consciousness I am constantly growing, constantly self-transcending. I am perfect even as my Father in Heaven is perfect because I am constantly becoming more as God is constantly becoming more through me.

Omega, I now meditate,
upon your throne in cosmic gate.
I'm born out of the figure-eight,
that Alpha and you co-create.

O Song of Life, you vitalize,
all hearts you truly synchronize.
O Sacred Sound, you alchemize,
turn earth into a paradise.

2. On this day, I choose whom I will serve. I am returning to the consciousness of Christ and the eternal life of the Christ consciousness. I am surrendering the sense of identity based on the consciousness of anti-christ. I am letting it die.

Omega, in your sacred space,
my cosmic parents I embrace.
I see that it is such a grace,
that I take part in cosmic race.

O Song of Life, you vitalize,
all hearts you truly synchronize.
O Sacred Sound, you alchemize,
turn earth into a paradise.

3. No matter what I have done in this world, no matter how far I have descended below the level of the Christ consciousness, I have the potential to turn around and start the upward journey that will bring me back to the Christ consciousness.

Omega in the Central Sun,
you show me life is cosmic fun.
And thus a victory is won,
my homeward journey has begun.

O Song of Life, you vitalize,
all hearts you truly synchronize.
O Sacred Sound, you alchemize,
turn earth into a paradise.

4. I am reconnecting to the immaculate concept, the image that was held in the mind of my Creator when my lifestream was first conceived. I am accepting my true individuality, the individual gifts that my Creator gave me when I was first conceived.

Omega, femininity
is doorway to infinity.
With you I have affinity,
to know my own divinity.

**O Song of Life, you vitalize,
all hearts you truly synchronize.
O Sacred Sound, you alchemize,
turn earth into a paradise.**

5. I am restoring my sense of self, my sense of identity, by once again becoming one with the immaculate concept. I am who I think I am, and because I envision and accept the immaculate concept, I *am* the immaculate being that God created.

Omega, in your cosmic flow,
my plan divine I clearly know.
My heart is now a lamp aglow,
as love on all I do bestow.

**O Song of Life, you vitalize,
all hearts you truly synchronize.
O Sacred Sound, you alchemize,
turn earth into a paradise.**

6. I am one of the beings who came to earth in order to raise their consciousness to the level of the Christ and thereby serve as the open doors for bringing the immaculate concept back into physical manifestation.

Omega, cosmic Mother Flame,
this is the light from which I came.
As I take part in cosmic game,
Christ victory I do proclaim.

O Song of Life, you vitalize,
all hearts you truly synchronize.
O Sacred Sound, you alchemize,
turn earth into a paradise.

7. I am transcending the illusion of anti-christ and realigning my vision of the earth with the immaculate concept.

Omega, I now comprehend,
why I did to earth descend.
And thus I fully do intend,
to help this planet to ascend.

O Song of Life, you vitalize,
all hearts you truly synchronize.
O Sacred Sound, you alchemize,
turn earth into a paradise.

8. The Ma-ter Light is rejoicing in outpicturing this immaculate concept rather than the current concept that is so heavily influenced by the mind of anti-christ.

Omega, I do now aspire,
to join the ranks of cosmic choir.
My heart burns with a Christic fire,
that is this planet's sanctifier.

O Song of Life, you vitalize,
all hearts you truly synchronize.
O Sacred Sound, you alchemize,
turn earth into a paradise.

9. I know that I descended into my present embodiment because I wanted to become one of the Christed ones who can help lift the earth out of its current limitations and bring it into a golden age in which all people share in the abundant life. I am embracing and co-creating this mission.

Omega, my heart is ablaze,
my life is in an upward phase.
Come teach me now the secret phrase,
so that I can this planet raise.

O Song of Life, you vitalize,
all hearts you truly synchronize.
O Sacred Sound, you alchemize,
turn earth into a paradise.

Sealing

In the name of the Divine Mother, I call to Omega and Mother Mary for the sealing of myself and all people in my circle of influence in the creative flow of the Divine Mother, the River of Life. I call for the multiplication of my calls by all representatives of the Divine Mother, so that we form the perfect figure-eight flow of "As Above, so below." Thus, I accept that this is fully manifest, because the mouth of the Lord, the Divine Mother that I AM, has spoken it. Amen.

About the Author

Kim Michaels is an accomplished writer and author. He has conducted spiritual conferences and workshops in 14 countries, has counseled hundreds of spiritual students and has done numerous radio shows on spiritual topics. Kim has been on the spiritual path since 1976. He has studied a wide variety of spiritual teachings and practiced many techniques for raising consciousness. Since 2002 he has served as a messenger for Jesus and other ascended masters. He has brought forth extensive teachings about the mystical path, many of them available for free on his websites: *www.askrealjesus.com, www. ascendedmasteranswers.com, www.ascendedmasterlight.com* and *www.transcendencetoolbox.com.* For personal information, visit Kim at *www.KimMichaels.info.*